The
Boxed Garden

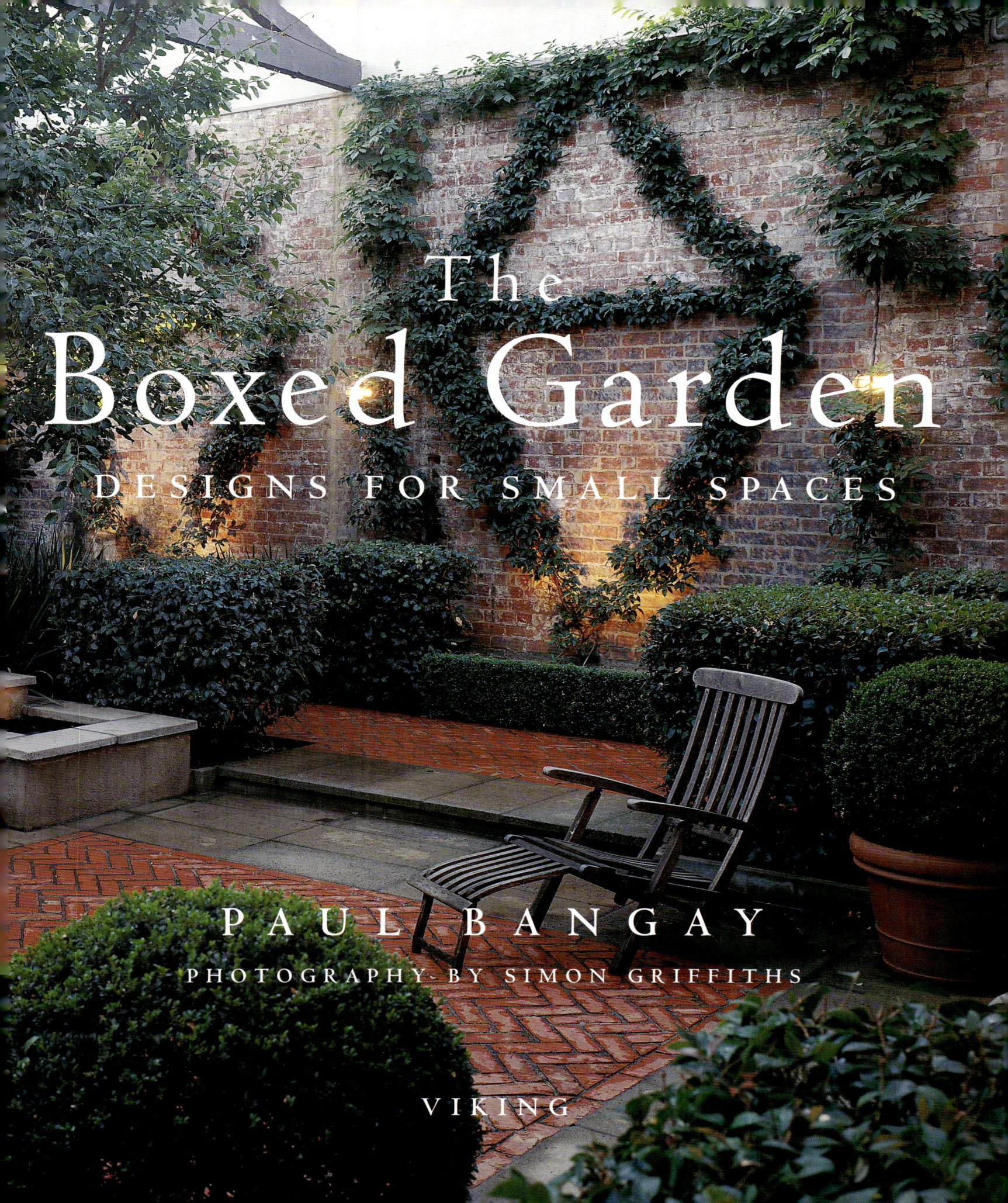

In memory of David Hicks, whose talent, energy and constant inspiration I shall miss

Viking
Penguin Books Australia Ltd
487 Maroondah Highway, PO Box 257
Ringwood, Victoria 3134, Australia
Penguin Books Ltd
Harmondsworth, Middlesex, England
Penguin Putnam Inc.
375 Hudson Street, New York, New York 10014, USA
Penguin Books Canada Limited
10 Alcorn Avenue, Toronto, Ontario
Canada M4V 3B2
Penguin Books (N.Z.) Ltd
Cnr Rosedale and Airborne Roads, Albany
Auckland, New Zealand
Penguin Books (South Africa) (Pty) Ltd
4 Pallinghurst Road, Parktown 2193, South Africa

First published by Penguin Books Australia Ltd 1998

10 9 8 7 6 5 4 3

Text Copyright © Paul Bangay 1998
Photography Copyright © Simon Griffiths 1998

All rights reserved. Without limiting the rights under copyright reserved above, no part of this publication may be reproduced, stored in or introduced into a retrieval system, or transmitted, in any form or by any means (electronic, mechanical, photocopying, recording or otherwise), without the prior written permission of both the copyright owner and the above publisher of this book.

Designed by Tony Palmer, Penguin Design Studio
Typeset in Centaur by Post Pre-press, Brisbane
Photography by Simon Griffiths
Printed and bound by South China Printing Co.
Hong Kong, China

National Library of Australia
Cataloguing-in-Publication data

Bangay, Paul.
 The boxed garden: designs for small spaces.
 Includes Index.
 ISBN 0 670 87796 4.

 I. Gardens – Design. 2. Landscape gardening.
 I. Griffiths, Simon (Simon John). II. Title.
712.6

Contents

Introduction vi

A Garden is Made 1
*Finding the Style 5   Developing the Ground Plan 7   Walls and Paving 11
Adorning the Garden 15   The Planting Scheme 19   Living in the Courtyard 25*

Fundamentals 31
*Levels and Retaining Walls 35   Hard and Soft Surfaces 38   Steps 44
Walls, Fences and Gates 45   A Paved Garden in the Grand Manner 50*

Ornamentation 56
*Urns 62   Statues 64   Busts and Niches 66   Sundials 67   Obelisks 68
Pots for Plants 70   Decorative Trellises 71   A Garden for Favourite Ornaments 74*

Water 83
*Ornamental Pools 86   Fountains 89   Swimming Pools 92
A Garden Built Around Fountains 98*

Plants 108
Special Problems 116   Useful Plants 117   A Picking Garden 130

Living in the Garden 138
*Outdoor Dining Furniture 144   Garden Seats 147   Poolside Furniture 149
Barbecues 151   Lighting 151   An Outdoor Room 154*

Acknowledgements 160

Index 161

Introduction

*A garden extends the possibilities of private life.
A house we need for shelter; a garden is pure pleasure.
It is true that it can be an additional room of the house,
in the sense that we can sit in it and eat in it and even bathe
in it, but it is not a room like any other. Though it may be
as psychologically enclosing, there is always an element of
change, of being at the whim of the weather, that makes it
seem more unpredictable, more open, more stimulating than
any room in a house. And it looks different. Its surfaces are
often harder, its changes of level more playful, and for its
adornment, it steals water and plants from nature and
displays them in ways not possible in a house.*

When I first started designing in the mid-1980s, the trend was towards larger gardens. A number of home owners were purchasing adjoining properties and demolishing the houses on them to extend their gardens. However, by the late 1990s, the encroachments of work on leisure time and a government policy of increasing inner-urban population densities had almost completely reversed this trend. These days I am increasingly asked to design courtyards for townhouses and converted warehouses, and gardens for the balconies and rooftops of commercial buildings turned into apartments. Even the gardens I design for large, inner-suburban houses are usually on smaller blocks than in the past.

The new small gardens present designers with tough environmental conditions. Their close proximity to neighbouring buildings creates problems of light and ventilation, as well as of privacy. Frequently owners are frustrated by the move from a large garden, with a great diversity of plants and many outdoor facilities, to a smaller property where every square centimetre is precious, and designers must deal with these frustrations. At the same time that gardens have decreased in size, the demands made on them have increased: now they must include terraces for drinks parties, alfresco dining and barbecues, and an area for growing herbs and perhaps some vegetables, while often still having to leave room for a swimming pool of some kind.

Gradually as I have experimented with, and gained greater experience of, designing to meet the new requirements, I have evolved a style suited to today's small urban gardens – a style that, while taking into account the diversity of architectural and other site-specific factors, nevertheless possesses enough constant features to warrant definition. In developing this style I have been influenced by the use of hard landscape and restrained planting found in the designs of David Hicks, with whom I had the great privilege of working during the last ten years of his life, and by the landscape design of the late Russell Page. In particular, Page's courtyard for the Frick Museum in New York has been a constant inspiration. The simplicity of its layout, its use of an overscaled lily pond as the main feature and its brilliant employment of the vertical surfaces continue to influence my thinking about the design of small gardens.

Any definition of the style that I have come to consider best suits restricted spaces would have to include the word 'formal' – a somewhat startling term, given that it is usually associated with the large, the grand and the traditional. What is a formal garden? In its most pure form, it is a symmetrical garden strung along a central axis. It depends on clarity of line for its effect: a clarity of line created by the employment of geometric patterns, hard landscape and highly stylised plantings, particularly clipped hedges of different heights. It is utterly reassuring in its regularity, and strongly directive in intent: its clearly articulated central axis and secondary axes carry the eye forcibly towards objects of excellence, with no time allowed for hesitation or digression. The result is a perfection that seems untouched by either nature or man – which explains why the great formal gardens remain so intriguing. There is something super-real – perhaps even surreal – about the symmetry of the design and the absoluteness of the execution; something utterly compelling about the high finish of the terraces and steps, the walks and ornaments, and the intensity of the clipped green hedges and topiary shapes. The eye looks and looks, but the design never falters, the garden never blinks.

What can such a tradition have to offer modern urban society? How can the formal style possibly be translated to today's small garden? Not by creating a mini-Versailles! And certainly not by arbitrarily filling a small space with what are commonly perceived to be the trademarks of the formal style: a line of topiary plants in pots here, half a dozen reproduction classical statues and fountains there. The type of formality I advocate is not at all the same as that found in the large-scale gardens of Europe. It is the essential visual elements and the underlying principles of the style — and not the elaboration of that style, as seen in the grand gardens of the past — that I find so applicable to small urban gardens. It is easily forgotten that there are many gardens in the European tradition — the Mediterranean gardens of Spain, Italy and southern France, for instance — that are formal in their organisation of space but quite modest in their scope. It is to these Mediterranean regions, with their similarities of light and climate and approach to outdoor living, that I frequently turn for reference.

A severely restricted space confronts the designer with two seemingly insurmountable problems: how to make the space seem larger and how to retain the viewer's interest. Many small gardens are like a box into which you look. Their width is the width of the house, and they are wholly visible from the main living rooms, which are often spread in a straight line across the block. A forceful central axis, with the main components of the garden symmetrically arranged along it or to either side of it, is a logical response to such an area. The creation of such an axis, intersected perhaps by a secondary one, introduces a strong sense of movement into the garden, which automatically suggests space. And the introduction of movement, by making space active rather than static, ensures that the garden holds the viewer's attention.

The utilisation of the central axis, in the formal manner, to create a long perspective reinforces these gains. The creation of a vista does not necessarily depend on endless terraces and flights of steps, on parterres and rows of trees, on lines of statuary and complex arrangements of pools, all stretching into the distance and carrying the eye with them. For instance, the tiny garden featured at the end of the second chapter in this book steals from the formal tradition three (minimal) changes of level, walls of dark hedging and one classical fountain in an ornamental pool, to sustain an illusion of a vista.

The formal style solves many of the practical problems of small gardens at the same time as it solves the visual ones. Its reliance on hard landscape to achieve purity of effect means, in terms of modern living requirements, that the paved area available for outdoor living can be maximised. (At the same time the clean lines and uncluttered horizontal surfaces create visual, as well as physical, space.) Again, the dependence of the formal style on a very controlled use of plants to underline the geometry of the design means that busy owners only have to work with a narrow range of hardy evergreens, not with a complex planting scheme and the diverse requirements of a wide variety of plants. In the gardens I design, fast-growing evergreens such as lillypilly, suited to Australian conditions and the modern need for instant gardens, have replaced slow-growing traditional plants such as yew, but clipped hedges remain the enduring structural element of the planting schemes. The robust plants still require regular trimming; however, they do not need applications of pesticides and fungicides, or excessive watering. As well as being easy to care for, an evergreen basis ensures that highly visible — and highly used — small gardens seem full rather than depleted of plant life in the coolest months of the year.

The formal style has yet more to offer than spatial and functional solutions; I believe it is a style that meets many of the psychological and aesthetic demands people make of gardens, though this may sound strange given that informality, not formality, is the signature of modern life. The restfulness of regularity, the promise of control, the intimation of perfection — these are all soothing qualities for people who spend long hours in the chaotic workaday world. But even these contributions would probably not be enough, in an age where change and diversion are also psychological needs, if the formal style did not also offer paradoxes, surprises and exciting variation.

For a start the formal garden is not, and never can be, a static, timeless world. Hedges, for instance, may be manicured until they seem utterly beyond nature, yet the clipping only encourages further vigour and growth. The transcendent nature of the style is an illusion, for a subtle tension must always exist between the ideal of a totally ordered and regular environment and the reality, which is time and change. Like many designers, past and present, I am interested in increasing the tension a little by introducing a touch of informality — and fascinated by the result, by the way in which a subtle loosening of the formal style, instead of undermining it, only reinforces its strength. A fringe of feathery wisteria around a door frame dramatises the hard purity of the adjacent masonry and paving, even as it softens it somewhat. The laxness of perennials and herbs highlights the restraint of an edging of clipped lavender, even as it challenges it. A tall, leafy hedge of lillypilly set behind a tight lower one of English box emphasises the severity of the design, even as it relaxes it a fraction.

The paradoxes of the formal garden extend further, to an engaging playfulness. A topiary fantasy or a seat composed of springy clipped hedges, suddenly encountered in the traditional formal garden, is always diverting. The viewer is charmed by the audacity of a highly serious style that can incorporate humour without breaking its own rules; that can use formality to introduce a quirkiness and a strangeness that would seem to be its antithesis. The wit and perversity of the tradition are easily translated to new gardens in ways that appeal to the modern sense of humour. For instance, the cushions of English box that seemingly support four huge oil jars in the courtyard featured at the end of this book are an amusing conceit — yet one that never detracts from the strength of the jars in the overall design.

If the style I have developed owes much to the basic elements of formal design, it is also very much a response to what people want from their gardens today and to the Australian environment, which in most cases allows us to enjoy our gardens throughout the year. Behind everything I discuss in this book lies an argument for simplicity; strong garden architecture; massed plantings largely restricted to evergreens; the use of native and other plants suited to the climate; and the adaptation of garden styles sympathetic to Australian conditions and patterns of living.

I have attempted to write a book that will help readers understand the principles underlying good design and the wide number of possibilities presented by even a small space. Throughout it I have taken gardens or specific aspects of gardens I have designed as examples and shown how I looked at the original sites, what factors I took into consideration and why I made the decisions I did. The book begins with a description of how I developed the ground plan for a small garden of my own, because I felt that was the most concrete way of explaining the design process and elements crucial to it such as perspective and proportion. It then goes on to discuss what I consider to be the essential components of small gardens — the hard landscape;

the decorative elements, particularly ornamental water; the plants and the planting scheme – and the requisites for pleasurable living in the garden.

I have tried in the book to offer all the tricks I have found best exploit the physical and visual space: the establishment of sight-lines and false perspectives; the fluid extension of the house into the garden; the introduction of small changes of level; the utilisation of the vertical plane; and the simplification of detail combined with an overscaling of the key elements in the design. At various points I have discussed the specific problems associated with different types of small gardens; however, I have not on the whole distinguished between the garden of a rooftop or balcony, the courtyard of a townhouse or warehouse, the traditional suburban quarter-acre block, with its separate small front and back gardens, and the individual compartment in a large garden divided into 'rooms'. Rather, I have tried to look at the conditions all limited spaces impose on the design.

Small gardens are a given. They are what we as designers and gardeners work with today – our opportunity. Designed effectively, they have the power to counteract the stresses of the working world and to enrich the private lives of all of us.

A Garden is

This is my first garden. For years I had built gardens for other people, gardens I became very attached to, but I had never made one for myself.

When I finally started to hunt for a house of my own, I looked for one I could use as both office and home. It needed to be close to the city, yet have enough space for me to create a garden for professional as well as private purposes – a showroom for landscaping, which would demonstrate my design principles and what was possible in a small area. It was also essential that the garden face north. I wanted the house to have a lot of sunlight; I wanted the garden to have a lot of sunlight.

The house I eventually chose was a tiny Victorian worker's cottage in an inner-urban area of old factories and warehouses. The walls of the adjoining properties loomed over it, and it faced into a side street of rundown buildings and parking lots. I liked it immediately. I liked the thought of creating a small oasis within the expanse of bitumen and red brick: a walled garden like the ones found in severe desert landscapes. I liked the thought of the surprise my visitors would experience entering from the narrow grey street into a private, totally enclosed green world.

The house faced east; however, it possessed a strip of land on its northern side, which gave the site the advantage of a short driveway and a back garden that was almost square – and sun-filled. The house was derelict, the garden a weed patch, with a Hill's hoist at its centre and a few token 'natives' straggling around the edges. Exactly what I was looking for! I could start my garden from scratch, using my favourite tool, the bulldozer.

Looking north from the added sitting room into my first garden: the area I had to work with was roughly square (8 × 9.5m), level and surrounded by high, old buildings. The fundamental design problems were, firstly, how to give the courtyard sufficient visual impact to sustain the observer's interest; secondly, how at the same time to keep the small space uncluttered; and, thirdly, how to deal with the dominating red-brick wall and huge ventilator overlooking the house and garden. This is how I overcame those problems.

Given the garden's size, I needed to utilise the vertical as well as the horizontal plane. A niche was added to the design of the side walls of the lower terrace to introduce ornamentation, in the form of two busts, without encroaching on ground space (opposite). Vines of Wisteria sinensis, trained on wires to repeat the straight lines of the French windows, decorate the house extension (below): elaborate architectural ornamentation would have weakened the strength of the façade. The summer sun added effects of its own, the colour of the walls bleaching to palest terracotta in full light, intensifying in the shade.

Finding the Style

The relationship of garden to house; different styles of design; the site and the space available; function; sight-lines and aspect: these are the things any garden builder must consider before arriving at a ground plan, let alone beginning construction. I believed this absolutely, yet the moment I took possession of my own property the excitement of the first-time home owner gripped me — for now I could have anything I wished; now I could try out all the ideas that had been buzzing in my head for years. Part of me wanted to get to work straight away: rip out the old; build walls and levels; add water and massed plantings; hunt down special ornamental pieces for special spots. The other part of me held back, knowing that I should practise what I always preach and take all the time necessary to analyse the site and develop a ground plan that was right for it. In the event, I spent nearly a year thinking about the design in unbidden moments and unexpected places, mulling over the possibilities and filling a notebook with my jottings and sketches. My office in the house had been in use for many months before I finally began work on the garden.

The property offered one of those rare opportunities to design (or rather redesign) the house and the garden together so that the architecture of the house and the architecture of the garden were one. I decided at the start that, since all the front rooms of the original cottage were needed for my work, I would add a wing, extending to the back boundary, to gain a two-storey living area facing north into the garden. I also decided that the new sitting room on the ground floor should have oversized French windows, and paving that flowed out to a terrace, because I wanted the room to feel as if it were part of the garden.

As to the style of the renovated and extended house, I considered myself free to choose, since the original structure was only a modest cottage in a largely non-residential side street – though I knew that I must keep it simple so that the architecture did not overwhelm the small space. I knew, too, that whatever the style I arrived at, it would need to be a formal one because my intention was to build a formal garden. A restrained garden style was essential given the area available – only 8 metres by 9.5 metres – but my decision was based on more than this. I wanted a garden that would reflect my conviction that, as we head into the hectic new century, we should embrace formal styles of design for, contrary to popular belief, these require far less maintenance than more informal styles.

The house and garden design that gradually evolved from my notebook scribblings had the formality found in the European tradition of design, though it did not belong to any one style. Rather, it borrowed elements from several styles – Spanish, Italian, even classical and Gothic – that answered the requirements of contemporary urban living. It is the formality common to all these styles that makes such an eclectic approach successful.

The fountain and water channel reflected a Moorish influence – because simplicity was imperative in a small space. Two busts in coral-filled niches hinted at Italian grottoes, but this ornamentation was chosen because it translated effectively to the vertical plane in a garden where space was limited. The upstairs window grilles and the terracotta colouring of the walls gave the house a slightly Tuscan feel; nevertheless, the strong colour was primarily chosen to suit the hard Australian light and the high red-brick walls that overlooked the property – and as an echo of the sheer cliffs along the Great Ocean Road. And although the house and garden offered relief from the surroundings, there was no

The terracotta colour of the courtyard walls was first used on the front of the house. It offered a warm welcome, reiterated by the embracing arms of two retaining walls. Plants added a sorely needed vitality to the drab street and were all that such a modest cottage could take for decoration. Springy cycads (Cycas revoluta) provided sufficient challenge from behind the retaining walls to make the house appear street-wise as well as inviting.

illusion that they belonged to another time or place. Instead of screening the bulky ventilator of an adjacent property, I left it visible as a constant reminder that we live in an urban environment and that the contrast between constructed garden and constructed city is a stark one.

Developing the Ground Plan

There is usually only one main sight-line in a small garden: that from the house to the boundary opposite. Certainly this was the case here, and my reason for devising a ground plan that placed the main feature, the fountain, in the centre of the far wall. Since I had the luxury of being able to design the new section of the house and the garden together, I reinforced this main axis by arranging the sitting room so that a massive sandstone fireplace would align with the fountain.

Because people probably spend 80 per cent of their time inside their house looking out, and only 20 per cent actually in the garden, what they see from the windows is of paramount importance. The garden becomes almost a theatre, and designing it almost like designing a set. In my own garden I decided to introduce a change of level to give the 'stage' a defined downstage and upstage, and to elevate the fountain so that, although at the far end of the garden, it dominated the 'set'. I divided the ground plan into two sections, both measuring about 4 metres by 9.5 metres, which would become an upper and a lower terrace. Before deciding to make the terraces roughly the same size, I ensured that the lower one, adjacent to the sitting room, would be large enough to accommodate a dining table and chairs comfortably. A crucial part of any landscape designer's work is to achieve a balance between the decorative and the functional requirements of the plan – no mean challenge when space is limited – and I would not have contemplated a design that did not allow me sufficient room to sit or eat outside with friends.

The change of level, by suggesting there was room for two gardens, would I knew add false depth to what was essentially quite a small area. However, I was careful to make the change in level (350 millimetres) a minor one: just two steps. Proportion is crucial in design. Any greater height would have brought the retaining walls visually closer to the house and made the lower terrace seem unpleasantly hemmed in, thereby achieving exactly the opposite effect from the one

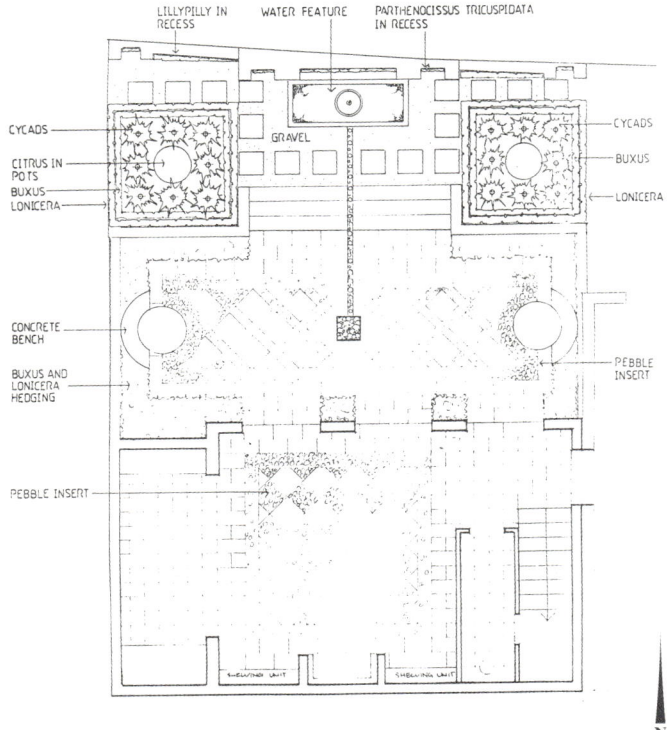

Two levels were introduced into the design to add variation and make the garden seem larger than it was (right). They were demarcated by different paving as well as the two wide steps between them. The lower terrace, for sitting and dining on, needed a hard surface; the upper terrace, whose purpose was to provide a stage for the fountain and a 'curtain' of green plants on either side, could take a less functional surface of stepping stones set within gravel. The main axis of the courtyard was strongly reinforced by a water channel built between the fountain and a small, square pool on the lower terrace. To visually stretch the space, a secondary, east–west axis was established by giving the lower terrace a rectangular paving pattern and placing a bay, consisting of a circle of artificial stone and a semicircular bench, at either end.

The ground plan initially showed, from south to north, the new sitting room, the lower terrace and the upper one (above). Not shown were the wing walls on the eastern side, which framed the opening from the upper terrace into the driveway. Using a scale of 1:50, suitable for a small area, I firstly drew in the givens: the house and perimeter walls. (If a tree or shed is to be kept, it should also be added, to scale, to the ground plan.) Since the site was flat, it did not need to be surveyed. The dimensions of the terraces were determined by the need, firstly, for the lower one to be large enough to dine on and, secondly, for the upper one to contain two generous square garden beds. The relationship of the sitting room to the garden dictated a central north–south axis, defined by a fireplace at one end and a fountain at the other.

intended. The steps I centred on the main axis of the garden and made particularly broad so that they would provide a rather impressive approach to the upper terrace and its fountain. I was then able to tie the width of both the apron in front of the fountain and a new wall behind it to the width of the steps, giving the apron and the wall more amplitude than one might have expected in a small garden.

The inclusion of steps in the plan automatically ensured there would be a strong movement along the main axis to the focal point, but I knew their breadth would also introduce a forceful east–west pull that would have the visual effect of widening the perspective. A secondary sight-line always adds a pleasing complexity to a garden, which helps further to create an illusion of space. To reinforce the secondary axis in my design, I decided to add two side walls to the plan of the lower level, both of which would be adorned with a niche. A wing wall was planned to abut the house wall on the east, while a high wall on the west was to mark the back boundary. The wing wall was to be matched by another on the upper level, so that together they would frame an opening on the east into the side driveway of the house. The curves of the wings were intended to soften the predominantly hard geometry of the overall design. They were repeated on the lower terrace in the outline of the niches and of the circular bays below that I had decided were needed both to strengthen the peripheral detail of the garden design and to further entice the eye to the sides of the garden.

The top level was to be where the real theatre took place in the garden. Here I planned to establish on both sides a symmetrical garden bed, which would reinforce the central role of the water feature in the design. To the same end, I decided the new northern wall must be a high, framing wall for the fountain, its detail matching that of the facing house. The extension of the house as I had designed it had little embellishment; it was really just a simple, barn-like structure. The only detail I had added was a plain, rendered band between the two storeys, and it was this that I copied for the capping of the wall. As well, three recessed panels in the framing wall repeated the lines of the three double doors on the ground floor of the house – though I planned to 'inset' them with clipped Boston ivy (*Parthenocissus tricuspidata*) instead of glass.

Walls and Paving

Once construction of the garden was underway, in accordance with the ground plan, I turned my attention to the finishes needed for the horizontal and vertical surfaces. The new brick walls of both the house and the garden were rendered in a terracotta colour that matched the finish already applied to the front of the house. The render was mixed three times before I got the strength of colour I felt was essential. If I was to achieve a small oasis within the built environment, I needed sufficient depth of colour to intensify the green of the climbers and the other plants. The depth of colour also strongly defined the framing wall of the fountain – the most dominant wall in the garden – yet at the same time merged with the red of the high building beyond so that neither wall closed in on the garden oppressively.

To achieve the effect of a sitting room set within the garden, I ran large (500 by 500 millimetre) pavers across the floor and out onto the lower terrace as one continuous surface broken only by the 15-millimetre drop in level between house and garden. I chose artificial-stone pavers

Walls constructed in inexpensive Besser brick and rendered in cement were built to abut the boundary wall, on the west (right), and the original back wall of the cottage, on the eastern side (far right). These became the side walls of the lower terrace. A circular niche was left in both walls and defined with a prefabricated moulding. Once these walls had been erected, a concrete slab was poured to form a firm base for pavers. Next, low Besser-brick walls were built to retain the soil that would form the upper terrace, a wide gap being left between them for the steps.

[11]

Three pairs of outsized double doors allowed the garden to seem part of the sitting room (opposite). The garden-room effect was reinforced by surfacing both the room and the adjacent terrace with 500 × 500mm artificial-stone pavers. Blurring the boundary between inside and out also brought the advantage that both room and terrace appeared larger. Tall vases, placed at either end of the wall of French windows, added their curves to those of terracotta pots and clipped balls of English box (Buxus sempervirens) beyond.

An expanse of pale pavers could quickly have become boring, so I varied it with two diamond patterns of inset black Indian pebbles, one inside and one out. The sitting-room pattern became a vibrant 'rug' of alternating paver and pebble diamonds, with a wide border of pebbles. The substantial sandstone fireplace was aligned with the fountain on the northern boundary to mark the main axis. The bust given central place on the mantelpiece influenced my choice of ornamentation for the side walls of the lower terrace.

The starting point for working out the paving pattern of the lower terrace was the centrally located sump for the small pool. The pattern chosen differed subtly from that of the sitting room: diagonally laid pavers, delineated by bands of pebbles, formed all the diamonds. A wider band of pebbles again bordered the whole. Small pebbles, 30–40mm in diameter, filled the narrow bands; larger, 40–50mm ones, the border. The pebbles had to be placed individually, like pieces in a jigsaw puzzle, on a slurry of wet cement, section by section; they were then tapped down, level with the surface.

in a soft tone that would not overpower the sitting room inside or compete with the strong terracotta-coloured walls outside. However, I was concerned that the finished work might look rather too bland. The solution was to separate the pavers with bands of polished black pebbles. The resulting pattern would add interest to the small space yet, being part of the horizontal plane, would not dominate the view.

Somewhat unconventionally, I began the interplay of pavers and bands of black pebbles in the sitting room. It is not common in Australia to incorporate pebbles in the paving of a room, although it is traditional in Italy. In fact the medium works particularly well inside: instead of an actual rug there is a lively rug-like pattern of pavers and pebbles that not only determines the seating arrangements in the room but also ties the interior to the exterior. Because the technique of laying the pebbles is not well known, I had to inlay the surfaces myself, with the help of family and friends.

Developing the paving pattern for the lower terrace presented me with quite a mathematical problem because it had to accommodate the water channel that would run down the centre of the steps to end in a tiny pool. The channel became the starting point for the design and construction of the paving. I devised a pattern of diamonds and triangles, based on full-sized pavers and half-pavers and edged with a wide border of pebbles, which would provide a sufficient area for a dining table and chairs. This in turn dictated the precise depth of the terrace.

The pavers were repeated on the upper level of the garden, but to quite different effect. There, to signal the fact that the area was a decorative rather than a functional one, they became stepping stones in an expanse of coarse gravel: the resulting pattern provided a fitting approach to the fountain. Loose gravel was chosen to soften the hardness of the terrace below as well as the austere lines of the ornamental pool and the two square garden beds on the upper terrace.

Adorning the Garden

Any garden of mine would have to include the splash and sparkle of moving water; in this garden, set in the midst of the noise and drabness of an inner suburb, it was imperative. Given the size of the garden, it was important, however, not to install an ornate fountain, so I merely placed a wide bowl on a low plinth in a sunken pool edged with plain pavers. I wanted the bowl to look as if it were resting on a mirror of water. A coating of black paint applied to the inner surface of the pool allowed the water to reflect its surroundings and gave the shallow pool a dark depth. The proportions of the rectangular pool, and therefore of the fountain within it, were essentially bound to those of the gravel approach and the framing wall (the proportions of which, in their turn, had been tied to those of the steps): in particular, the length of the pool was fixed by the width of the central section of the wall.

The ornamental pool was designed to release water into the channel descending the steps to the small, unadorned square pool set in the lower terrace. Here, as in the fountain, water jetted from a simple spout. In the channel and this pool I often placed loose black stones. As it trickled along the channel, the water hypnotically shined and shifted the stones. And whenever I removed the stones, so that just a clear channel of water remained, the mood of the garden was subtly altered again.

Visiting Spain, which has a climate similar to Australia's, I had been struck by the Moorish use of water channels in the old gardens of that country. In whatever hot climate they lived — not just Spain, but their native North Africa and parts of India also — the Moors had channelled water through their gardens. On a hot summer's day, the moving water in these enclosed gardens is as cool to the hand and eye as any stream, and its constant evaporation makes the air soft and moist. In every way a perfect use of water for an Australian courtyard.

I restricted other ornamentation in the garden largely to the

The design included a break in the paving of the steps and the upper and lower levels for the water channel. Water was to overflow from the bowl of the fountain and run down the channel into the pool on the lower terrace; a pump installed there would then return the water to the fountain. Eventually, when this became a reality, I would often place in the channel and the smaller pool more of the pebbles used for the paving, only loose this time, to add to the smooth flow of the water the fascination of a little turbulence.

The crescent benches on the lower level were constructed of brick; limestone tops were added later (far left). A space was reserved in the paving for a prefabricated artificial-stone circle, to define each bay. Once the lower terrace and the steps were finished, work began on the fountain (left). A framing wall, with recessed panels, was constructed, and a slab poured at ground level for the base of the pool. The fountain bowl was temporarily placed on a stack of bricks to establish its correct height.

vertical plane. As soon as the backing wall of the fountain was installed and rendered, I realised that it required something further — something that would bring it more into proportion with the towering red-brick wall behind it; something that would be a culmination of the strong vertical movement created by the wall. Often it is hard to find original ornaments suited to a garden: in this instance it was six to eight months after the fountain was completed before I found something sufficiently unusual. When finally I spotted two large griffins in an antique shop I knew instantly they were right. Statues of griffins are not often found in Australia, despite their rather Gothic appeal, and these two were made in the United States. Curiously juxtaposed with the ventilator, they create a small, unexpected fantasy high above the fountain.

I intended from the start to place busts in the circular niches of the garden's side walls. I wanted neo-classical busts that would relate to the large bust I had placed on the mantelpiece of the sitting room. Again it was a matter of patience. In the end I discovered two inexpensive cement busts in a nearby shop. The mock coral that I installed behind them immediately gave both the air of a Neptune, while its pocked and veined surface lent depth to recesses that themselves had been added to make the garden seem more substantial: a flat surface behind the busts would have revealed how shallow the niches in fact were. Although the busts were an embellishment, their simplicity and position made them a restrained embellishment. Wreaths of delicate *Wisteria sinensis* around the niches increased the classical Roman influence while at the same time paradoxically lightening its effect.

The only other sculpture I added was a headless draped figure placed in the opening between the wing walls. The mysterious figure, tantalisingly turned not towards the garden but towards the half-glimpsed driveway, provided a further classical reference, though it was in fact an old, abandoned religious statue that I had found in a junkyard years before.

I had hoped to add two eighteenth-century sphinxes to the centre of the square garden beds on the upper terrace, partly as counterweights to the fountain and partly to extend the fantasy created by the griffins. Sadly, I was the unsuccessful bidder when they went to auction. I had a strong sense of how the beds were to be treated and what would suit the garden, so concrete imitations of the sphinxes – or any other kind of statuary – were out of the question.

The Planting Scheme

Natural elements such as water and plants are less likely than manufactured objects to make a garden seem over-adorned, which often ensures them a key decorative role in a small space. By introducing the two large garden beds, I was able to enhance the upper level, as I had the lower, with a geometric pattern, while avoiding the severity of an extensive hard surface. I defined the two beds with an edging of deep green *Lonicera nitida*. Somewhat taller, lighter green inner hedges of English box (*Buxus sempervirens*) repeated the lines of the lonicera, and surrounded the spiky, dark green fronds of cycads (*Cycas revoluta*) planted in the middle of each square. Tall hedges of

Hard-clipped double hedges became a strong decorative element on both terraces of the garden (opposite). Lonicera nitida formed the low, outer hedge; English box, the taller one. From a distance the double hedges of the lower terrace, planted against the retaining walls, merged with the double hedges outlining the garden beds immediately above, to create a textured wall of vivid green.

clipped lillypilly (*Acmena smithii*), grown in a panel of the walls built on either side of the fountain framing wall, provided a glossy background to the beds.

Since eighteenth-century sphinxes were no longer an option as centrepieces for the beds, I decided to draw on the strength of the natural elements and the Mediterranean features in the garden. I placed a large terracotta pot, elevated on a concrete base hidden by the cycads, in both squares, and in each planted a lemon tree (*Citrus limon* 'Lisbon'). The shiny leaves, abundant lemons and forceful growth of these trees added a wonderful vigour to the garden. To prevent the trees growing too tall and obscuring the panels of lillypilly behind, I trained their branches to extend horizontally on 'baskets' of canes. This is a rather unusual treatment in Australia, but quite common in Italy. As the trees grow, the branches require regular trimming and wiring to the canes.

The square beds set the style for planting in the rest of the garden. Narrow bands of severely clipped lonicera were grown against the risers of the two broad steps leading to the upper level, their dull green softening the long central view of hard surfaces as well as punctuating the transition between levels and linking the two beds. Double hedges of lonicera and English box planted in front and to the exact height of the retaining walls linked the lower terrace with the upper one and its square beds.

Similar double hedges were grown against the house wall to break the abrupt conjunction of rendered wall and paving, and vines of *Wisteria sinensis* were trained up the wall for the same reason. I always train wisteria against a house if I can. It flows perfectly with the lines of a building, and helps to integrate house and garden.

To repeat the curves of the rendered-brick benches that formed the side bays, and those of the niches above, and to modify the effect of the hard surface, I added two terracotta pots of English box clipped into balls at both ends of each bay, and beside these placed smaller terracotta pots of *Sedum* 'Autumn Joy', a handsome plant with fleshy mid-green leaves, and pale green heads in spring. Pots displayed on a terrace such as this should always have a simple shape that complements or repeats a shape used in the garden design. Like the circle of paving I had laid to delineate each side bay, the conical pots chosen worked well with the diamond pattern of the terrace paving.

The predominant tones of the planting were green: the contrasting greens of double hedges; the electric combination of old and new growth on a flourishing evergreen plant; the changing greens of foliage, from pale leaf buds in spring to dark maturity in summer. When you are using green as the major colour in a planting, it is important to achieve contrasts, so that the variation normally created with different flower colours is duplicated by different shades of green.

Although the plants were chosen for their foliage rather than their flowers, touches of colour other than green marked the seasons of the year. In spring the bare wisteria vines wreathed windows and niches with drooping blue racemes. In summer the green of the sedum heads was streaked with a pink that slowly turned to rust as the season waned. In autumn the delicate leaves of the wisteria were a buttery yellow against the terracotta walls, and the Boston ivies on the far side of the garden turned as red as the building towering behind them. And in the coldest months of the year waxy yellow fruit hung on the boughs of the lemon trees.

There are just eight kinds of plants in this courtyard: English box, lonicera, lillypilly, cycads, lemon trees, wisteria, Boston ivies, and the sedum in pots. Massed planting, using a restricted number of plants, always looks more striking than a hundreds-and-thousands sprinkling of many different plants, no matter what the size of the garden.

All the plants were chosen for their hardiness as much as for their form and foliage. This was a hot courtyard in summer, the strong sunlight seeking out most corners in the course of a day, the hard surfaces soaking up heat and releasing it into the garden: only a plant as resilient as lonicera could have survived planted against the steps, in narrow strips of soil. Yet because of the surrounding walls, the small area could be a place of deep shade, too. English box and lonicera, which take both

Trained and trimmed to fill the framing-wall panels of the fountain, Boston ivy (Parthenocissus tricuspidata) became an important detail of the garden's central feature. The leaves added the freshness of green to the heat of the terracotta colouring in summer, yet their autumn red was equally effective, intensifying the earthiness of the wall so that the garden retained a sense of warmth even as the days grew cooler.

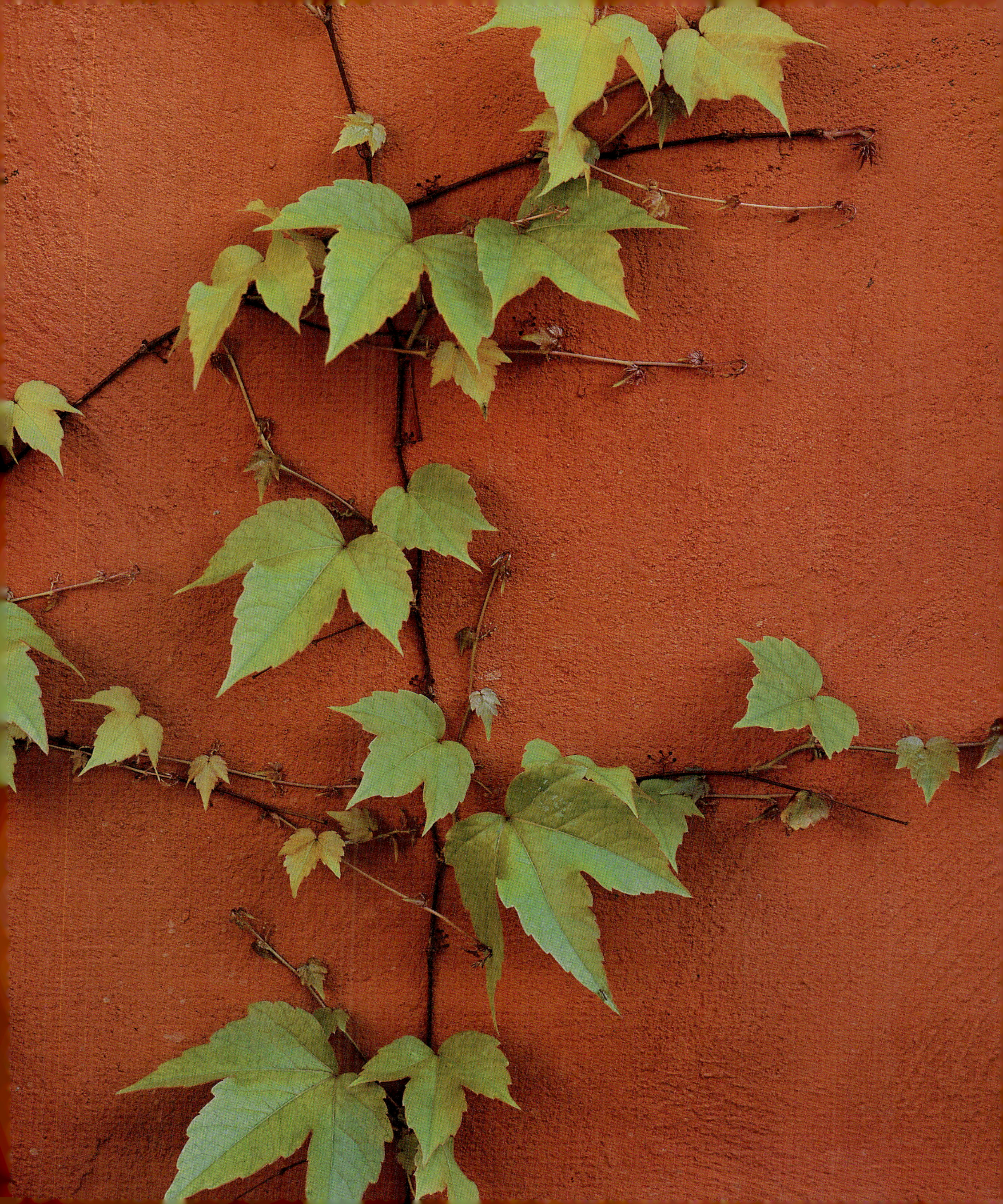

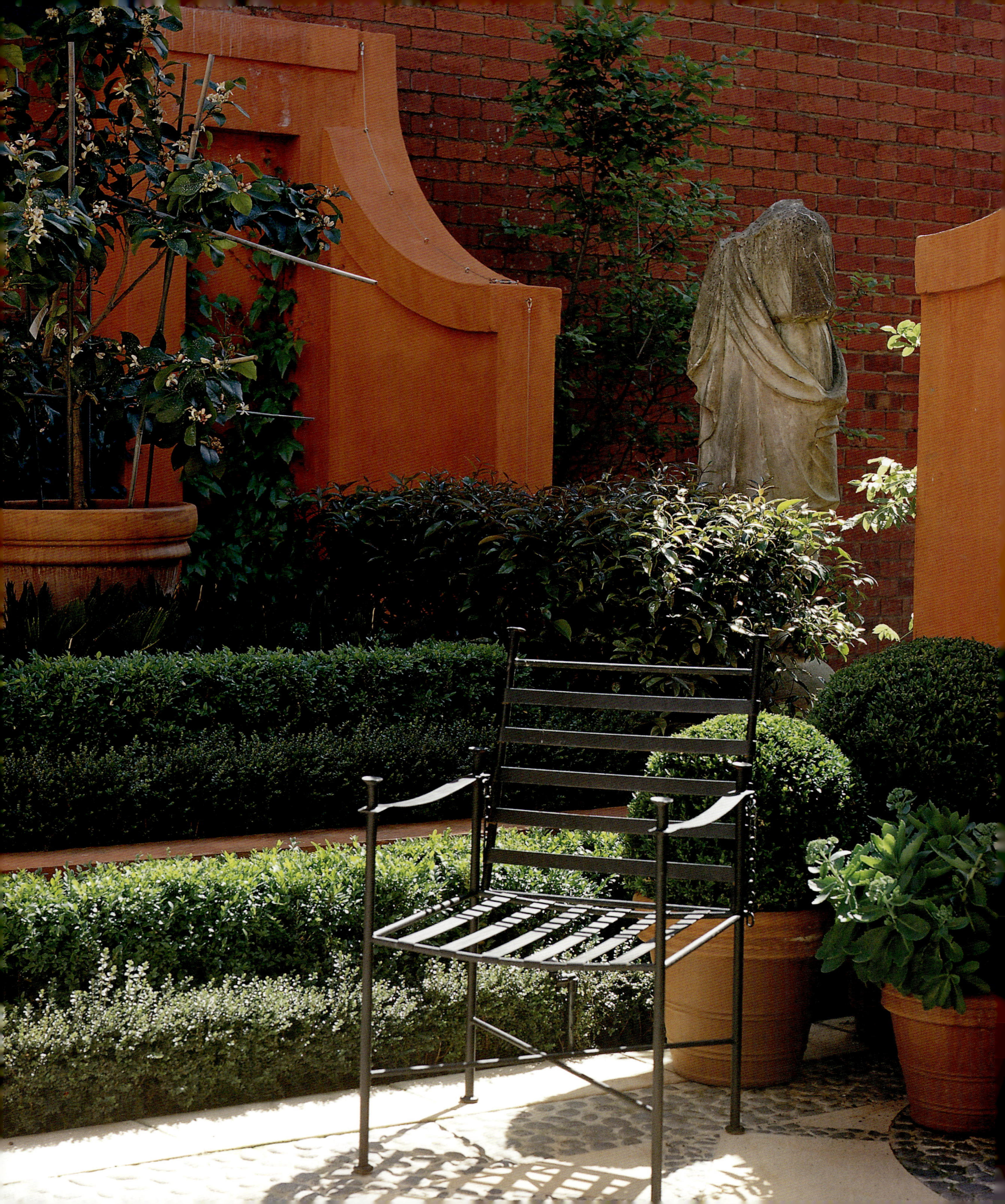

This photograph, taken in spring before all work on the courtyard had finished, shows the plants already fulfilling their intended roles; to achieve this, I had used well-advanced plants (opposite). The double hedges of lonicera and English box were about to be trimmed: at this stage I was clipping them every six weeks or so. The boughs of the lemon trees (Citrus limon 'Lisbon') planted in huge terracotta pots at the centre of each of the two garden beds were trained on a 'basket' of canes to grow horizontally. On the east side a hedge of native lillypilly (Acmena smithii) linked the wing walls of the upper and lower terraces and acted as a partial barrier between the courtyard and the driveway beyond, without obscuring the enigmatic statue in the opening. Behind the figure rises a hornbeam (Carpinus betulus), one of four that I planted in the corners of the short driveway because they are light, slow-growing trees. However, their leaves burn easily in the sun, so they are not suited to some Australian gardens.

full sun and full shade — not to mention hard clipping — were obvious choices for the double hedges.

As for the lillypillies, my other often-used hedging material, they reflected a general resolution on my part to combine Australian native plants with exotics. I would never want to be restricted to using only native plants in a garden — I would always want to choose the best plants for a particular space, irrespective of their origin — but equally it would be absurd to ignore the variety and suitability of Australian flora. Contemporary Australian gardens should be like contemporary Australia itself: an integration of many influences.

The cycads were chosen because their palm-like fronds contrasted well with the small, neat leaves of the double hedges — and hinted at my oasis — and because they, like the vigorous lillypillies, thrive in courtyard environments. *Cycas revoluta* is often assumed to be Australian (perhaps because it is widely cultivated and Australia does have a number of cycads), but in fact it is a slow-growing native of Japan.

Most of the plants chosen were evergreens. When a garden is small, it needs a strong foundation of permanent green if it is not to look blighted in the coldest months. The new beauty of the stripped climbers — the only deciduous plants in the garden — was sufficient reminder of change and time passing. Glimpsed through the windows of the house on wintry days, the green leaves of this garden, glistening with raindrops rather than sunlight, offered a constant surprise.

Living in the Courtyard

Soft light playing on jetting water and the contorted faces in the shadowy niches, dark walls closing in, the indigo city sky beyond — at night the drama of my garden took hold of the viewers on the terrace or in the sitting room. The lighting of a small garden is all-important for it makes it as much a night place as a daytime pleasure. Knowing this, I installed concealed, 12-volt lights beside the steps, at the base of the ornaments and beneath the water of the fountain and the channel.

Although I had carefully ensured that the design of the lower level allowed enough room for dining outside, I never intended to have a permanent table and chairs on the terrace: I wanted the water channel and the square pool to be the focus. Permanent dining furniture would have been too heavy for the space and obscured the view of the fountain from the house. I had always loved the European tradition of taking a table and chairs outside for a meal, so when I invited people to dine in this garden I simply carried my dining-room furniture out onto the terrace — after I had turned off the water spout!

The benches adjoining the side walls of the lower terrace had been added primarily to enhance the design, but I had also had in mind that the bays could become places where small groups of people could sit and rest cups of coffee or glasses of wine. As well, a few black wrought-iron chairs — more comfortable than the backless benches to sit on for an extended time — were designed by my brother Benjamin to stand on either side of the terrace. The lightness of the metalwork, its dark colour and the simplicity of design ensured that the chairs did not overpower the terrace, while the curves of their iron strap armrests echoed the lines of the fountain.

No garden exists that does not require care. Plants are living things, so gardeners must regularly feed and water, trim and train, plant and pull out — must try to dominate nature even in the mildest of gardens. My garden was designed to be genuinely low maintenance, but

At night carefully positioned lighting gave the space the atmosphere of a Roman courtyard. Two uplights below each niche threw the busts, with their artificial-coral backing and wreath of wisteria, into strong relief. To give the statue in the opening and the potted lemon trees three-dimensionality, uplights were placed at both their front and back. Ambient light from the different uplights and the house was sufficient for sitting, or dining by, in the garden.

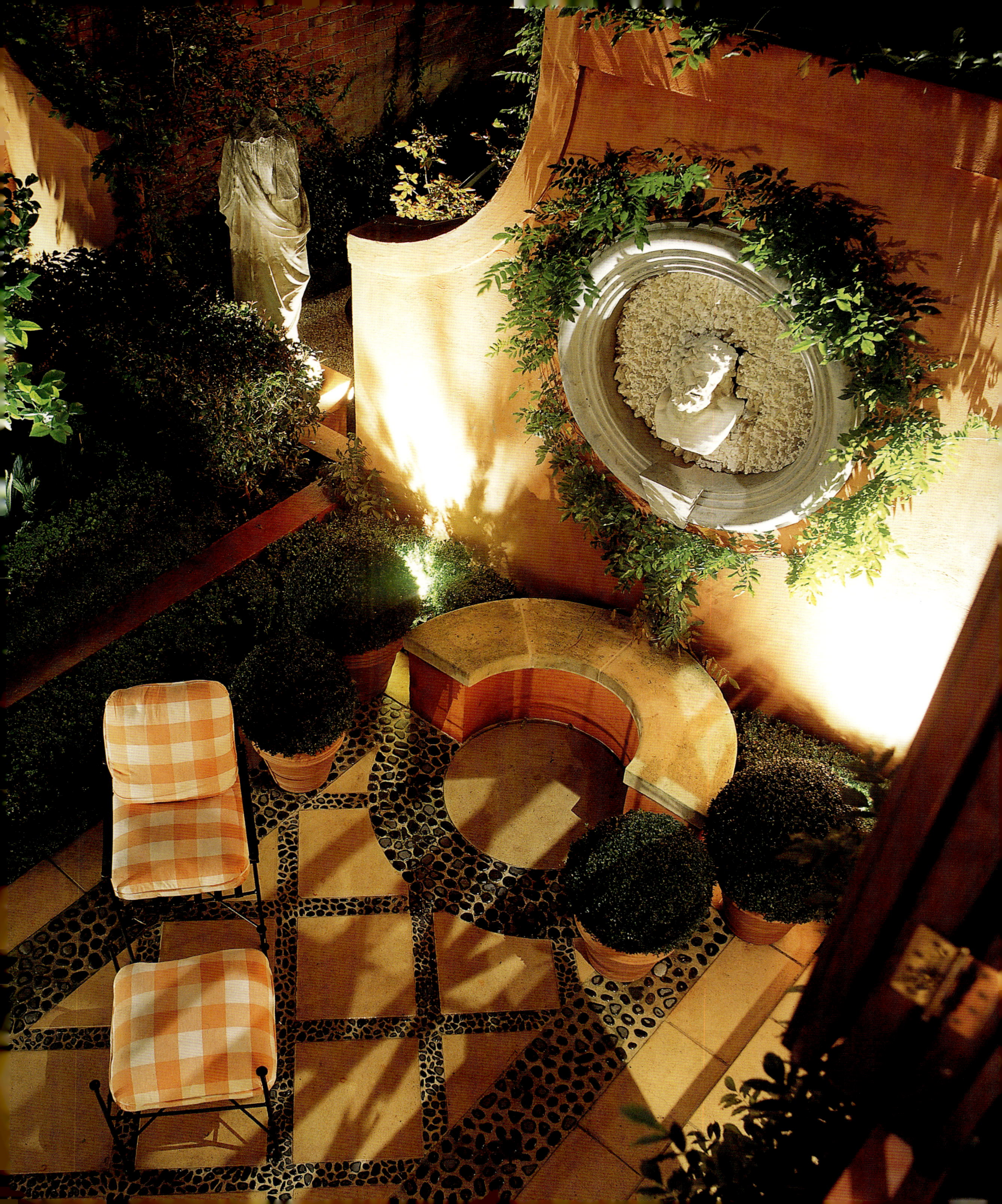

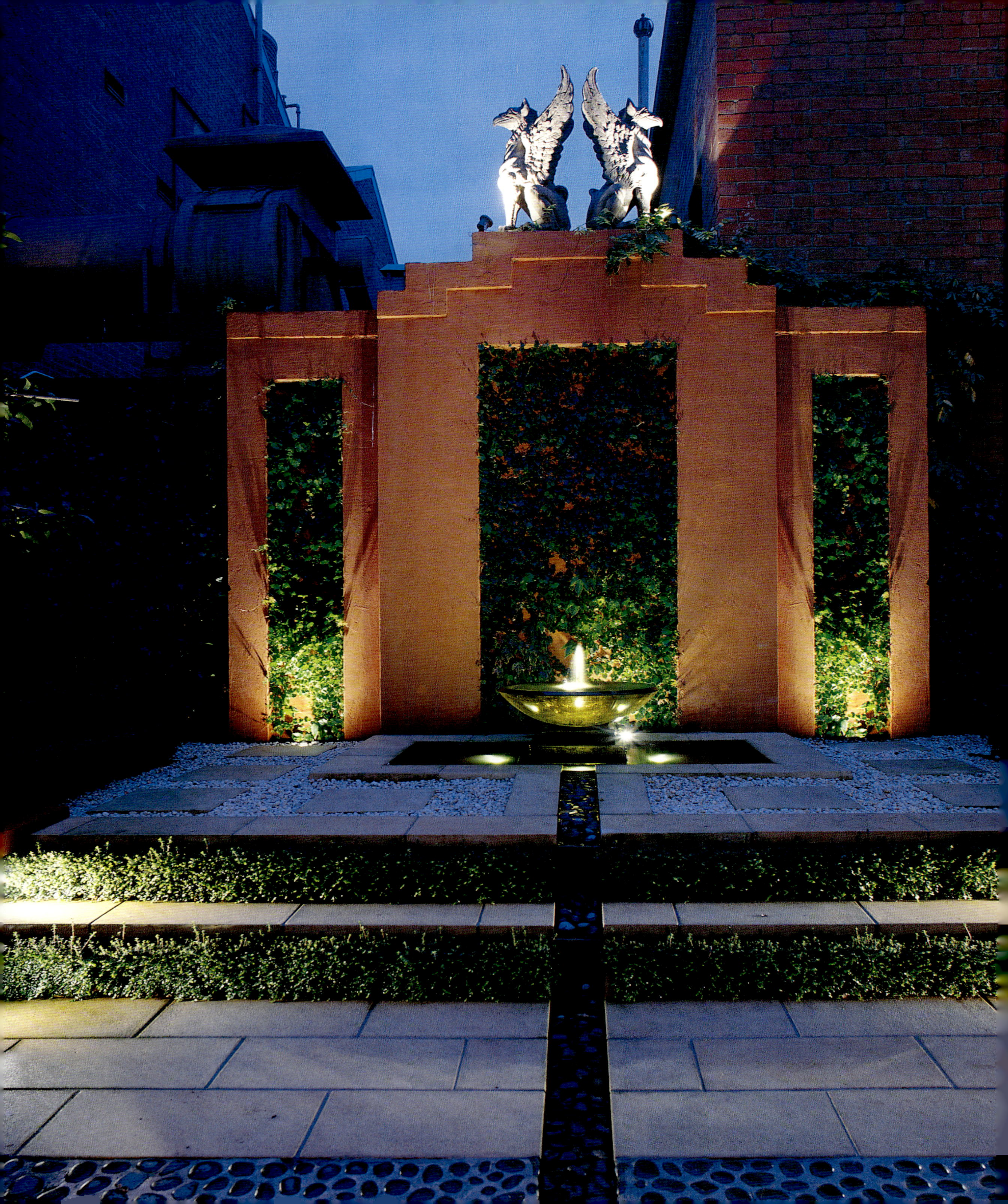

The base of the steps and the tread of the first step were lit from either side for safety. The light also ensured that the tight bands of lonicera, which delineated the risers, were as dramatic at night as in the daytime. Three lights positioned in the top pool caught the underside of the fountain bowl; the bowl itself required only one light placed within it to illuminate the single jet of water. At night, uplit, the heraldic griffins – those two stone flights of fancy – finally triumphed, the brooding ventilator and harsh brick wall retreating into darkness.

even if it had been possible to do away with maintenance altogether, I would not have wanted a garden I could not work in. What a garden has to offer – peace, fresh air, beauty – can only be fully experienced by working and living in it. Therefore I designed the garden so that the pot plants had to be watered by hand, the lemon trees needed occasional training, the hedges had to be periodically clipped and the whole garden fed regularly: just enough work to occupy my spare moments and prevent me from tinkering with elements of the design.

Like every owner, once the garden was finished I felt tempted to add just a few more things, even though I would never dream of doing this in a garden I had designed for a client. But there must always come a time when the garden itself is complete, and any addition – another statue, a birdbath or an impulse buy at a nursery – can only mar the clarity of the original design.

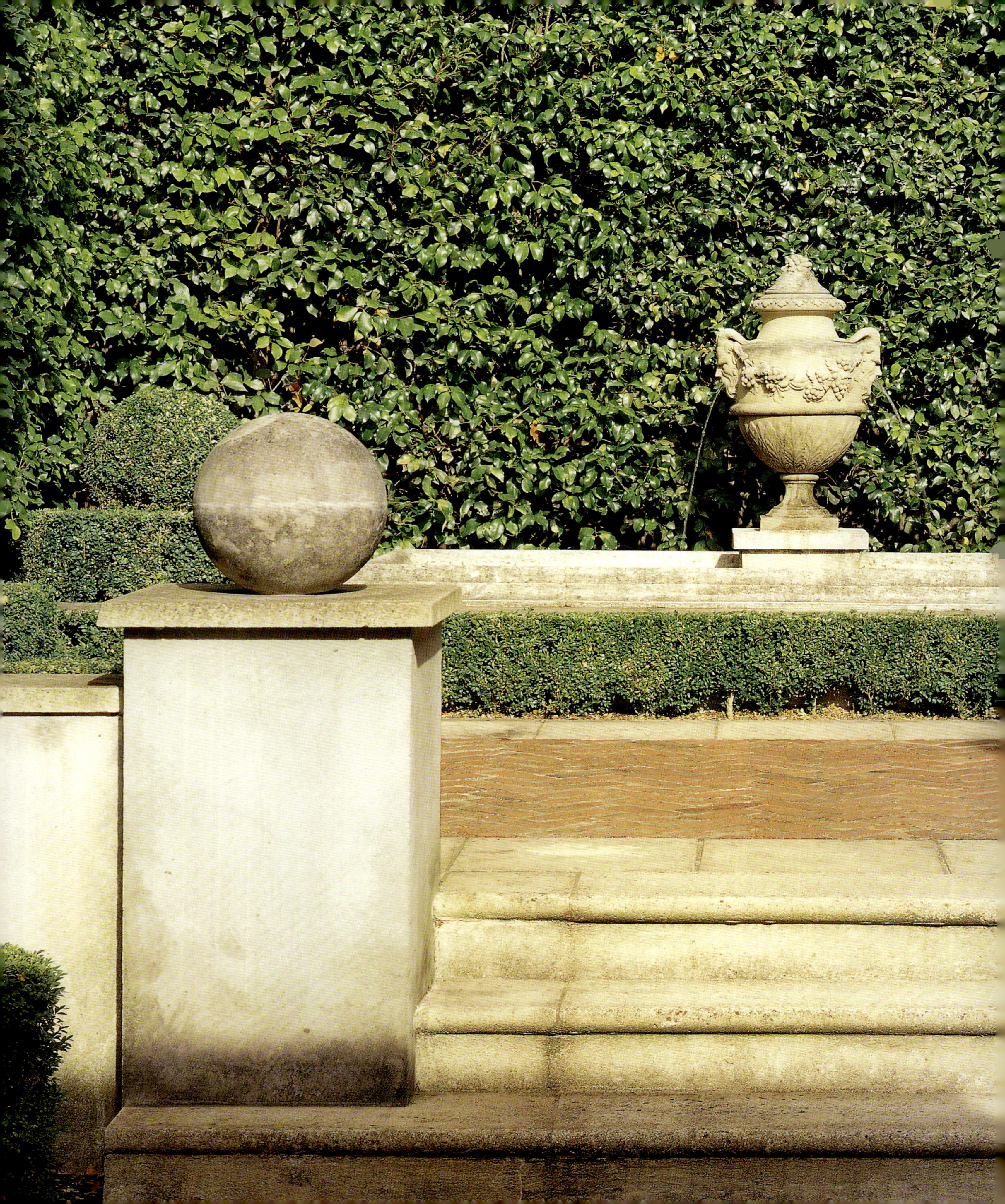

Fundamentals

*A garden is like a house: just as the interior
cannot be furnished before the building of the house
is finished, so the plants and ornaments cannot be added
until the structure of the garden is complete. Yet often
garden builders in their enthusiasm to see plants
growing, or one part of the garden looking good,
plunge in before they have laid the foundations and
erected the framework for the whole. Levels, steps, paving,
walls: these are the fundamentals – the architecture – of
the garden. Their construction is costly and the results
are permanent or difficult to change, so developing a
ground plan is crucial before any work is begun.
The better you plan, anticipating problems before
they occur rather than solving them afterwards, the
fewer the setbacks you will experience once
construction has begun.*

A sloping site meant this garden had to be divided into several sections (right). Circular steps softened the retaining walls' brickwork, but required space – contributed by both the upper and lower terraces. This was a garden where it was appropriate to tie the horizontal surfaces, of for example a seating bay (left), as well as the vertical, to both the brickwork and detail of the house.

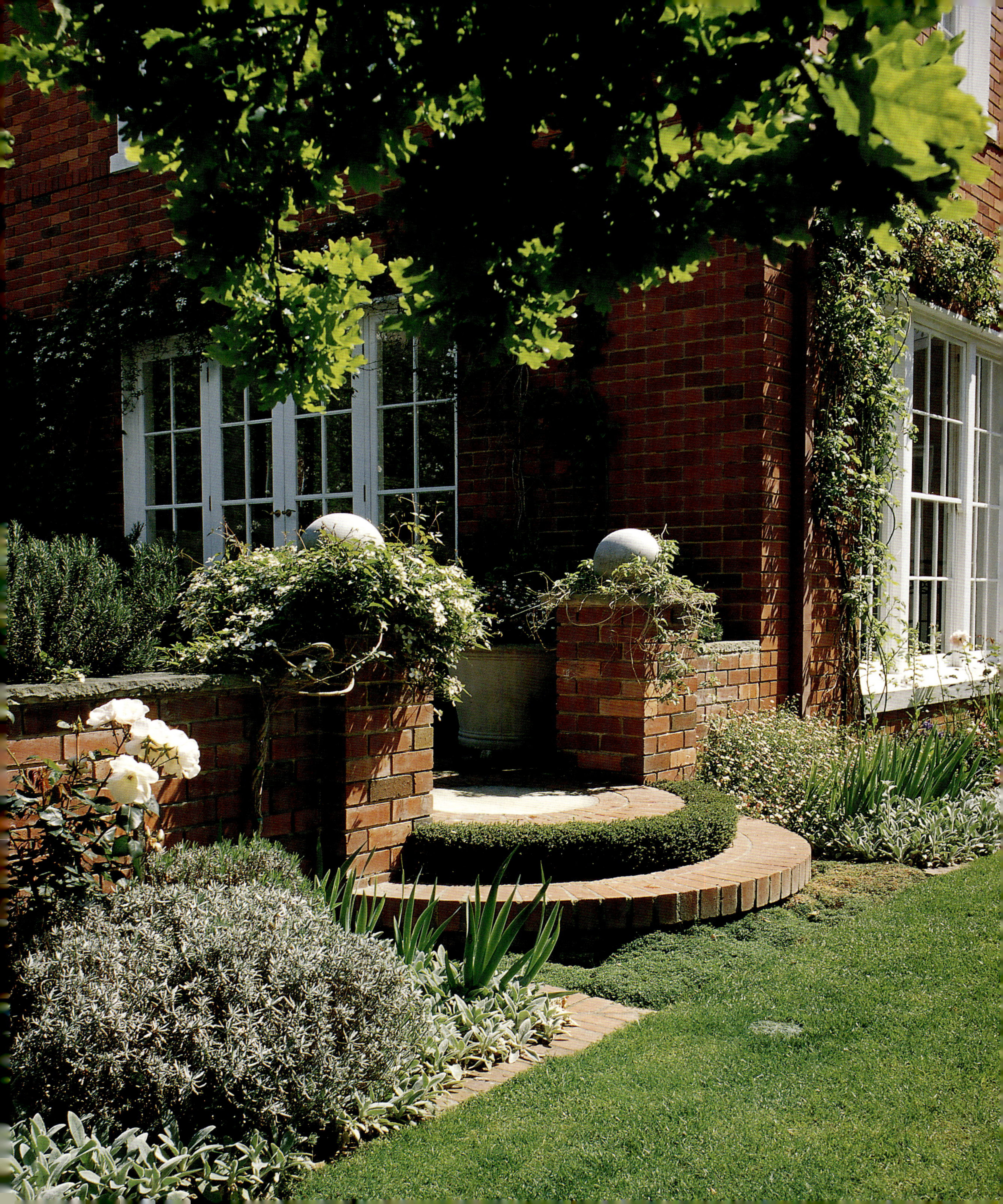

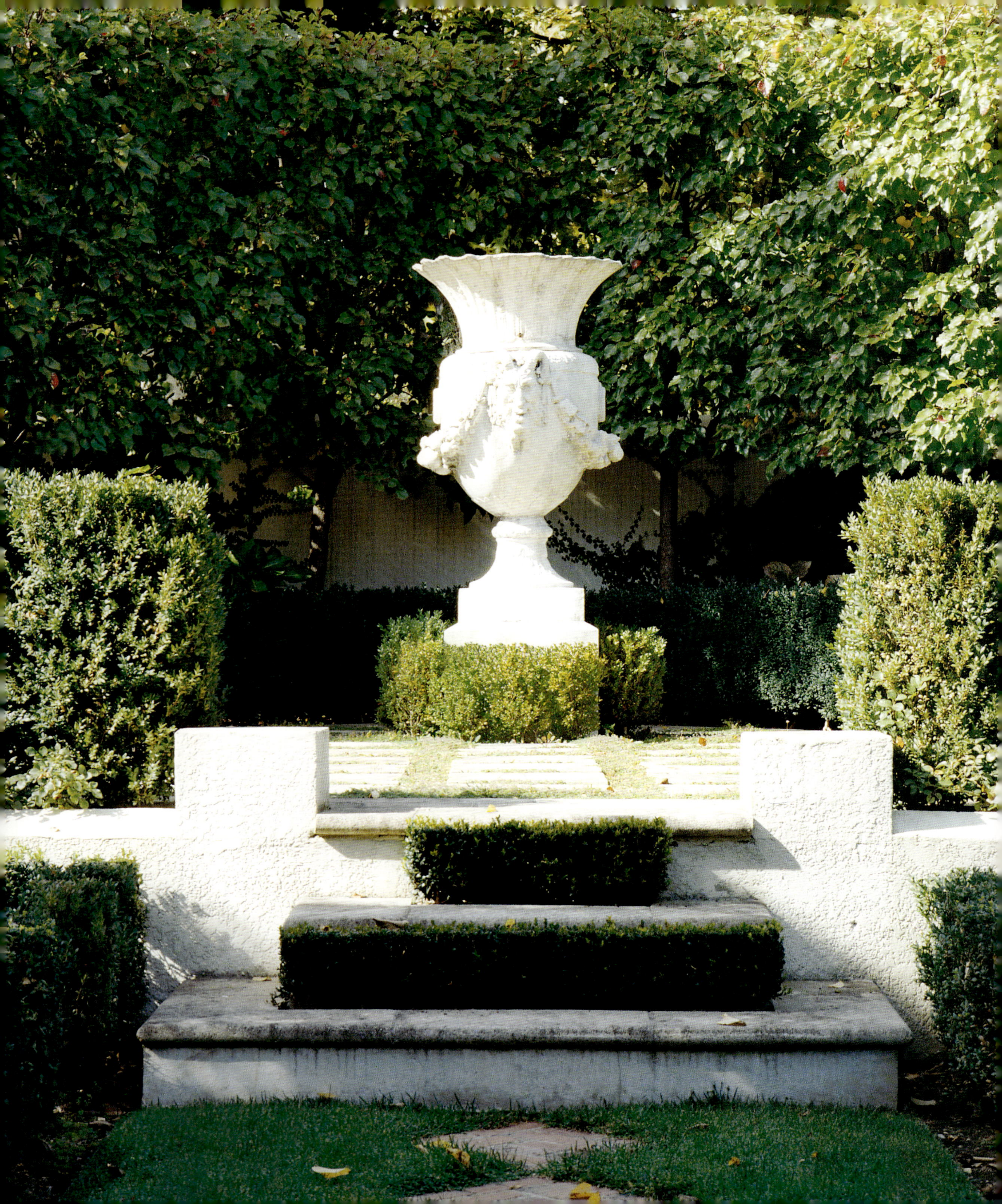

LEVELS AND RETAINING WALLS

A change in level, by suggesting that a garden is large enough to have two or more separate areas, creates a sense of space. Since creating an illusion of space is all-important in a small garden, I often introduce a change of level if one does not exist naturally. An artificial level is achieved by building essentially a box, with retaining walls as sides, which is then filled with screenings and topsoil.

Gardens are rarely entirely level, and even a slight slope can be exploited to advantage. This is particularly the case with a small garden, where no change of level should be great. A steep rise or descent between two small areas would make the garden seem precipitous, and there is insufficient room in a small garden for a long flight of steps. To roughly gauge the change of level your garden can take, sit on the lower level and assess whether you will be able to look across the upper level to the focal point when the upper level is completed. (This also automatically ensures that the prospect will be the same from the ground-floor windows, given that the house lies at a greater distance from the upper level.) Divide your rough estimate of the rise between levels by 175 millimetres – the ideal height for risers – to establish the number of steps you can have, slightly adjusting your rough estimate as need be.

When I am choosing the building material for a retaining wall, I like to take my cue from the house: I nearly always use the material employed in its construction (although if plants are to cover the wall entirely, I am happy to use a cheaper material such as sleepers). A red-brick house dictates a red-brick retaining wall; a rendered-brick house, a rendered-brick retaining wall in the same colour. In this way the retaining wall looks like an extension of the house's architecture – and the garden looks as if it has been designed at the same time as the house even when it has not. I prefer not to use the same material as that employed on the horizontal plane of the house and garden, although there are a number of small gardens in which the paving, too, has to be matched to the house, as discussed below. Where possible, I like to emphasise the complexity of the three-dimensional space by making a clear distinction between the horizontal and the vertical surfaces.

A level, three steps up from the rest of this garden, was introduced to display the main feature, a substantial reproduction French urn (opposite). 'Layered' hedges of English box (Buxus sempervirens), made possible by the level change, part on either side, like stage curtains, to reveal the urn. Since steps automatically carry the eye forward, they should be aligned with the chosen feature: here, to further fix attention on the drama of the urn, I made the steps very narrow. In a complex interplay, the different box hedges mimic the sharp lines of the steps and piers – and vice versa.

Retaining walls should usually not be made a major feature of the garden; it is the change of level itself that is important. Certainly in an austere design retaining walls, like hard surfaces, become a dominant characteristic; however, in a small garden a muted change between upper and lower levels, created by growing a bed of plants in front of the retaining walls, is often more appropriate. The retaining walls become an inconspicuous backdrop to the plant life. Even a low planting at the base of a retaining wall, though it does not obscure the whole wall, blurs the hard juncture of wall and paving. And what is true for the base is true for the top. In many cases planting on the upper level, rather than paving, is needed to soften the severity of the wall — a lawn, for example, can seem to float delightfully on the top of a retaining wall.

Retaining walls are closely regulated by local councils, so you need to find out from your council what its building regulations are and whether you need a permit before beginning construction. Councils have become increasingly concerned about the safety of walls, particularly those on street boundaries, which could collapse on passers-by. Council regulations relate to matters such as the material, reinforcement and depth of the foundation, the number and nature of the uprights supporting a wall, and the provision of drainage.

The foundation is the most important part of a retaining wall. How deep and strong it needs to be depends on the size and weight of the wall it is to support and on the amount of pressure the soil behind the wall will exert. A brick or stone retaining wall needs to sit on a concrete foundation or slab. Only a wall constructed from sleepers or timber does not require a foundation: the lengths of wood are simply bolted closely together. If your retaining wall is to be over a metre high, you will probably need to have an engineer assess the project and provide drawings and specifications for your council to approve and your builder to follow.

Every retaining wall should have drainage. Water built up behind a wall both adds pressure and erodes the building material. An agricultural drain installed behind the structure, at its base, and running the full length will carry away any water that collects in the soil retained by a wall. Weep holes placed at regular intervals, near the base, will ensure that any water that seeps into the wall escapes.

This front garden was originally flat. A semicircle was excavated to create a sunken garden and give the house presence. The retaining wall matches the masonry; the sandstone steps, the front entrance. These semicircular steps repeat the graceful line of the sunken garden, but equally importantly lend a welcoming expansiveness to the rather formal front entrance. Gravel further softens the approach to the front door (although visitors have to be careful not to carry it into the house).

A lawn or garden bed that is retained by a wall needs to have effective drainage. A lawn requires a herringbone system of agricultural pipes; a garden bed, a circuit of agricultural pipes. The depth at which the drainage is laid depends on what is to be planted: the pipes will need to be about a metre below the surface if trees are planned, because of their extensive root system; 300–400 millimetres below if small plants are to fill the area; and only about 200 millimetres below if a lawn is to be sown.

Hard and Soft Surfaces

The smaller a garden, the more important it is to have an attractive, functional surface covering in the most used parts. A small garden is often viewed as another room of the house and is used more intensely than a larger garden. The one confined space that comprises the garden is going to be employed for dining, parties and sitting on. The traffic on it will be heavy, so the choice between a soft surface such as gravel or lawn and a hard surface such as pavers or bricks needs careful consideration.

Gravel is generally not an option for a much-used area adjacent to the house: loose stones need to be kept at a sufficient distance to ensure they are not transported inside – not always possible, when the garden is small. However, larger, heavier pebbles, over 30 millimetres in diameter, are less likely to be carried indoors than the fine gravels, so may be more suitable for heavy-traffic areas next to the house.

Apart from the high maintenance a lawn requires, it wears out quickly in a small space no matter how tough the grass chosen. And if children or pets are to use the garden, making the whole area a lawn is usually not advisable. In many cases, children will want to ride their bikes around or use their skateboards, so a hard surface will be necessary. For all these reasons, full paving may be more practical and attractive. A central paved area with lawn restricted to a less used part of the garden is another solution – though there is a point beyond which a pocket of lawn ceases to be a lawn and becomes merely a token gesture that weakens the design.

Every garden, large or small, should have a terrace adjacent to the house for outdoor living. Not only should the area be close to the house for convenience, it should also suggest a natural progression from the interior to the exterior. As a consequence, the surface material chosen needs to be in keeping with the flooring used in the interior. If the floors are timber, timber decking will relate well to the interior; if the floors are paved in stone or artificial-stone pavers, the same type of material will look effective outside. If there is dark wall-to-wall carpet inside, a dark material may look good outside; if the flooring is straw-coloured, a correspondingly light-coloured material may work best. However, it is often not possible or appropriate to take the cue from the floors; for example, small children playing outside may stain a pale surface material. In such cases matching the outside horizontal surface to the house itself may allow you to still achieve unity of house and garden. If the house walls are rendered, consider paving materials in a sympathetic colour. When the house is constructed of red brick, the same bricks used as paving will make the garden look as if it belongs. Stone or artificial-stone pavers or timber decking makes a suitable surface adjacent to a weatherboard house.

Paving patterns give visual messages. I usually lay bricks side-on over a concrete slab, particularly for a tight, strongly directional pattern, such as herringbone (top left). When I want a path to take on some of the irregularity of age, I lay them on a base of crushed rock, and face-up (top right) if a ground cover, such as Nierembergia repens, *is to be planted between them. Sections of inset black pebbles (middle left) alternating with pavers produce a bold chequerboard pattern; a subtler variant is small diamonds of pebbles inserted at every corner where the pavers meet (middle right). Similar pavers set diagonally in loose washed river pebbles make a soft-toned yet eye-directing path (bottom left). A more informal path can be achieved by growing a ground cover, such as* Ajuga reptans, *between stepping stones (bottom right).*

By ensuring that the horizontal surface appears to flow from inside to out without the distraction of abrupt change, you in effect increase the space of both the room inside and the terrace beyond. Only rarely does a dramatic contrast between internal and external surfaces work aesthetically, particularly when the garden is small, because it creates too jarring a visual division between house and garden. However, an unbroken expanse can be rather dull. A border or pattern set within the paving, perhaps formed by bricks that match the house, adds strength while avoiding a glaring contrast. The subtle textural variation between gravel and pavers is also pleasing. Some materials, however, do not combine well: the difference between slate and terracotta, for instance, is just too great; and stone and timber usually do not work happily together, either. Nor do similar materials complement each other if their colours are different: cream-brick paving can look ugly with a red-brick house.

The introduction of detail also makes paving look more complex, and hence larger. A herringbone pattern or a diamond design can actually be used to visually stretch the paved area. Similarly a border elongates a rectangle of paving. Small tricks like these make a garden seem deeper or wider than it is — but the detail must be kept simple, because over-complexity confuses the sight-lines and has the opposite effect to the one intended. Both the unity and the variation that a garden needs can often be achieved simultaneously by having the paving detail reflect the shape of another feature in the garden or house. This is a most effective way of linking a garden to its house when it is made later than the house. It may be that the house has arched windows, or the garden is going to use round pots prominently, so a circle becomes the motif; or the chimneys of the house

A mosaic gives a paved area great vitality. Marble chips have been used here because they fit together closely so are ideal for a pattern that requires precision. They are often cheaper than other materials such as imported pebbles. When two colours are used, the darker one is normally used for the pattern and the lighter one for its background.

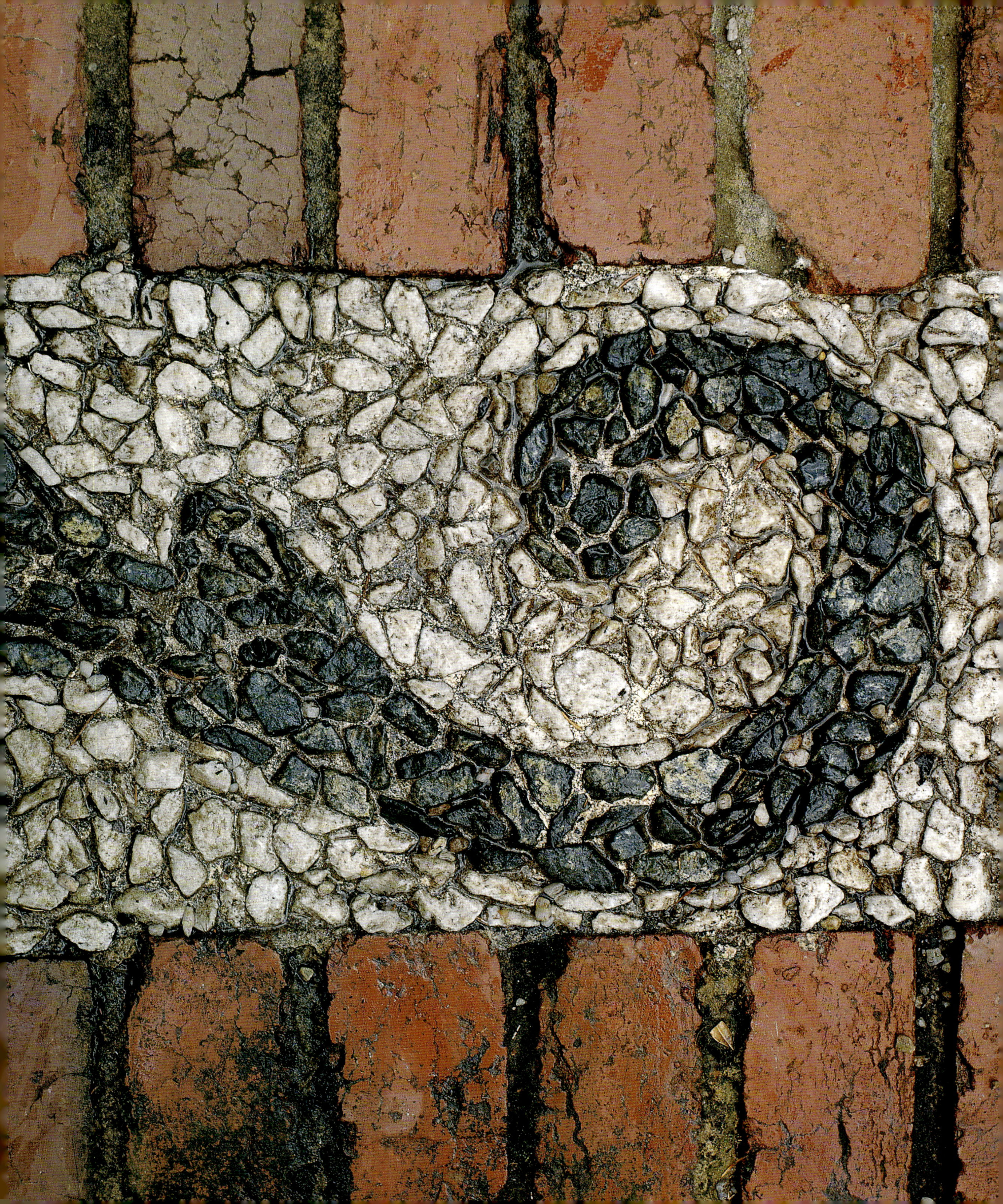

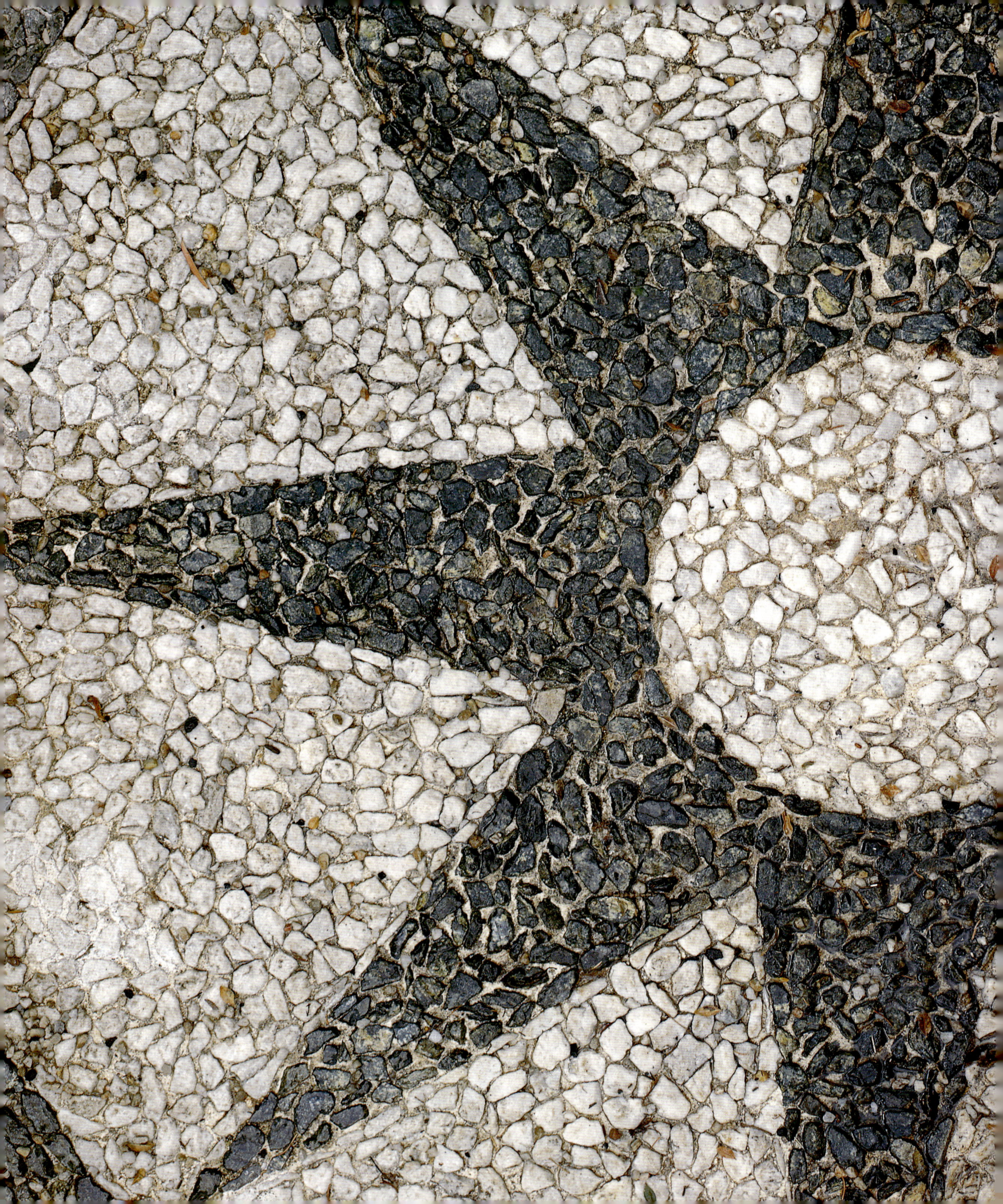

Mosaics are laid on concrete: in this instance, to create a vibrant section of paving set within gravel (opposite). Every marble chip in the star and the background had to be laid by hand, but only took a morning. Artificial-stone pavers (above) were laid in a solid sheet on a terrace, then star shapes cut out with an electric grinder. The difference between the stars and the pavers is a subtle, textural one: the stars were inlaid with pebbles in tones close to the colour of the pavers to achieve a pearly glow.

may have an interesting detail, or the walls a brick pattern, that can be replicated in the paving.

Design detail in the paving can be employed to lead the eye towards the focus of the garden. It can also be used to establish a second sight-line; for example, in a garden where the main axis extends from the house to the centre of the far wall, a paving pattern set parallel to the house creates a secondary axis that suggests the garden has breadth as well as depth. In the same way a line of paving stones laid in a soft surface such as lawn or gravel can be used to direct the eye towards a statue or fountain.

Although bricks and pavers can be laid on a bed of crushed rock, I prefer to lay them on a slab, particularly in a small garden where the traffic will be heavy. The slab should be 100-millimetre-thick, steel-reinforced concrete, and slope slightly away from the house to a drainage line on its far side. As the slab is the basis for the paving, the more even its surface is, the more even the paving will be.

Pipes for watering systems, lighting and so forth should be laid before the concrete is poured. Again this highlights the need to draw up a garden plan that includes all plumbing and electricity requirements, at the start of the project — and the need to keep the plan for future reference. Often I include a 100-millimetre conduit beneath the hard surfaces and retaining walls so that I have the flexibility to run smaller pipes to any part of the garden at a later stage.

Paving does not need to be given an edging where it meets a soft surface such as lawn, earth or gravel. In contrast, two abutting soft surfaces do require a timber edging: usually 15-millimetre-thick jarrah is employed. The edging, positioned flush with the ground, is invisible but provides an effective barrier between the two surfaces.

Steps

I make all risers of steps 175 millimetres in height because that is the change I have found most comfortable for people moving from one step to the next. There are local council regulations concerning steps: usually the variation allowed for risers is 150–175 millimetres, and the minimum depth for the tread is 300 millimetres. For aesthetic reasons, if you decide to have very broad steps, you should make the treads a little deeper; and if you make the treads a little deeper, you should make the risers a little shallower. When the garden area is limited, you can create an illusion of greater space by recessing the steps in the retaining wall, rather than building them out from the wall.

I frequently use steps to accentuate a sight-line because the eye automatically travels up or down a set of steps. In a small garden this generally means placing the steps in the centre. Both the risers and the treads of steps, particularly in a small garden, usually look best constructed in the paving material chosen for the rest of the garden. Rarely would I add steps that contrasted with the paving material, or give a contrasting edge to the treads, because steps should seem tranquil, not over-busy. People ascending or descending want to feel absolutely certain about where to place their feet and confident that they will not trip on something unexpected. And steps should look as if they are a transition, not a focus in themselves.

The sharp lines of steps can be confronting; therefore I often like to camouflage the base of the risers with a low row of hardy plants such as *Lonicera nitida*, so that viewers see alternating horizontal bands of hard paving and soft green. In this case the measurement of the risers remains 175 millimetres, but a width of 50 millimetres for the planting strip is added to the 300 millimetres allowed for the width of the treads. If there is not sufficient space for a narrow strip, plant creeping fig (*Ficus pumila*) or English ivy (*Hedera helix*) at the side of the steps and train strands across the risers, keeping these hard clipped as you would a tiny hedge of lonicera — any greenery introduced needs to be severely restrained so that people feel they can step over it easily without their feet becoming entangled.

WALLS, FENCES AND GATES

Privacy becomes a prime consideration when gardens are small; most people do not want neighbouring houses or apartments looking into their back gardens, or passers-by staring into their front rooms. High boundary walls or fences would seem to be the solution, except for one problem: they can be overpowering and make a small garden look even smaller than it is. The trick therefore is to make the walls or fences seem to disappear, or to merge with plantings beyond the boundary lines, so that the garden actually looks larger. This can be achieved by using dark materials or paint when the walls or fences are built, and by planting in front of them. Black and dark green are colours that recede and become indistinguishable from foliage at a distance.

Sometimes, however, walls and fences are made a feature even when the garden is small. Walls are often a prominent part of a severely architectural design that restricts vegetation to a limited number of rigorously clipped plants, for example. And, perversely, although it would seem

The main part of the garden featured in the next chapter gives onto a narrow driveway. There was no room in which to plant an attractive hedge along the boundary line, so the fence itself had to become the screen — though of necessity a light and decorative one, since it had also to be a backdrop to the garden. A series of trellis arches, their verticality both emphasised and softened by climbers, provided a graceful barrier that also relieved the boredom of the long driveway. Rather than have the garden give lamely onto the driveway, I introduced a fence and double gates that make visitors pause to take in the view, yet are sufficiently low and open not to box in the driveway oppressively.

common sense that the smaller the garden, the lower its walls should be, gardens do not always work that way: high walls can give a small courtyard an intimacy that becomes more important than a sense of space. However, dominant walls (with the exception of trellis screens) should be constructed from the same building material as that of the house, because anything different will make the walls too distracting.

Local councils have strict regulations concerning the height and construction of boundary walls and fences. The standard height for a rear wall is 2 metres, which is generally as high as most people want to go. Climbers can be grown along horizontal wires on top of walls and fences if extra height is desired. There are no regulations about what trees can be planted on boundaries, so I often use pleached hedging; that is, a row of light trees pruned so that their trunks are branchless

The owners of the garden featured in the chapter on 'Water' commissioned a number of beautiful wrought-iron gates from a designer when they renovated their house. I was happy to include the gates in the garden design because they were exactly the kind that small gardens need: open in pattern so that tantalising vistas are glimpsed, not obscured, and no area of the garden feels completely confined. One gate, set between high brick walls, provided an entry from the paved driveway to the grassy front courtyard (below left). It allowed the garden, though enclosed, to have an extended view across the driveway to pencil pines (Cupressus sempervirens 'Stricta') and euphorbias; and visitors, who must enter the property from the driveway, to catch sight of a fountain at the far end of the garden itself. A second gate was set at the entry to a side walkway leading from the front to the rear courtyard (opposite). It helped to create a tiny additional garden of Hydrangea quercifolia.

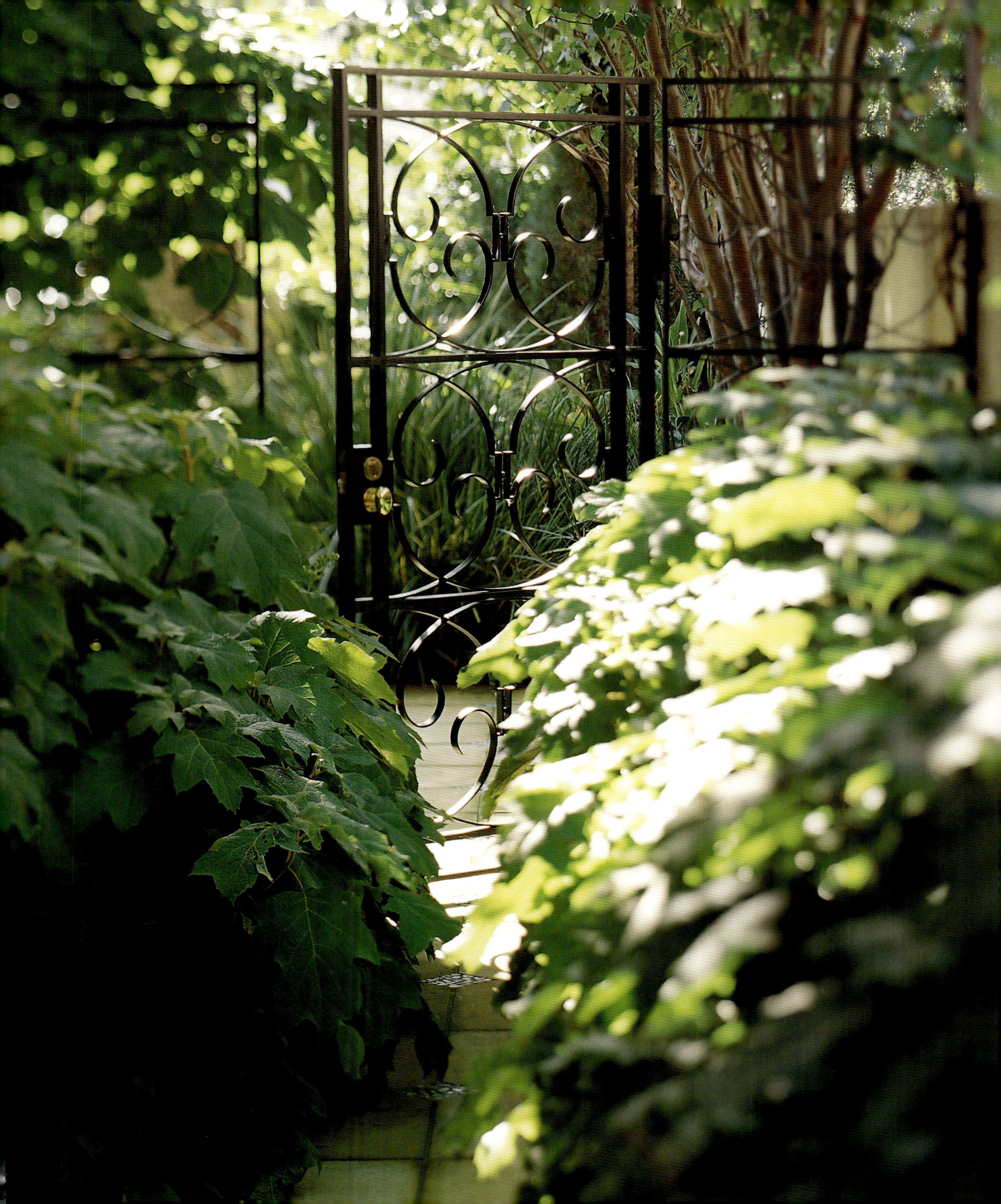

to a certain height. The canopy blocks out the building next door, while the trunks take up little space in the garden below. Solid hedges planted along a boundary also give extra height (and disguise an ugly fence), but they take up more space at garden level than a row of pleached trees.

Some local councils permit owners to add a trellis to the top of a boundary wall or fence, but always check local regulations before you increase the height in this way. I prefer a full-length trellis on a free-standing frame to one attached to the fence because the weight of any climbers grown on it can be considerable. A trellis screen also looks better than a band of trellis added to a fence or wall of a different material. A trellis can be a simple support for a covering climber or an elaborate feature in its own right, depending on the style of the garden. A plain trellis, painted a dark colour so that it recedes into the background, suits a simple garden such as one in the Mediterranean style, or an informal garden perhaps built around Australian native plants. An intricate trellis is particularly suited to an elegant, finely detailed garden reminiscent of a Parisian courtyard, as I discuss in the next chapter.

Panels of trellis are readily available commercially and are much less expensive than custom-made trellises. They come in different patterns, so basic ones may be alternated with more decorative ones. The open woodwork of a trellis necessitates a respectable backdrop. If the fence that will be behind the trellis is unsightly, the trellis can be attached to cement sheeting, painted two shades darker than the trellis itself so that it recedes into the background. Cement sheeting can be attached to a sturdy frame, or to existing paling fences or sheds provided these are in good condition: since the support will have to take the weight of the trellis and perhaps some climbers, as well as that of the cement sheeting, it must be strong. Whether the trellis is attached to an existing wall or fence or to cement sheeting, a gap of approximately 10 millimetres should be left between the two surfaces so that the trellis stands out. Before a high trellis screen or a cement-sheeting frame is erected on a boundary adjoining a street or public space, council regulations need to be checked and permission gained if appropriate. The neighbour's approval must always be sought before a trellis screen or cement-sheeting frame is built on the dividing line between two properties if it is to be higher than a standard fence.

One of the gates hung in the low fence delineating the driveway and garden shown on p. 45: for the design of the timberwork, I copied the detail and dimensions of the balustrade surrounding the cupola on the roof. The result was a lower than usual (about 600 mm high) fence and gate that created a sense of enclosure in the garden without presenting a visual barrier — most important in a small area.

Fences and walls — and pleached or solid hedges — can be used to create divisions within a garden as well as to enclose it. Although high, solid walls or hedges that effectively divide an area into 'rooms' are only for large gardens, in small gardens walls or hedges that allow glimpses over them or through breaks or arches in them can suggest that another, more extensive part lies beyond.

Gates opening into the garden from the street can either be treated as a focal point or disguised within the wall or fence. The gate may be aligned with a fountain or ornament or with the main windows or doors of the house to create an axis. A special wrought-iron or wooden gate set in a handsome brick wall also beckons viewers with a promise of intriguing things beyond. For that reason a fake gate (or arch) added to a wall or fence can suggest that there is more to the garden than meets the eye. On the other hand, a gate of the same colour or material as the wall or fence becomes almost indistinguishable from it, and the eye is free to rest on other features in the garden; similarly a gate painted dark green will merge with a hedge. In this way you can also create a secret gate, one which visitors only discover when they explore the garden. However, often you have little choice about where you site an entry — for practical reasons it may need to be adjacent to a driveway or the kitchen door — so its position may preclude your making it a focus of the garden.

The construction work in a garden can certainly be done by a skilled amateur with the time to do so. Quite often I devise a ground plan for people who want to implement it themselves. However, unless you are very experienced and certain that the end result will be sound and attractive, it may be better to have professional help with the major tasks such as excavation, laying the slab and building walls. Fences and walls, steps and surfaces are the most enduring — and the most exposed — elements of a garden, so the hours and money spent on careful planning and construction will be repaid by a garden that is a pleasure to look at and to be in, at all times.

A Paved Garden in the Grand Manner

In this garden narrow steps lead the eye from the first paved terrace to a second, which gives onto a third where a large urn spills water into an imposing ornamental pool. The second terrace is partly obscured by wing walls; on the third the pool seems to float on a sea of clipped box. High, unbroken green walls of hedge disappear into the distance. At night, light dances on the dark surface of the pool and shadows flicker across the urn. The formality of the paved terraces and steps, the rows of hedges, the long vista — all suggest the grand garden of a mansion in the European manner.

The reality is somewhat different, for this is a small — 12 metres by 6 metres — garden set behind a red-brick Federation townhouse, and the grandeur a deception of the eye. The owners were people whose occupation required them often to work long hours outside the normal business day so they wanted a low-maintenance garden, with strong, restrained lines, yet a garden also that they could frequently entertain in. The solution seemed to be to design a garden that depended on the beauty and strength of hard surfaces and on changes of level for its effect.

Because the existing garden was quite scrappy, I could completely clear the whole block and start anew. The land had a natural fall of about 800 millimetres from the back boundary to the rear of the house, which I utilised to the full by introducing three levels, the first, nearest the house, occupying roughly half the space and the other two about two-thirds and a third of the remaining half. The rendered brick and the coping of the retaining walls were matched to details of the Federation house.

Although the largest terrace was designed to be the main entertainment area, the second terrace was also envisaged as a place where

Only one sight-line was possible in this very small garden: from the house to the centre of the back boundary. The focus became a reproduction English lidded urn — converted to a fountain — as I indicated by elevating the urn on a small terrace of its own before a plain but vivid backcloth of lillypilly (Acmena smithii).

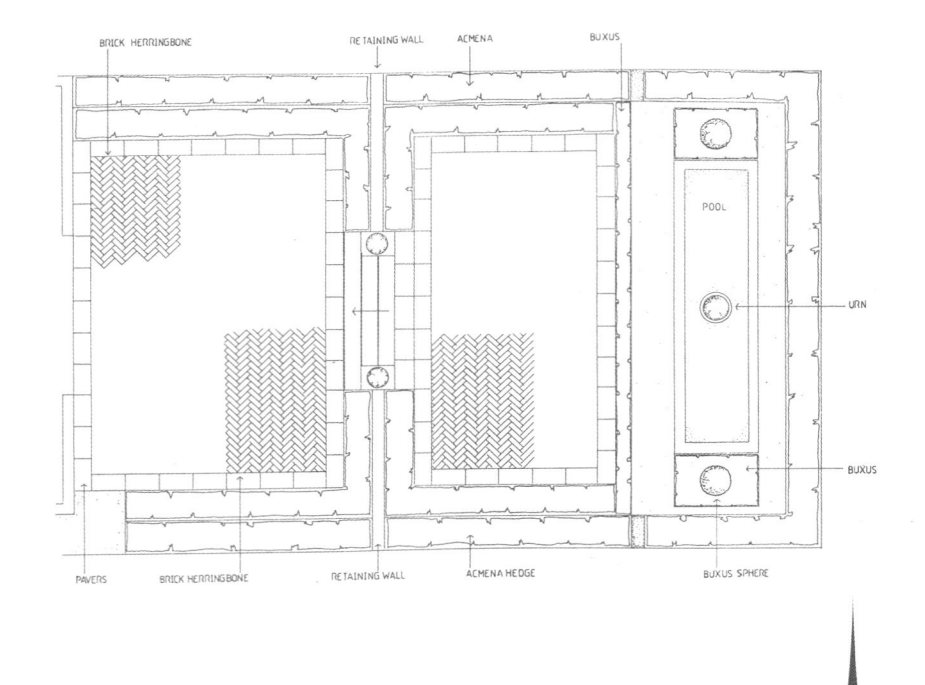

As this early sketch (not to scale) shows, I decided from the start that the only approach with such a limited area was to boldly divide it into three levels ascending from the house, helped by the natural east-to-west slope of the site down to the house. Such an approach could only succeed if the design was kept severely restrained and dependent primarily on its hard landscape for effect — which was very much in accordance with the owners' desire for a courtyard for parties. To this end, not only the first and largest terrace, adjacent to the house, but the second one also was designed to be wholly paved. The third terrace was little more than a dais for the fountain and the pool, but its importance to the design, and the imposing proportions of the pool, could be relied on to suggest a greater change in level had occurred.

people could sit or stand, so both needed to be entirely paved. I knew that, as a consequence, they could easily become dull mirror images of each other. It became imperative therefore to add a little mystery. Accordingly, I restricted the view from the first level to the second somewhat by increasing the height of the retaining walls to about a metre to create low wing walls on the second terrace. The steps between these two levels were kept deliberately narrow to further entice visitors to explore hidden parts of the upper garden.

The narrow steps were also intended to tightly frame the focus of the garden, the fountain. To exploit the full length of the short garden, I had decided that the fountain must be placed at the very back of the property. It was vital therefore to ensure that the fountain did not lose impact because of its distance. I overcame the problem by, firstly, giving its ornamental pool a level of its own; secondly, raising the pool itself; and thirdly, elevating the urn that formed the fountain on a square plinth. The third level was actually only a podium, one step higher than the second level, but because I designed a rather monumental pool to fill it, and

The open mouths of the two fauns and the effort expressed in their furrowed brows made this an appropriate urn to convert to a fountain.

effectively cut it off from the second terrace by planting an unbroken hedge of English box (*Buxus sempervirens*) in front of it, the podium is easily read as another terrace. The hedge is kept to only about 200 millimetres in height, allowing the pool to rise above it so that, from the house and the first terrace, its elegant moulded lip looks like a retaining wall. Given its importance to the design, the water feature needed to be of the finest quality. The vessel chosen for the fountain was a copy of an English stone urn, which I had converted.

Once the levels were designed, I gave considerable thought to the paving, because in a garden that has few plants the hard surfaces are all-important — and very exposed to the critical eye. This was one garden where it seemed appropriate to match the horizontal surfaces as well as the vertical ones to the walls of the house. Consequently, red-brick paving was bordered by artificial-stone pavers that, like the retaining walls, matched the colour of the house's rendered sections. However, the bricks were laid in a herringbone pattern, instead of repeating the brickwork of the house. The herringbone pattern was chosen because of its restrained, traditional nature, and because it did not confuse the eye, but rather 'stretched' the paving and worked in conjunction with the steps to carry the eye towards the fountain. The bricks were laid on their side, not flat as is often the case: this is the way they are meant to be used; the way they are always laid when a house is built. The pale border was made the width of a single paver, 500 millimetres.

Planting was severely restricted to just two kinds: lillypilly (*Acmena smithii*) and the English box. Lillypilly, grown to a height of about 3 metres, was used for the hedges that completely enclosed the garden and screened neighbouring sheds. The use of one, all-enveloping plant makes the boundaries indeterminable, so that any sense of where they start or finish is lost: the tall, shadowy hedge in the background might be just the wall of yet another compartment in the garden.

Within the walls of lillypilly, hedges of English box, grown to a height of about 500 millimetres, define the sides of each terrace, like a plush trim. The wings of English box that flank the pool give the fountain further presence. Topiary balls rest on each, their luxuriance suggesting space where there is little. Cement spheres placed on top of the piers on either side of

The tiny garden depends on several elements for its impact: level changes; a central feature of quality; and excellence of hard surfaces. The three level changes (left) add complexity without confusion in a severely constrained space and visually lengthen the perspective, while the sections of herringbone brickwork persuade the eye that the terraces have breadth. The urn chosen for the fountain (below left) was sufficiently fine to need only a long, restrained pool and low hedges of English box (Buxus sempervirens) to display it. The retaining walls were constructed of rendered brick, to match the rendered parts of the house, with the artificial-stone pavers used on the terraces employed for the steps and the capping of the retaining walls and piers (below right).

the steps echo the shape of the topiary balls. Spheres are an excellent choice of ornamentation in a garden intended to be classical in effect but lacking the space for any elaboration of the style. The different spheres, confined to their separate realms of hard masonry and soft greenery, make a strong statement in a garden of such restraint.

The garden was meant to be viewed from two points: the terraces where entertaining takes place and, even more importantly, the interior of the house. Since the back of the house contains both the kitchen and a large informal living area, the owners spent much of their time at home there. Concertina-doors along the length of the house open directly onto the first terrace, allowing parties to spill easily into the garden. The garden was subtly lit, so that looking into it from the house at night is like gazing into a serene, ordered world specially arranged to revive the spirits of people who spend many hours at work.

ORNAMENTATION

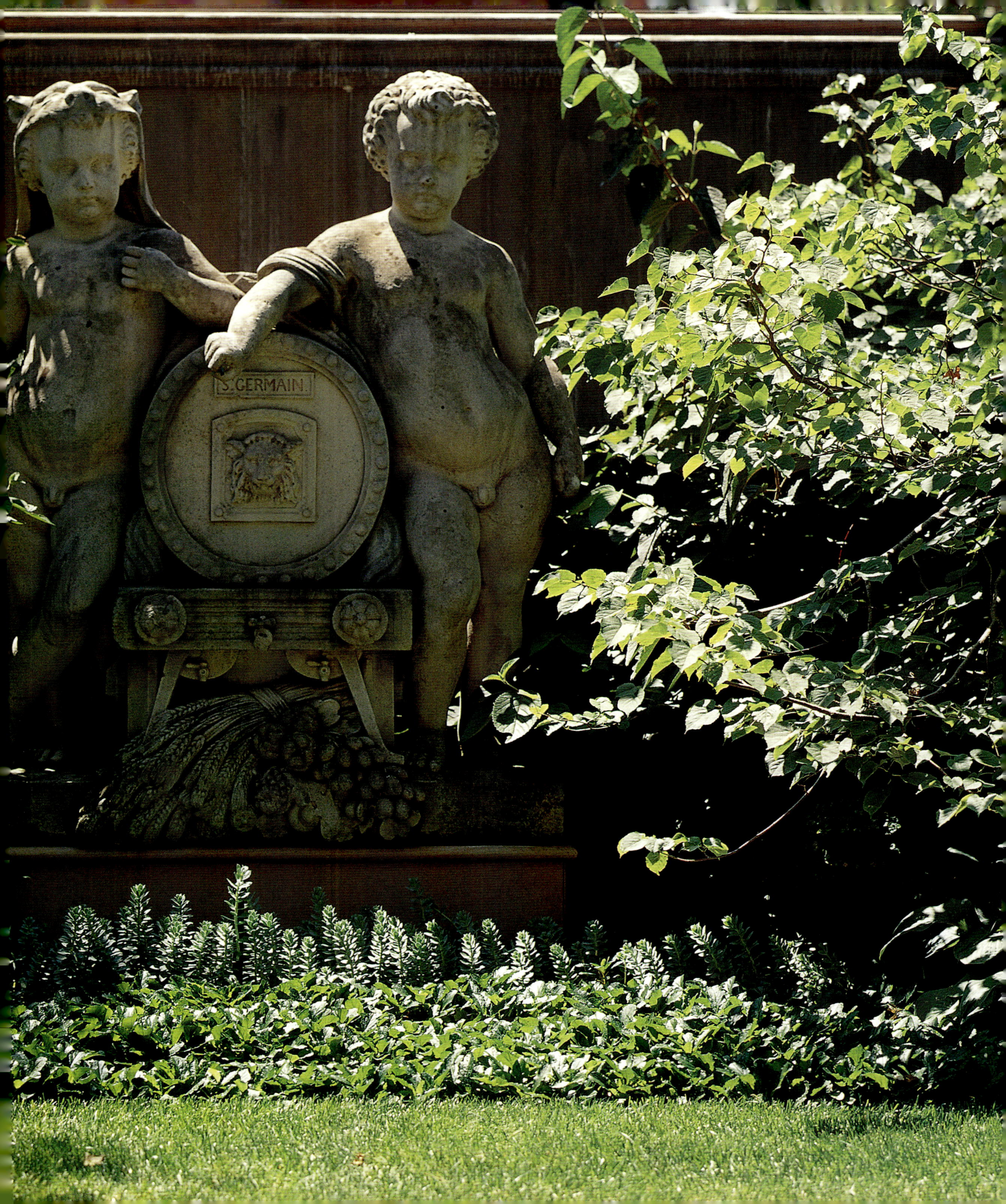
S. GERMAIN

We have gardens because we want to replicate a little of the beauty and change we find so exhilarating in the natural landscape — we want our eye to be able to wander around a miniature landscape of our own, stimulated by its variation and its highlights. A crucial means to achieving such variation and highlights in the garden is the establishment of focal points. Focal points help the eye to read the garden; they signal the axes along which the eye needs to travel to discover the garden. In effect, they create movement in the garden. A specimen plant or a group of plants is an obvious choice of feature for a setting intrinsically devoted to plants. Yet ornaments in a garden are perhaps an even more effective focus, for to the beauty of living things they add the art of finely made objects.

For me, water in a fountain or pool is the most ornamental feature of all, but before I discuss water in the next chapter, I want to talk about how to choose and place any ornament, whether it is a fountain or a statue or a found object. It is easy to fall in love with a number of ornaments and want to have every one in the garden, but restraint is vital, particularly in a limited space. A small garden cannot offer many vistas. Usually only a major axis and a secondary one are possible, in which case only three ornaments may be needed to focus the eye: the most prominent one at the end of the major sight-line, and a lesser one at either end of the secondary sight-line. It is much better to perfectly place a few special ornaments than to dot the garden with a confusing number of objects.

An ornament placed at one end of this side garden creates a vista (opposite). A lidded cement urn was elevated on a matching plinth, but kept just below eye level to make the perspective seem longer. A path of rectangular cement pavers set in loose gravel, and bordered on either side by the lacecap flowers of Hydrangea macrophylla *'Blue Wave', carries the eye to the urn.*

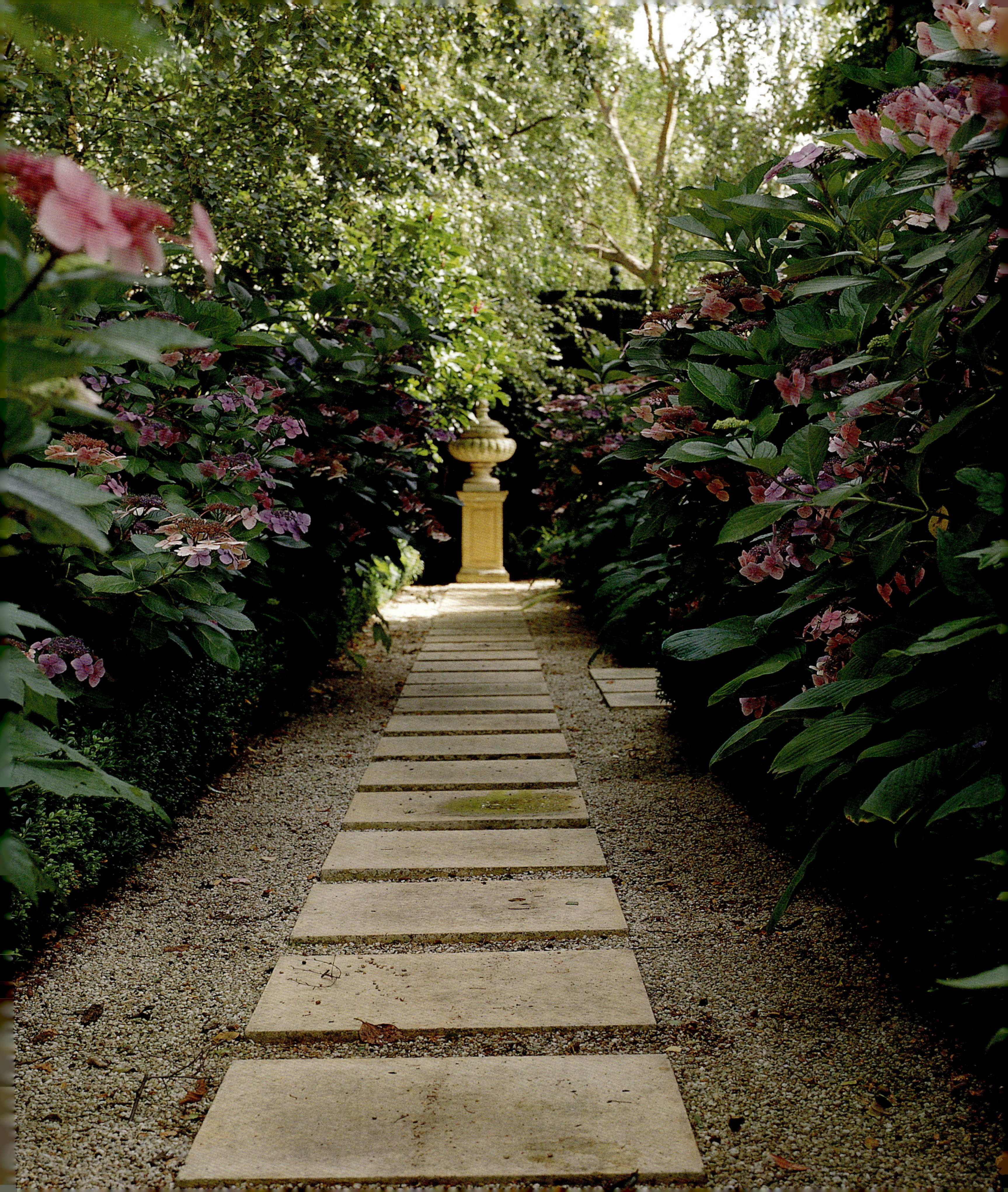

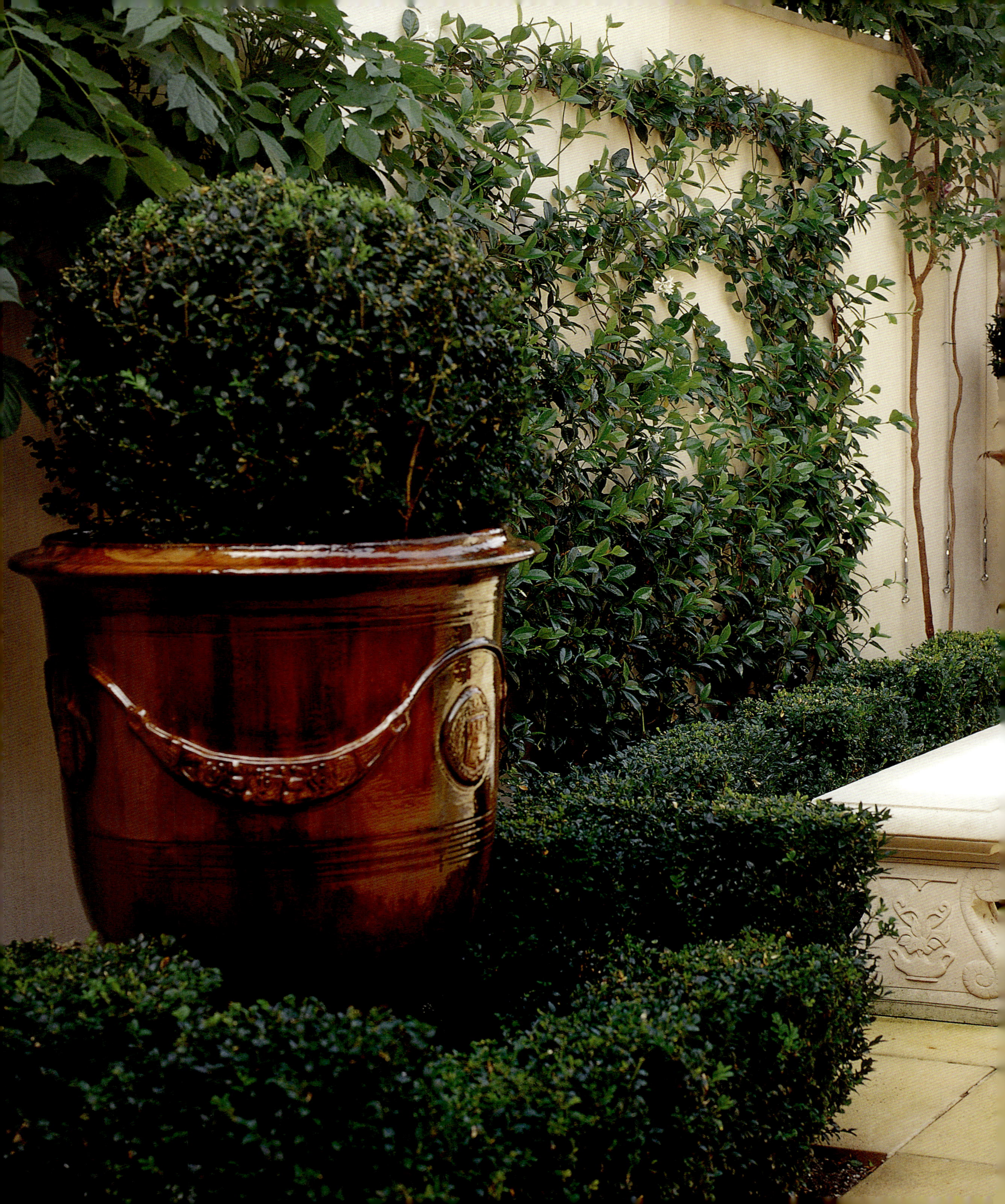

All the living areas of the house looked into this broad courtyard so I arranged the design around a tableau, composed of two French Anduze vases on either side of a reproduction bench, rather than a single feature. The three objects are linked by a low hedge of clipped English box (Buxus sempervirens) that winds around them, and framed by panels of star jasmine (Trachelospermum jasminoides) trained on wires and a line of Wisteria sinensis along the top of the wall. Domes of box give the vases both height and further solidity. To ensure the vases did not appear too earthbound, I placed them above ground level so that they seem to float on the box.

The secret to choosing ornamentation that enhances rather than detracts from its surroundings is to match it to the style of the house and the garden. Simple architecture requires simple ornamentation; avant-garde architecture, avant-garde sculpture; architecture in the European tradition, neo-classical adornment. And all ornaments that are a focus need to be finely executed: you will soon become bored or irritated with an inferior piece. Ornaments, too, must be large enough to be seen from the house or an important part of the garden. Choosing the right-sized ornament for the space is another key to a garden's success.

Where you want the eye to look is where you place an ornament. If you want people to look down rather than up because there is a particularly ugly view beyond the boundary, place your ornament at a low level. If you want people's eyes to travel upwards, as I did in my garden to take advantage of the vertical plane, elevate your ornament. Remember, though, that a feature by definition is highly exposed: it always needs a good backdrop. There is no point in putting an outstanding sculpture against a paling fence. This does not mean, however, that you must necessarily erect a costly brick wall: a climber grown over the paling fence or a tall hedge planted in front of it may make an equally fitting background for the sculpture. Nor does the backdrop have to be an introduced one: the sky, trees beyond the garden, the chimneys on a neighbouring house or the spires of a church in the distance can be borrowed.

The view to a featured ornament must be unimpeded; however, this is not to say that nothing must be placed in front of the object. Creating the setting for an ornament can be like layering: the object is placed prominently against its backdrop, then lower plants are grown in front of it, and paving extended out from the plants so that the view to the feature takes on a new depth.

Urns

Garden urns are essentially a traditional form of ornamentation. Often incorporating the styles and motifs of earlier periods, they were used extensively and mass-produced during the Victorian and into the Edwardian era. Consequently these urns, and earlier, Georgian ones, either in their original form or reproduced, look particularly appropriate in the gardens of houses built in the architectural style of those periods. There have been twentieth-century styles of garden urns, so you may discover one from the 1950s or 1960s to match a post-World-War-Two house, but finding an urn to suit contemporary architecture is trickier: a simple vase is best.

Garden urns should never sit on the ground. Traditionally, they were designed to sit on top of an architectural feature such as a gate pillar or their own plinth. It is important that an urn and plinth belong together: apart from being made in the same style, colour and material as the urn, the plinth needs to be in proportion. Most reproduction urns today come with their own plinth.

Many urns traditionally were designed without lids so that they could hold plants; however, I tend to use urns with lids, as ornaments rather than containers for plants. Any plant grown in an urn needs to be particularly hardy and able to do without much water because urns are often placed in inaccessible or easily overlooked spots. This is probably why people in the Victorian era so often planted cactus and other succulents in them.

Another consideration when choosing between lidded and unlidded urns is whether the urn is to be a major feature or a more muted element. If the latter, a graceful trailing plant may suggest that the urn

When I was asked to demonstrate what could be done with small city spaces for Sydney's 1997 Splendiflora exhibition, I designed a rooftop garden around an elevated, 2m tall, reproduction nineteenth-century French urn framed by very high partitions (opposite). The vertical movement and monumentality achieved by overscaling key components in a severely restrained design makes a space appear larger. A small story was invented by filling a Victorian cast-iron urn with stems of Magnolia grandiflora and Euphorbia wulfenii and setting it on a French nineteenth-century table beside an old watering-can (below) — one idea for a rooftop or balcony garden.

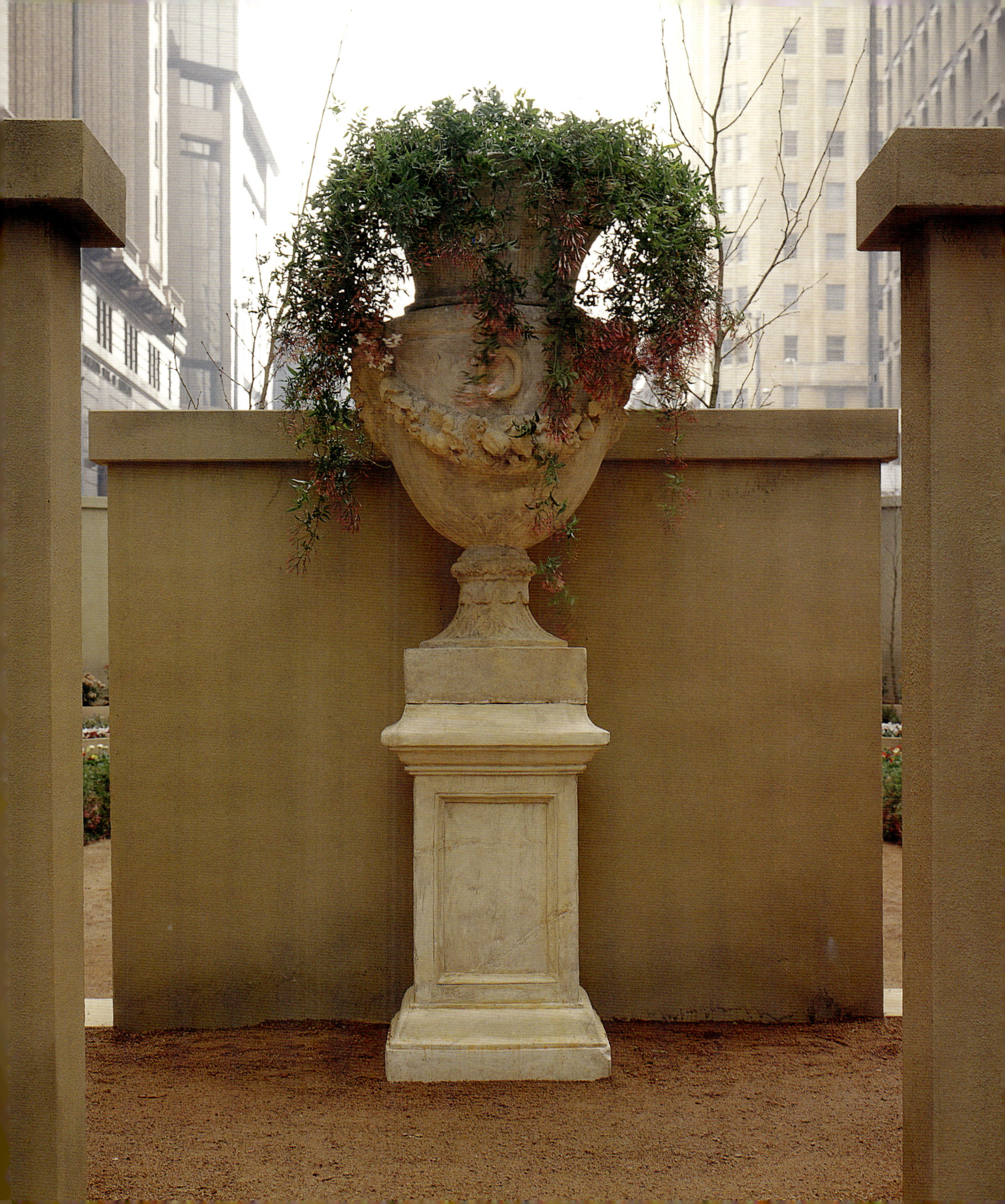

has been in the garden so long that it has become part of it. If you want the urn to be a stronger focal point or its effect to be more masculine, add a clipped plant. However, no plant in an urn should be so large or attention-seeking that it overshadows its receptacle. It is there only to enhance the urn. A plant grown to about a third of the urn's height achieves the right balance.

I tend to plant around the base of a plinth. Traditionally, urns on plinths often nestled into garden beds, and they can look awkward standing on a hard surface. Urns rising above *Erigeron karvinskianus*, an ivy (*Hedera*) or clipped hedges of English box (*Buxus sempervirens*) are a delightful spectacle. The plants soften the hardness of the base and link the feature to the larger garden.

Urns on plinths need a firm, level base. All soil moves, so any heavy object placed directly on it will eventually fall over. A permanent solution is to pour a small concrete slab. Alternatively, you can level the area, then add a solid paver.

Statues

Statues, unlike urns, do not necessarily have to stand on a plinth. A statue, after all, is like a human being. Just as it seems natural to find a person walking around the garden, so it seems natural to find a statue standing on the ground. However, neo-classical statues, being based on a style of sculpture that represented the ideal rather than the real, often look right somewhat elevated above human life. Whether raised on a plinth or placed at ground level, statues can stand alone on a hard or soft surface, without necessarily needing to rise from a bed or edging of plants. Statues — and modern sculptures, also — often look particularly good placed on lawn or gravel.

Choosing a free-standing figure is a very personal matter. I often go hunting for statues with clients, and they always know what they like and do not like. Some people will not like a particular face, or will want a female figure not a male one, or vice versa. I myself don't like anything too cherubic: I like my statues a little more realistic, a little stronger — even a little grotesque — because it makes them more interesting. It is very much a matter of individual taste, and it is important to have what you like. After all, as I have said, having a statue in the garden is like having a real person in the garden all day long, so before you acquire it you must feel

Before acquiring a statue, make sure it is suitable for the position it is intended for. The statue above has a definite front and back, so it would be well placed, on a low plinth, in front of a wall. The statue on the right is meant to be viewed from all sides and would sit well, on a higher plinth, in the centre of a garden. A plinth (or a slab) prevents ground moisture from eroding the stone of fine originals.

sure you will not grow tired of its expression or pose. I also tend to choose oversized statues: there is nothing worse than a small figure lost in a garden. I don't think you can ever have too large a figure, no matter how small the garden.

A free-standing figure will always be a dominant feature in a small garden; therefore no matter how attractive your planting scheme and hard surfaces are, an inferior statue will mar the total effect of the garden. Consequently, if you do decide to have a statue, you will need to accept that the decision entails buying a well-executed piece, which will not be inexpensive. A badly cast or sculpted figure is easily recognisable: it will look crudely made and lack facial detail. This does not necessarily mean that you have to acquire antique garden statuary, which is horrifically expensive, because luckily good reproductions are being made. These certainly cost more than inferior ones but are not as expensive as antiques. The advertisements in garden magazines are an excellent source of information when you are seeking reproductions — or unusual sculptures — and good antique shops often sell fine reproductions.

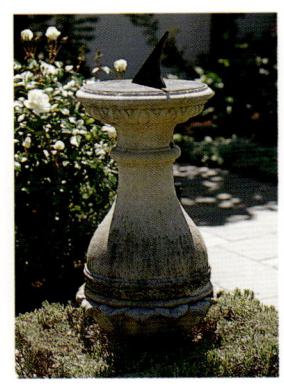

I created a recess, in effect, for a Georgian bust (above left) in a neo-classical fountain-back I designed for the fountain shown on p. 89: since eighteenth-century busts were elevated, in niches or on pedestals, this seemed an appropriate position. A sundial, another appropriate ornament for a small garden, must be placed in full sunlight if it is to fulfil its function (above right). This reproduction nineteenth-century English one is easily read: a fringe of clipped French lavender (Lavandula dentata) at its base does not prevent people approaching from any side.

BUSTS AND NICHES

Niches in garden walls have long been used to display busts, urns or half-urns. Consequently, they are always recessed at eye level. Because they use the vertical plane, they offer an ideal means of ornamentation in gardens that are hard-pressed for space. However, think carefully about the style of your garden before you introduce niches into the architecture, for they automatically impart a classical look. They are well suited to houses and gardens in the formal style of old English,

French or Italian manors, but not so well suited to contemporary architecture. Your design also has to be one that can accommodate substantial walls in parts of your garden where the niches can be properly viewed. Since niches catch the eye, their walls must be suitably handsome, and they themselves need to be finished with a decorative moulding: ideally one that repeats a detail of the house.

Niches give depth to walls, but they are in fact only shallow recesses; it is their ornamentation that creates the illusion. Further depth is created when the back of the recess is given a decorative surface such as lattice-work, a patterned render, or even a mirror. The decoration should be kept quite simple so that it remains a background to the bust or urn in the forefront.

Sundials

Sundials are appropriate to any style of house and garden, traditional or contemporary, formal or informal, and can be designed specially to match a house and garden. Free-standing and wall-mounted sundials are usually light and graceful, and therefore admirably suited to a small garden. However, certain conditions should prevail when you are installing a sundial. Firstly, it has to be made specifically for your area because small variations in the path of the sun affect the telling of time. Secondly, the sundial must receive full sun throughout the day if people are to tell the time by it, as they should be able to – it jars to see a functional object placed so that it cannot fulfil its role. And, thirdly, it needs to be placed so that the user is able to draw near to it. A free-standing sundial is ideally set in an area of lawn, paving or gravel; its base can be softened with a ground cover or a few plants, but the user must be able to get close to it to tell the time.

A free-standing sundial is often the central feature of a garden. It looks particularly good set at the centre of a circular garden of grass or paving surrounded by flower beds. However, as long as there is sufficient space for it to receive day-long sunlight and be viewed from all sides, a free-standing sundial can also be placed in a side section of the garden.

Obelisks

There are three types of obelisks – timber ones, metal ones and stone ones – and they are used in quite different gardens. Timber and metal obelisks are hollow, can be seen through and, at their simplest, can be constructed by any gardener. They are often used to display an especially lovely climber or to introduce climbers into a garden that has no other suitable place, and as a consequence they are placed in garden beds. A timber obelisk can be as simple as three bamboo poles tied together, around which sweet peas, clematis or jasmine twine, or as elaborate as a highly worked construction on which to show off a rose.

Because they are surrounded by plants, wooden obelisks that are used to bear climbers introduce a softer, often more informal, element into a garden. Stone obelisks, in contrast, sit on a surface such as paving or gravel. They – and also the most finely fashioned wooden ones – are important enough to stand on their own, and require space around them to be seen to effect. They are only suited to the classical-style houses with which they have been traditionally associated. You certainly would not want to put one with a timber house; the house needs to be made of stone, brick or rendered brick.

All obelisks, whether functional or not, are inherently decorative when placed properly, because they add a distinctive geometric shape to the garden. The clean, tapering lines of these needles make them a light, uncomplicated ornament particularly suited to small gardens. By carrying the eye upwards to a disappearing point, they introduce a strongly vertical movement that counteracts the flatness of many small spaces.

This small garden was designed around two beds of roses. By giving each an obelisk, the garden simultaneously gained two structures, in full sun, that allowed climbing roses to be grown – and two ornamental features that took up little horizontal space. A rose arbour, although appropriate to the style of the garden, would have been too large to incorporate gracefully within the limited area. The open white timberwork of the obelisks is in keeping with two wooden seats placed on either side of the path that separates the beds, and the iron lacework of the verandah.

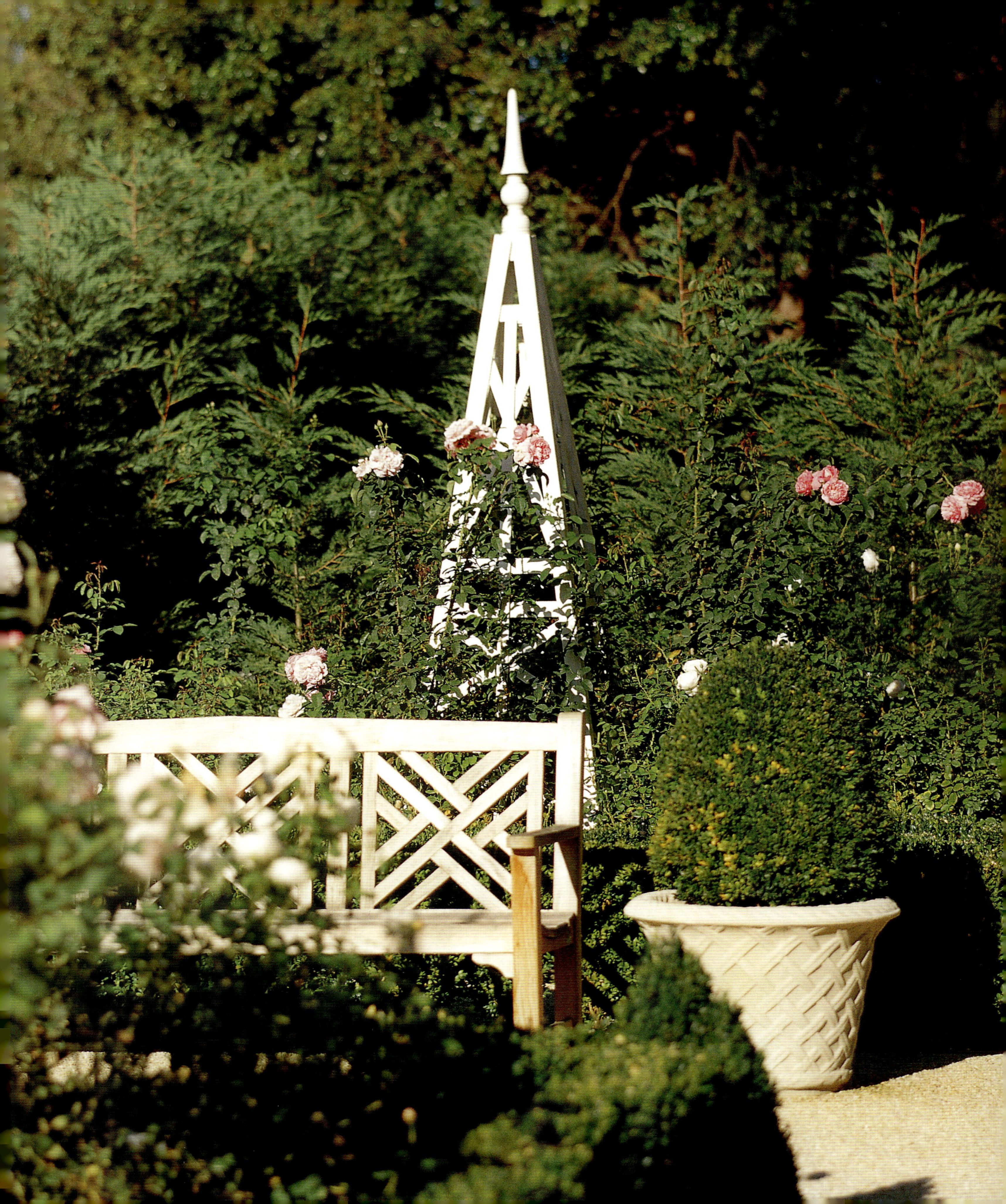

Pots for Plants

Pots are the opposite of urns. Pots are made to sit on the ground and to show off plants. Plants in pots are grown to add greenery to gardens that lack planting space or to parts of gardens not designed for planting. For instance, groups of pots spilling over with plants soften the severity of a terrace in a way that an urn on a plinth could not. I like a plant to occupy about two-thirds of the total height of pot and plant.

Plants in pots give a small garden great flexibility. Where you might be reluctant to dig up plants in a garden bed and rearrange or replace them, you can happily move pot plants around or change them. Pots can contain annuals, replaced two or three times a year so that there are flowers constantly in bloom, or topiary plants offering visual relief from the hard architecture of a garden year round. They can be arranged symmetrically or informally, according to the plants grown in them and the style of the house and garden. Pots lined up in a row on a terrace, or

Artificial-stone pots, and the spheres of English box in them, were chosen to echo the shape of a porch (below left). An evergreen cone of star jasmine (below right) can be achieved by training the climber up the centre of an iron frame inserted in a large, round pot. The stems of star jasmine are pulled through the frame and kept clipped. The circumference of the pot at its top provides the measurement for the frame's height.

placed on either side of steps, suit clipped English box or *Lonicera nitida* and a formal setting. Pots of flowering plants such as daisies, hostas or hydrangeas enhance a less formal arrangement and a more relaxed setting.

The number of pots you use depends on the effect you wish to achieve. People who are passionate about plants, or live in an apartment, often fill their terrace or balcony with a myriad plants in pots and the result is quite wonderful. And in Spain and Italy and Greece geraniums in pots cascade down every window sill and stairway. On the other hand, pots of topiary may need to be restricted to one placed at either end of the terrace or balcony for their form to be seen to advantage: any more might overwhelm the space. Before you decide on the number of pots, consider how you want to use the area to which you are going to add them: if it is a terrace on which you wish to dine, don't add so many pots that not enough space is left to fit a table and chairs.

Pots of plants are ideal positioned so that they emphasise major features of the house and garden: a doorway; the top or foot of a flight of stairs, or the steps themselves; the end of a terrace or a walk. However, they need to harmonise with those features. Their colour should never dominate or clash with the surface they are placed on. They should always be secondary to their surroundings: terracotta pots should not be set on slate; light-coloured pots should be chosen for light-coloured paving; dark pots for dark paving.

Decorative Trellises

Sometimes in a small garden there is not sufficient space to display a sculpture or some other large ornament to proper effect, yet the garden looks as if it lacks adornment. In these instances decorative trellis-work can be the solution, particularly if the area is a courtyard and the house a two-storey one like those found in the old parts of Paris. Trellises were used by the French to make courtyards look bigger than they were.

Trellises take up less space than three-dimensional objects and are less confronting. Both the design of a trellis and the patterns of its woodwork can create a *trompe l'oeil*: repeated shallow arches, for instance, create a false perspective and confuse the eye so that viewers find it hard to guess how far away the wall really is. Overscaling a screen, using panels of trellis 150 millimetres by 150 millimetres, also suggests that a garden is larger than it is, where an equally large but solid wall would suggest the opposite. The paint chosen for a trellis, too, can be used to help achieve the desired effect. Deep green makes a trellis recede; a lighter colour brings it forward, in those rarer instances when it is required to be a dominant feature.

Like any other form of ornamentation, trellises need a good backdrop: if an ugly paling fence is likely to be visible through the trellis-work, a cement-sheet backing may be necessary, as discussed in the previous chapter. Nor should decorative panels that are a major form of ornamentation in the garden be heavily covered with plants.

It is possible for many objects to become an ornament in a garden so long as they are appropriate to the style and design of the garden, in proportion to the space available and properly placed. Something as simple as a row of old watering cans can be decorative. However, it is probably better to avoid kitsch — unless you are a master at arranging quirky objects interestingly — and popular pieces that you and your visitors may grow tired of. Whatever you choose, make sure that it has been designed specifically to go outdoors: apart from the fact that they may weather badly, objects that are meant to be displayed inside somehow always look out of place in a garden.

Finally, remember that it is all too easy to go overboard with ornamentation. So often after the garden is finished, you think you will just stick in a sundial that has taken your fancy, but the result always undermines the unity of the design. Subjugating the detail of a garden to the good of the larger plan is one of the most important disciplines of design.

This courtyard was more like a sideway than a garden, so creating visual space and exploiting the vertical surfaces became the main aims. A decorative panel of trellis and an artificial-stone ball-fineal urn were employed to create a false perspective. The urn draws the eye to itself and hence to what appears to be an archway behind. From a distance, the urn seems to float in an indeterminate space because it has been placed on a green trellis-covered stand, not a matching plinth. Overarching 'boughs' of wisteria complete the deception.

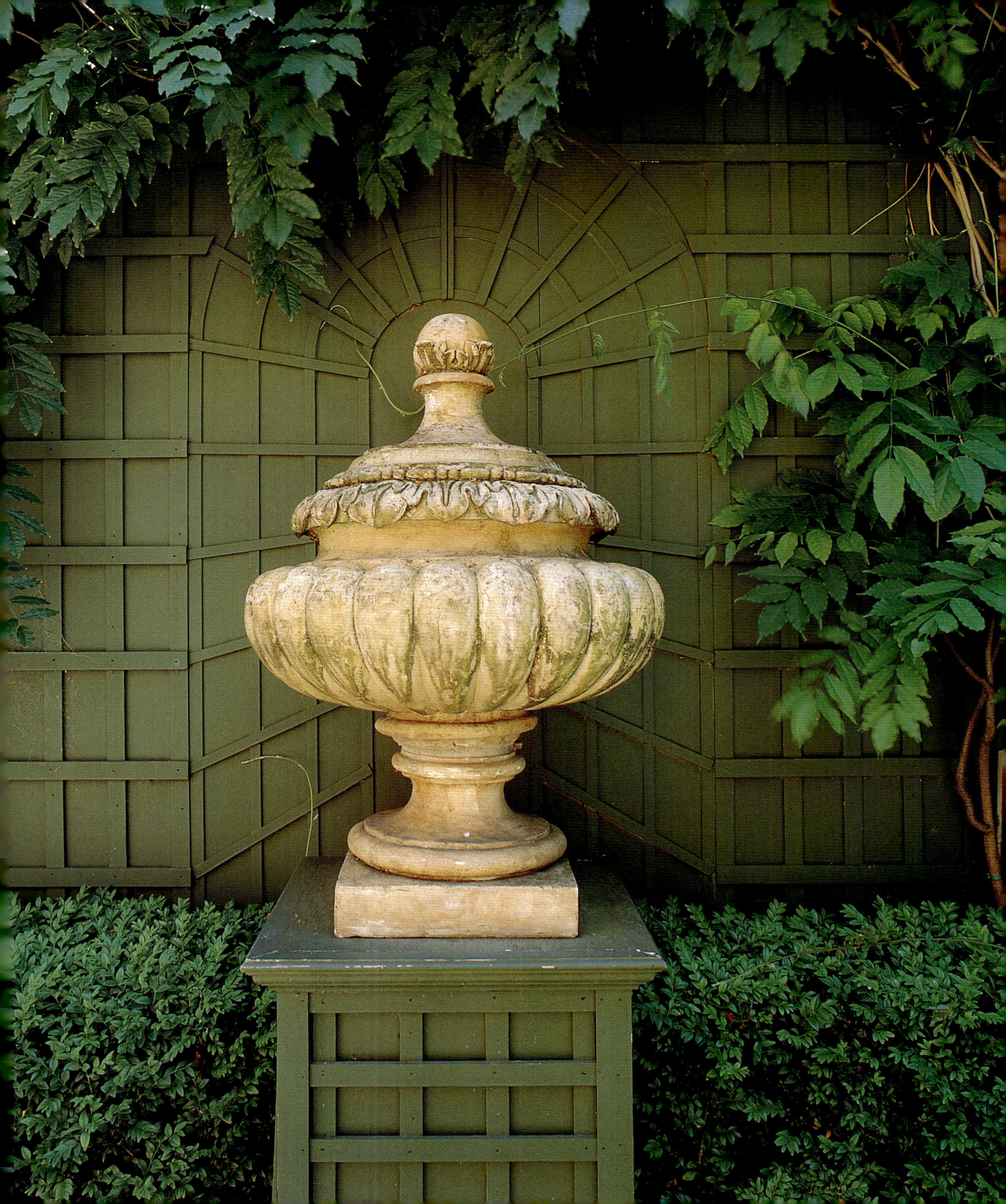

A Garden for Favourite Ornaments

The owners of this garden fell in love with two sandstone sculptures that had originally adorned façades in the St Germain area of Paris. They determined to buy them and make them the centrepieces of the garden they were planning for their new townhouse. As well as the French sculptures, the owners brought with them to the new home a few much-loved pieces from their previous one. Around these ornaments I designed the garden. Usually the process is the opposite: as a design evolves, a certain kind of ornamentation suggests itself. However, when works of art or very special outdoor ornaments are to be placed in a garden, it is appropriate to design the garden so that it displays them to full advantage.

The owners' new townhouse occupied much of the block; nevertheless, they wanted the illusion of a large garden. For that reason they asked me to design a somewhat wild, somewhat overgrown informal garden. The space on either side of the house was narrow: only sufficient on one side for a long driveway, and on the other for a strip of garden. The main garden, measuring 18 metres by 7.5 metres, lay at the front of the house and was entered from the driveway, as was the house. The owners knew they wanted the two French sculptures placed so that they became the central views from the main living rooms: the sitting room, which looked onto the front garden, and the dining room, which opened onto the narrow side garden.

The front boundary of the property was marked with a low rendered-brick retaining wall, on top of which I planted *Viburnum odoratissimum*, kept clipped, and *Trachelospermum asiaticum*. A metre behind this, another, much higher, rendered-brick wall was added, about 2.5 metres in height, to hide the street from the garden and to act as the backdrop to one of the French sculptures. The work was quite large

A detail of the French sculpture that is the main decoration of the front garden: the smiling lion's head adorns a plaque displayed by two putti, which reads 'St Germain'. The sculpture, like a second one placed in a narrow side garden, originally decorated a façade in the St Germain area of Paris. Both are unusual, finely executed sculptures well worth designing two gardens around.

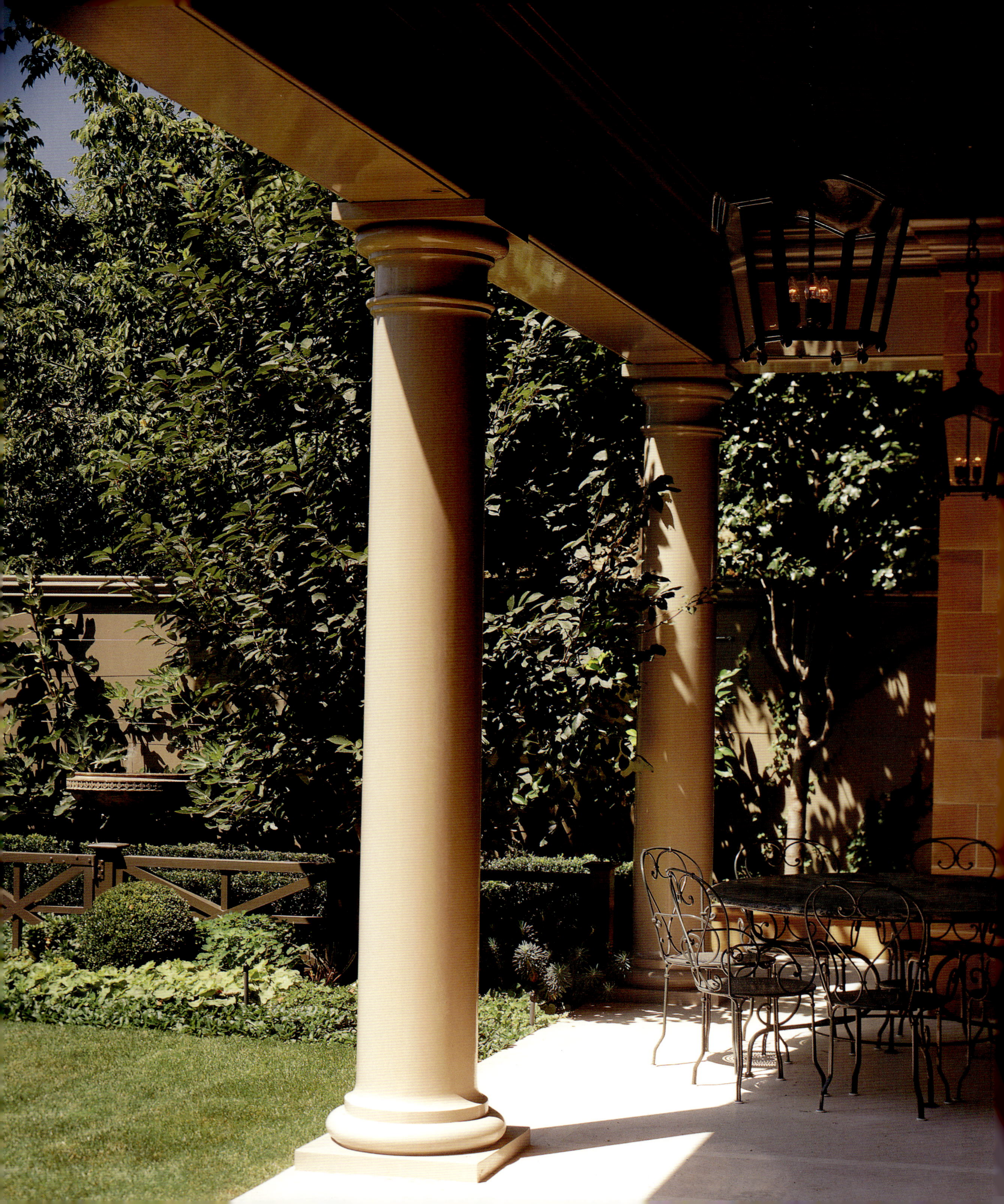

(about 2 metres by 2 metres) and depicted two putti leaning on a plaque that read 'St Germain'. Although the work could have stood on its own, it had been sculpted to be placed in front of a wall and I felt it was important for the integrity of the piece to display it in the same way. For that reason, and to emphasise its centrality to the garden, I elevated it on a plinth set in front of the wall. On either side, for further punctuation, I planted a lime, or linden, tree (*Tilia × europaea*). These, with two prunus placed at either end of the verandah, are the only trees in the front garden, and were carefully chosen for the beauty of their form and shape, a prime consideration when a garden is small and its trees a major focus. Lime trees have handsome trunks, a fine branch structure, delightful catkins in spring and soft foliage. They are light trees, unlikely to swamp a small garden, and can take a lot of pruning. Viewed from the street, the different layers of the garden — plant-covered retaining wall, high inner wall and canopy of tree tops — suggest further pleasures to be discovered and a garden of some size.

The house is constructed of Australian sandstone, so to complement it I chose French limestone for the paving of the wide verandah and carried it into the garden, in a relaxed manner, as stepping stones that form an irregular edge between a lawn and the long garden bed. Although the space available was quite limited, the owners very much wanted a soft garden, almost a country garden, so it became one of grass and ground covers pushing between pavers and deep beds full of flowering plants. Because plants of the same kind are more effective in beds when grouped together, the planting scheme was largely restricted to euphorbias, hostas, irises, lavenders, *Alchemilla mollis* and *Ajuga reptans*. Parts of the north-facing garden are shaded, and here the hostas do particularly well; in other, sunnier parts the euphorbias thrive.

The sculpture in the front garden was placed centrally against a specially built wall so that it could be viewed from the house and verandah (top). In the sideway the second French sculpture had to be raised higher so that it could be enjoyed by people as they dined (bottom). The view from the verandah also takes in the fountain set in a small picking garden to one side of the front garden (opposite).

The ornamental trellis-work (right), also shown on p. 45, is as important to the front garden as it is to the driveway. The trellis panels were painted the greyish green of the house trim; the rendered backing wall, seen through the arches, was made the colour of the house itself. Wisteria sinensis was trained up the trellis-work between the arches, then along the top of the wall; star jasmine (Trachelospermum jasminoides) filled the panels. The low fence and the double gates were matched by ones on the other side of the front garden that separated but did not cut it off from the abundant plants that filled the picking garden.

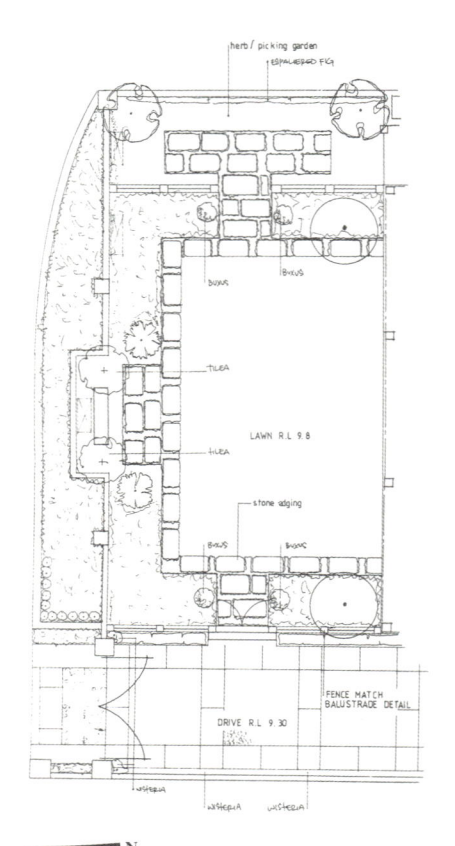

The front garden (left) measured 18 × 7.5 m, including the 3 m deep picking garden on its eastern side. The two obvious sight-lines — from the house and verandah across the width of the garden, and from the driveway down the garden's length — were confirmed by placing the larger French sculpture against a wall of its own a little in from the low front wall, and a small fountain (not indicated on this drawing) in the centre of the picking garden at the far end of the garden. Each object was recessed in an abundantly planted garden bed and given an approach of sandstone stepping stones to both signal its importance to the design and visually lengthen the view. Further stepping stones — less visible in photographs than on this plan because Ajuga reptans grows about them — were added as an informal edge to the garden bed that wraps around the lawn on three sides.

[78]

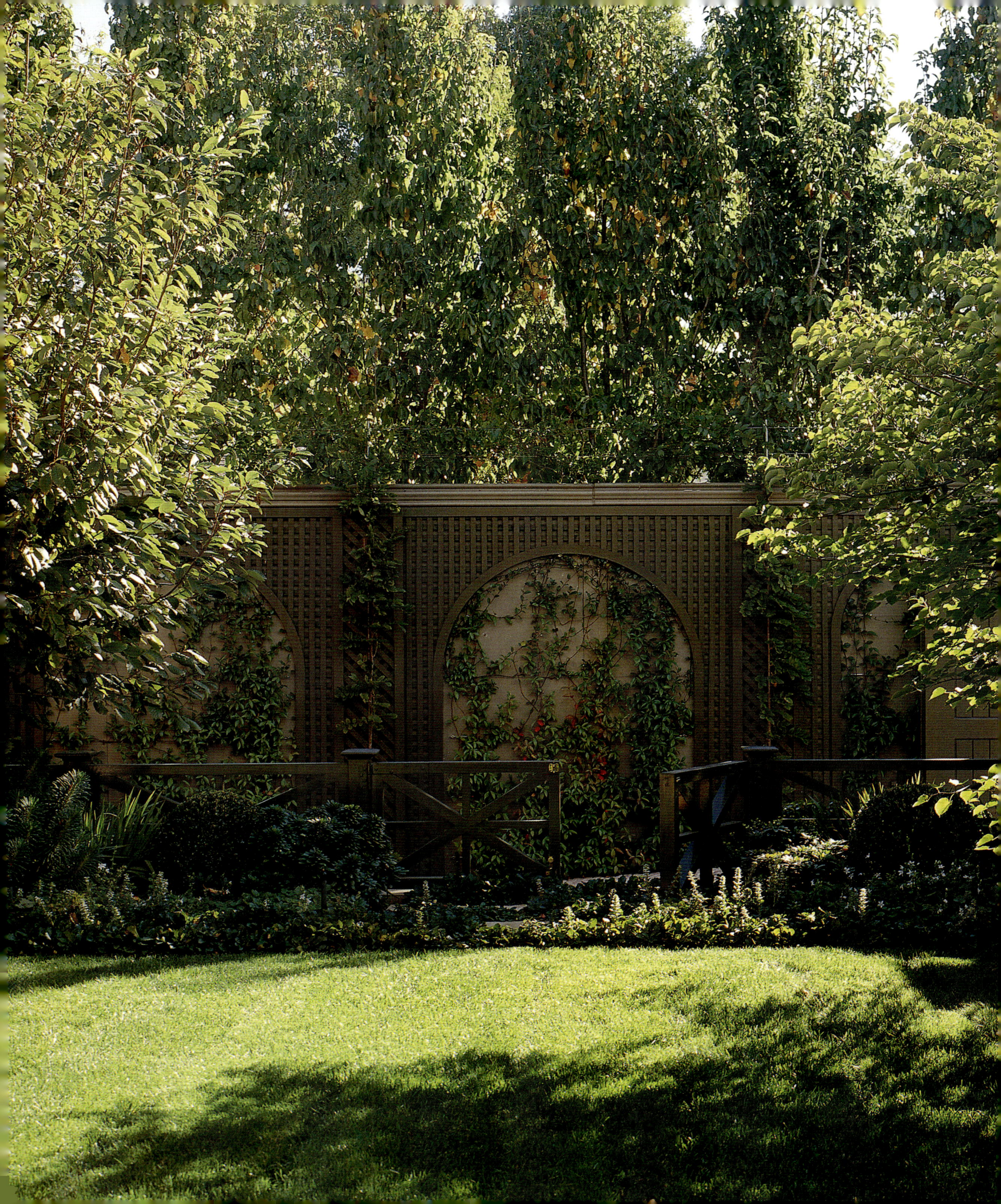

The owners and I agreed that the front garden should not open directly into the driveway, but rather be announced in some way. Consequently, I erected a low (only about 600 millimetres high) wooden fence with a double gate, copying the balustrade surrounding the cupola on the roof. I repeated the fence and double gate at the opposite end of the front garden to create a separate part, only the width of the narrow space running the length of the house on that side. Here the owners, who are great food enthusiasts, have established a picking garden for the table. Annual herbs abound in beds outlined in English box (*Buxus sempervirens*). A couple of lemon trees (*Citrus limon* 'Lisbon'), and espaliered fig trees (*Ficus carica*) on the wall, yield abundant fruit for the house. The focus of this small garden is the simplest of fountains — just a wide bowl, set in front of the espaliered figs, from which issues a single jet of water. The bowl is actually a Victorian sandstone urn, converted into a fountain by the addition of a small pump and spout: a special ornament from the owners' old garden, which they had brought with them. From the gates into the front garden, the visitor looks across an oblong of lawn to the picking garden — the stretch of grass, the low fence, the abundant planting and the fountain all adding a complexity of composition that lengthens the sight-line.

The second French sculpture I placed against the boundary wall facing the curved glass wall of the dining room. I set it on a somewhat higher plinth than the one used in the front garden, in full view of people seated at the dining table. There was room only for an English box hedge to flank the sculpture, if sufficient space was to be left for paving to put a little distance between the boundary wall and the curved glass wall. Strands of *Wisteria sinensis* trained along the top of the sculpture blended it a little with its background and provided extra privacy.

The long, narrow driveway was difficult to make attractive, yet it was essential to do so because it is the first view visitors have when they arrive. My solution was to belie the problem by erecting a trellis that gracefully decorated the driveway — and provided a fittingly beautiful frame for the front garden — but without taking up precious space. To create a false perspective, I designed the screen as a series of trellis-work arches, traced in *Wisteria sinensis* and separated by trellis-work panels filled with star jasmine (*Trachelospermum jasminoides*). The climbers bring spring and summer flowers and autumn colour to the driveway.

Two steps up to the front garden gates were needed as the driveway sloped (below left). To hide the retaining walls, low hedges of Portuguese laurel (Prunus lusitanica) were introduced. The fountain in the picking garden on the other side of the front garden (below right) nestles among the distinctive leaves of espaliered fruiting figs (Ficus carica). It was converted from a precious nineteenth-century urn. The picking garden was contained by a clipped hedge of English box (Buxus sempervirens), as well as a low fence, adding a little formality to the front garden. Herbs and flowers are planted in box-edged compartments.

I inlaid the driveway itself with large, coral, tumbled-granite pebbles edged with the same French limestone pavers I had used for the steps into the front garden, the verandah and the stepping-stone border of the garden beds: the inlay gives the driveway paving a signature of its own; the French limestone pavers give it unity with the rest of the garden. Against the side of the house I espaliered heavy-scented *Magnolia grandiflora*. Because of their size, these trees are not often used in this way, and yet they respond well to training and pruning. At the end of the driveway I placed a statue that the owners had also brought from their previous home, to complete the decoration of a garden designed specially to display fine ornamentation.

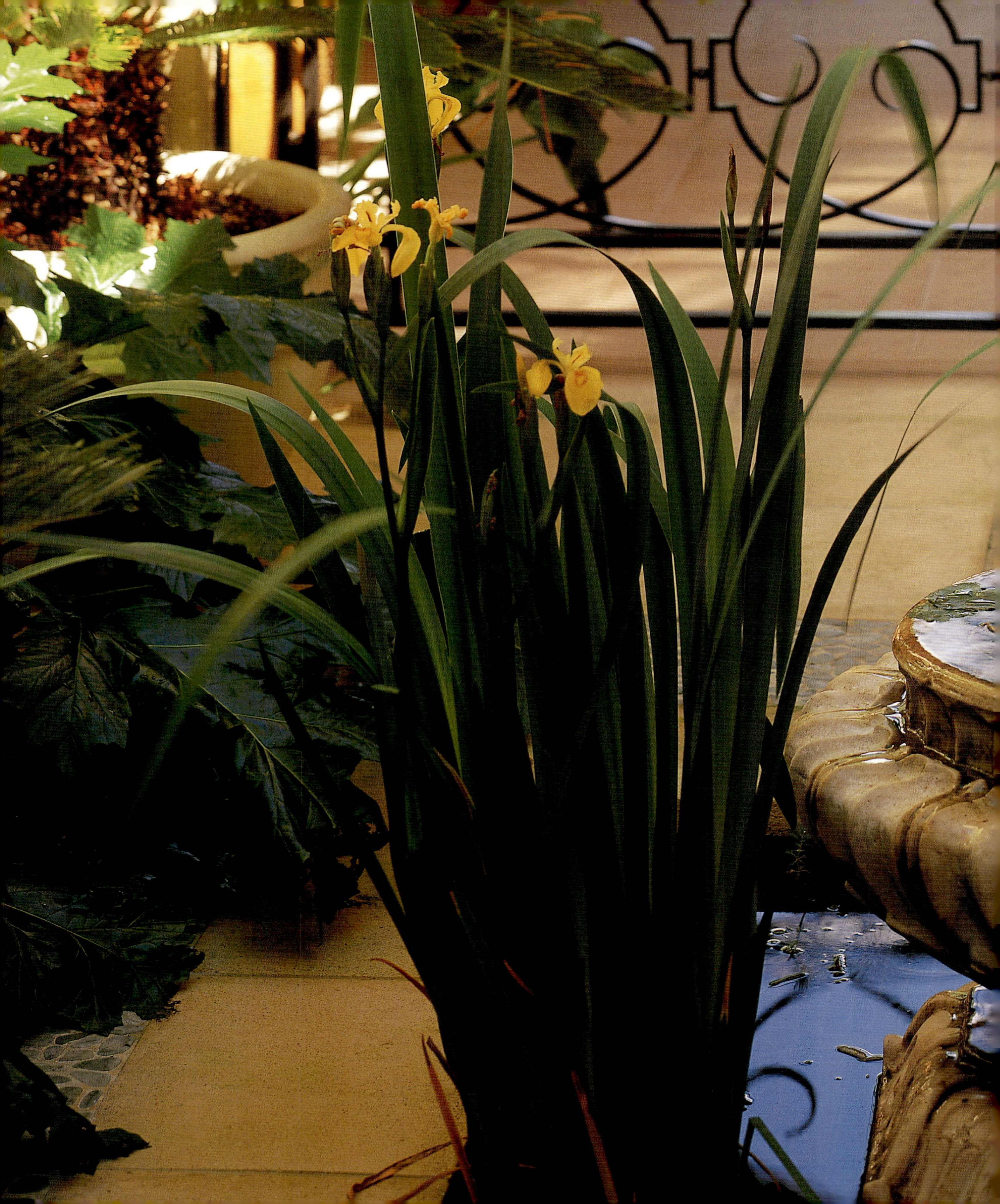

Water

No static ornament can compete with the drama of water jetting and leaping at the heart of a garden. I could never live with a garden that did not have ornamental water. Perhaps it is because water is the essence of life that ornamental water seems fundamental to a garden. The sight and sound of running water is so subliminally soothing, so emotionally satisfying that even the smallest garden should have at least a water spout. Australia's cities are often difficult environments — places of hard surfaces, glass and steel, pollution and noise — and the country itself is such a hot, parched land that its gardens need the coolness of water splashing and evaporating as well as the shade of well-watered green life.

Water is the focus of many of the gardens I design, with other ornamentation secondary to it — though water can certainly also be an intriguing minor feature kept somewhat hidden so that visitors hear it rather than see it at first. To me, water is of critical importance in turning small urban gardens into places of tranquillity and respite: people focus on the sound of the water and mentally block out the background noise of the city. I am also excited by the interaction of light and moving water and the ways one can use natural and artificial light to play with water — by the fine rainbow spray of water from a fountain on a sunny day, and the moody ripples of light and shadow across a pool at night.

Water spouts from a single jet into a bowl, overflows into a rendered-brick trough and trickles down a channel in the paving, finally to end in a round, sunken pool: an appropriately simple way to ornament a small internal courtyard. Such a courtyard is inevitably an extension of the house; a run of terracotta tiles and a wall of glass recognises this.

[84]

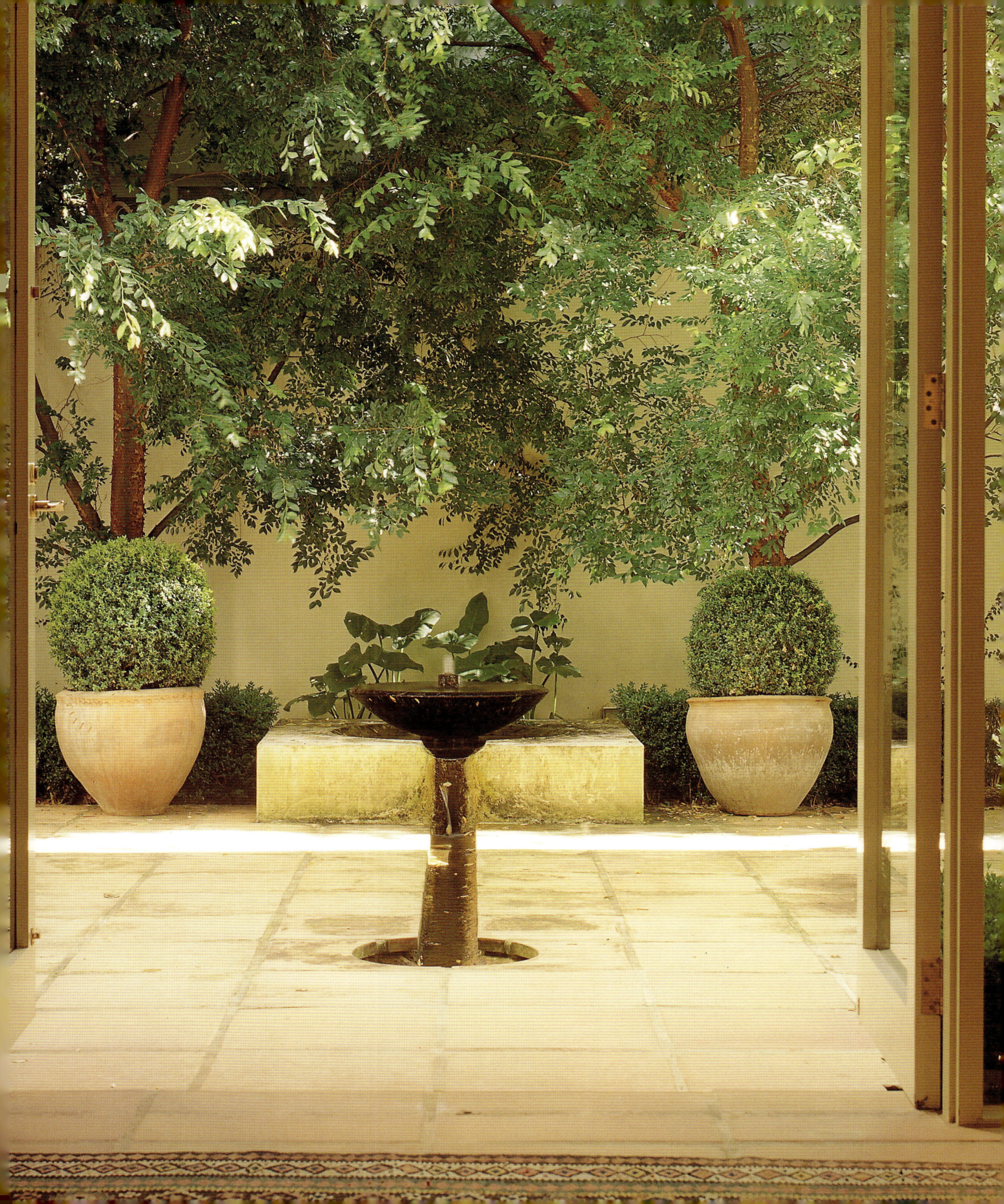

Ornamental Pools

Whatever its position, an ornamental pool should always seem an integral part of its garden. This means, firstly, keeping it in style with the house and garden. A wall fountain with water spouting into a trough suits an Italianate setting. The garden of a mock-Tudor house can be given a classic lily pond, a low pool with a very simple moulded edge. And if the house is contemporary, a sunken pool, edged only with the overhanging pavers of the terrace, will be effective.

Pools that pick up a detail or a material used on the house will look right in their setting: a stone house may suggest a stone coping; a moulding around a door or window frame may be copied for the edge; or the colour of a brick house may be repeated in the surrounds of the pool. Alternatively, the water itself can mirror the world around it: if the inside is painted black, the water will reflect plants and sky and the architecture of the garden nearby.

It is also important to get the proportion of an ornamental pool right in relation to its house and garden: the balance of a small garden can be easily destroyed by the introduction of a pool that is too high, too large or too ornate. Dark water in a low, simple pool, by mirroring its surroundings, can suggest that a garden is more spacious than it is, while at the same time giving the pool a depth and presence that makes it a focus without overwhelming the garden.

I always design, then build on the spot, all the pools in my ground plans because I want the flexibility to have whatever shape and size suits the space best; I don't want the form to be dictated by a prefabricated pool. A 100-millimetre-thick, reinforced-concrete slab is poured for the base and the sides are bricked to the required height or depth. The pool is usually finished with a moulded edge — sometimes one made specially, which if it does not copy a moulding found on the house will repeat a paving material used in the garden. To seal the pool it is lined first with a waterproof render, then with a black bitumen paint, which will not affect any water plants or fish that might be added later. The allure of an ornamental pool at night is enhanced by the addition of submerged lighting, as discussed in the final chapter.

Most pools need a reticulation system both to conserve water and to prevent it from becoming stagnant. This is achieved by submerging a pump in the pool. Water is pumped

The strong, contemporary feel of this converted warehouse dictated the style of the courtyard, and particularly the main focus, a fountain. The courtyard had the space and scale to take a series of rectangular, hard-edged troughs. Three wall-mounted bronze bowls, commissioned from a sculptor, added a sinuousness that prevented the troughs and the hard surfaces of the warehouse from becoming too confronting — as did the falling water itself.

through a fountain or simply released as a jet, returns to the pool and is pumped to the surface once more. The movement aerates the water so that it remains clear and plants and fish can thrive in the pool.

The depth of water a pool requires depends on its purpose. To grow water lilies a pool must be at least 600 millimetres deep. If water plants are not wanted, 300–400 millimetres of water is sufficient to hide a pump. Remember, however, that young children can drown in 100 millimetres of water in an ornamental pool as easily as in 2 metres of water in a swimming pool. Consequently, a strong mesh needs to be installed just beneath the surface of the water and firmly attached to the sides when the pool is being constructed. If both the pool and the mesh are painted black, the mesh is not visible. Plants can grow through the mesh, fish can come to the surface, but children will not drown if they fall in.

A channel of water, such as the one I constructed in my own garden, is an excellent way of adding moving water to a small garden without compromising its simplicity. Channelled water seems very controlled, very peaceful. Now and then a small change, a little white water, can be

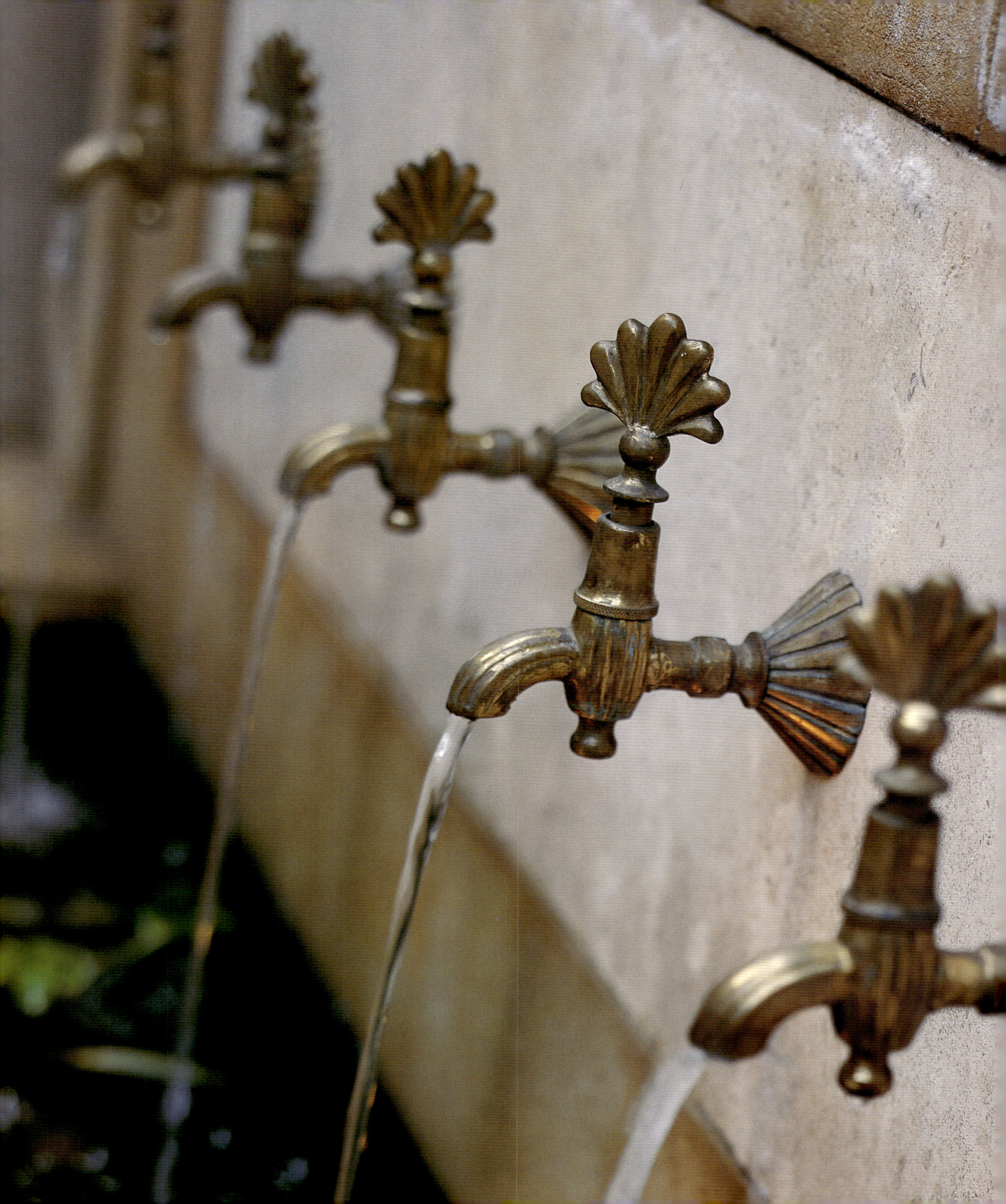

Again the architecture, this time of a monumental neo-classical apartment, determines the style and proportions of the components in a courtyard, particularly the water feature (below). Although the courtyard is not large, its main elements such as the wall fountain, columns and beams were overscaled — a decision made possible by the restraint of the design. Water runs from a line of bronze Persian taps mounted on the limestone inlay of the fountain-back (opposite). The innate simplicity of taps and the size of the fountain (3m in length) allowed me to have water issuing from more spouts than I would normally advocate for a small garden.

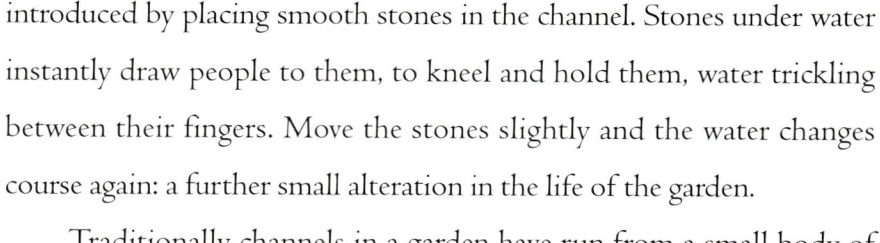

introduced by placing smooth stones in the channel. Stones under water instantly draw people to them, to kneel and hold them, water trickling between their fingers. Move the stones slightly and the water changes course again: a further small alteration in the life of the garden.

Traditionally channels in a garden have run from a small body of water, which may have just one jet, to a larger one, but there are no hard and fast rules: a simple channel can start from a large pool, or terminate in a small bowl without a water spout. Even the chlorinated water of a swimming pool can be allowed to flow through the garden, ultimately to return to the pool: the water of the channel spilling, like a natural stream, into the pool turns the pool from a functional feature into an ornamental one.

Fountains

A fountain, by adding a strong vertical element, automatically becomes a focus of a garden. Therefore you need to decide from where in the house or garden you wish primarily to view it: any fountain you install will establish the major axis or at least a secondary axis of the garden.

A small private garden is no place — and definitely has no space — for a cascade or a sheet of water or one of those monumental fountains found in public foyers and squares. A garden of a hectare or two may be able to incorporate a rocky outcrop with a waterfall, but owners of a small garden will have to be content with water trickling down a few steps or from one bowl to another. The soft background sound of a fountain is enticing; the constant noise of a large body of water at close range soon becomes annoying!

A fountain, like the receptacle into which it feeds, should take its cue from the architecture of the house. A Victorian two- or three-tiered cast-iron fountain is appropriate to the symmetrical ornateness of large Victorian houses but immediately looks glaringly out of place when placed near the architecture of any other period. An extrovert Edwardian house can take the theatricality of a neo-classical male or female statue spilling water into a large pool, while an Italianate house is enhanced by Roman dolphins or a gargoyle mounted on a garden wall. On the other hand, a plain concrete bowl or sphere with just one jet of water often suits the clean lines of many modern houses — or modest Victorian cottages — far better.

Just as the size of an ornamental pool should be in proportion to the space around it, so a fountain should neither dwarf nor be dwarfed by the receptacle. As well, the distance water from the fountain can carry needs to be taken into account: water should not be able to splash or spray onto the paving or a lawn or garden bed. If you can, choose your fountain first, then add a receptacle that harmonises with it in style and size.

A wall-mounted fountain, which utilises the vertical plane rather than taking up terrace or planting space, is particularly appropriate to many small gardens. It should be kept simple to suit the size of the garden: water should spout from only a few outlets on the wall. There are a number of prefabricated ones on the market, made of metal or resin; however, you can create your own ground-level trough in the same way as a free-standing pool, by laying a reinforced-concrete base, then building rendered-brick sides. The fountain support must be sturdy: a brick wall is ideal, although a well-constructed timber fence may be able to bear the weight of the fountain and its back. Water itself is surprisingly heavy, and adds considerably to the weight of a wall fountain.

Getting the proportions right is always fundamental when a free-standing fountain is added to a pool: the area of the pool must be sufficiently greater than the widest part of the fountain not only to catch all the water but also to avoid any suggestion that the fountain is sitting in a dish of water. Here a correctly proportioned lily pond, with a figure for its fountain, becomes a whole landscape. Given the dimensions of the courtyard, the pool needed no more than a square-edged rim set flush with the gravel surface. The bronze reproduction cherub, displayed against a drapery of lillypilly, and the reflections on the water of the black-lined pool hold the eye's attention in a very small courtyard.

A bronze ram's head, purchased in Paris, became the starting point for a small wall fountain (right). The scrolls of the bronze bowl specially made for it repeat the curves of the horns. The ram appears to graze happily in a meadow of Erigeron karvinskianus, beneath an arch of Wisteria sinensis. A walkway between two parts of a garden (below right) is able to take a large fountain because it is set against the wall, allowing it to be displayed across paving and a band of grass. The fountain was designed around two Roman dolphins mounted on a panel, and its flowing lines repeat those of the house's bay windows. The fountain seems to have drawn plant life to it, its placement allowing space for wisteria, erigeron, English box (Buxus sempervirens) and even two silver pears (Pyrus salicifolia) to grow.

The wall to which a fountain is to be attached must be attractive: never draw attention to an ugly wall by adding a handsome fountain. A free-standing masonry fountain-back, with tall hedges or thick climbers grown either side of it, offers a practical and aesthetic solution to the problem of an insubstantial fence. A fountain set against a free-standing trellis can also look most attractive. On the other hand, if the wall behind is strong and pleasing, a contrasting marble, stone or rendered panel can be attached to add variation and to highlight the fountain. A pattern, or a different pigment from that of the wall, can be worked into a rendered panel.

Swimming Pools

Swimming pools are difficult to integrate into any garden gracefully, but in a small garden where they will take up much of the space it becomes a huge challenge to make them an ornamental as well as a recreational feature. You need to ask yourself before you install one whether you will use it frequently enough to be able to overlook its disadvantages, for swimming pools as well as occupying a great deal of space are costly to build and require a lot of maintenance.

A second question to ask yourself is how you are going to use the pool. Are you going to use it for swimming laps or just to cool off and relax in? If the latter, you might consider following the recent trend towards smaller swimming pools, rather than the standard ones, or even just installing a plunge pool. Think hard before you add a spa, as well: spas take up extra room and require a lot of upkeep and three or four hours to heat.

A third question you must ask yourself is whether you have sufficient space to comfortably include a pool fence as well as the pool itself. Any new or existing swimming pool built in Australia has to be enclosed. The actual requirement is that the pool be isolated, so in theory the windows and doors of a house are acceptable as a barrier as long as they comply with the regulations; that is, they must be permanently locked with a childproof lock installed at a specified height, and any door must shut instantly behind the adult who has unlocked it to pass through. However, this approach needs to be checked with the local council first, and is in any case not relevant to many people because they want their own or visitors' children to be able to go freely

The head of a Roman god, mounted on a garden wall, spills water into an eighteenth-century carved travertine bowl set in a simple trough (opposite): this is a fountain that contrives to be both refined and rustic — and very economical of space. A trim of English box adds to the refinement; moss-lined slates to the rustic setting; and a garland of wisteria to the vitality of the small garden.

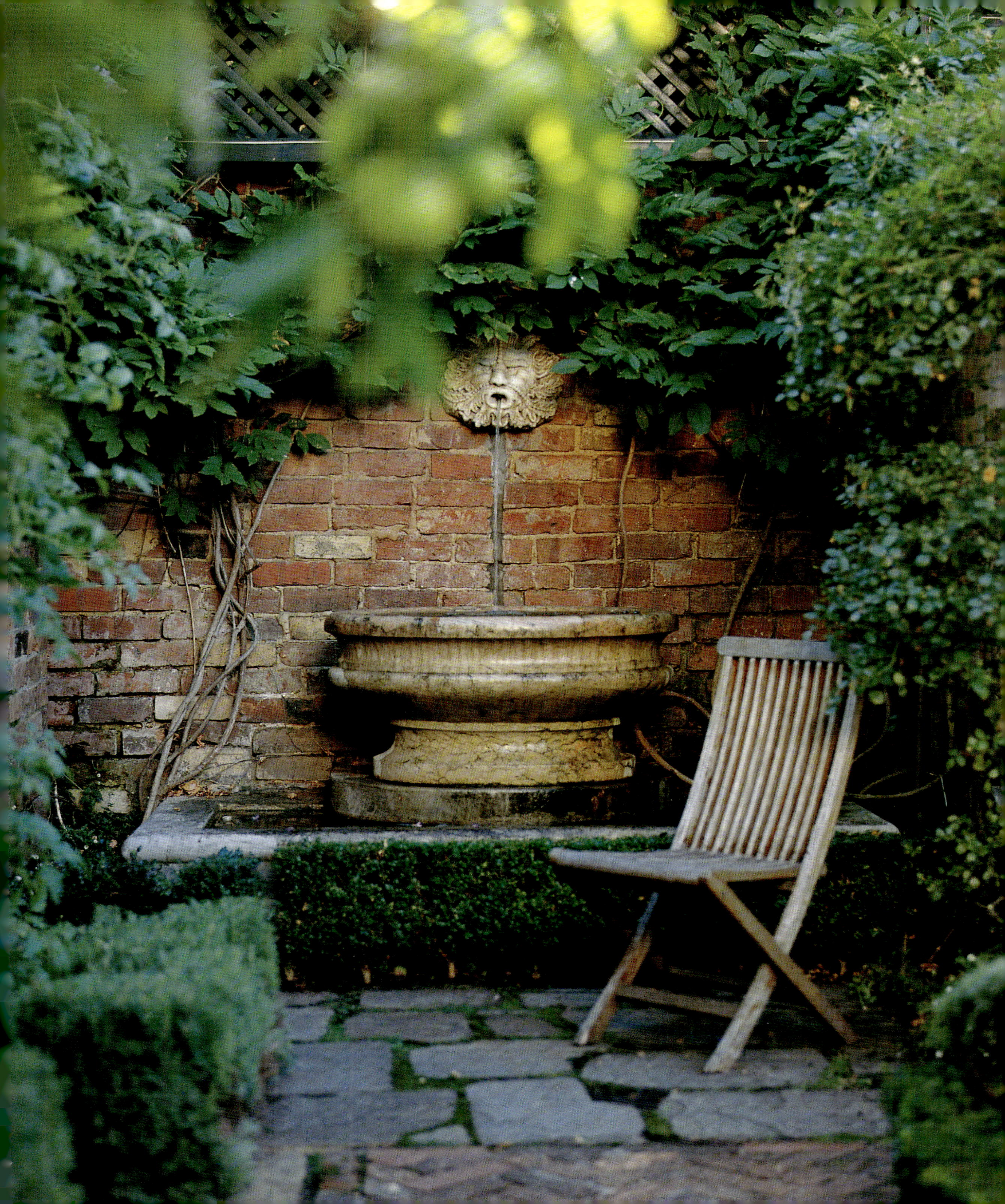

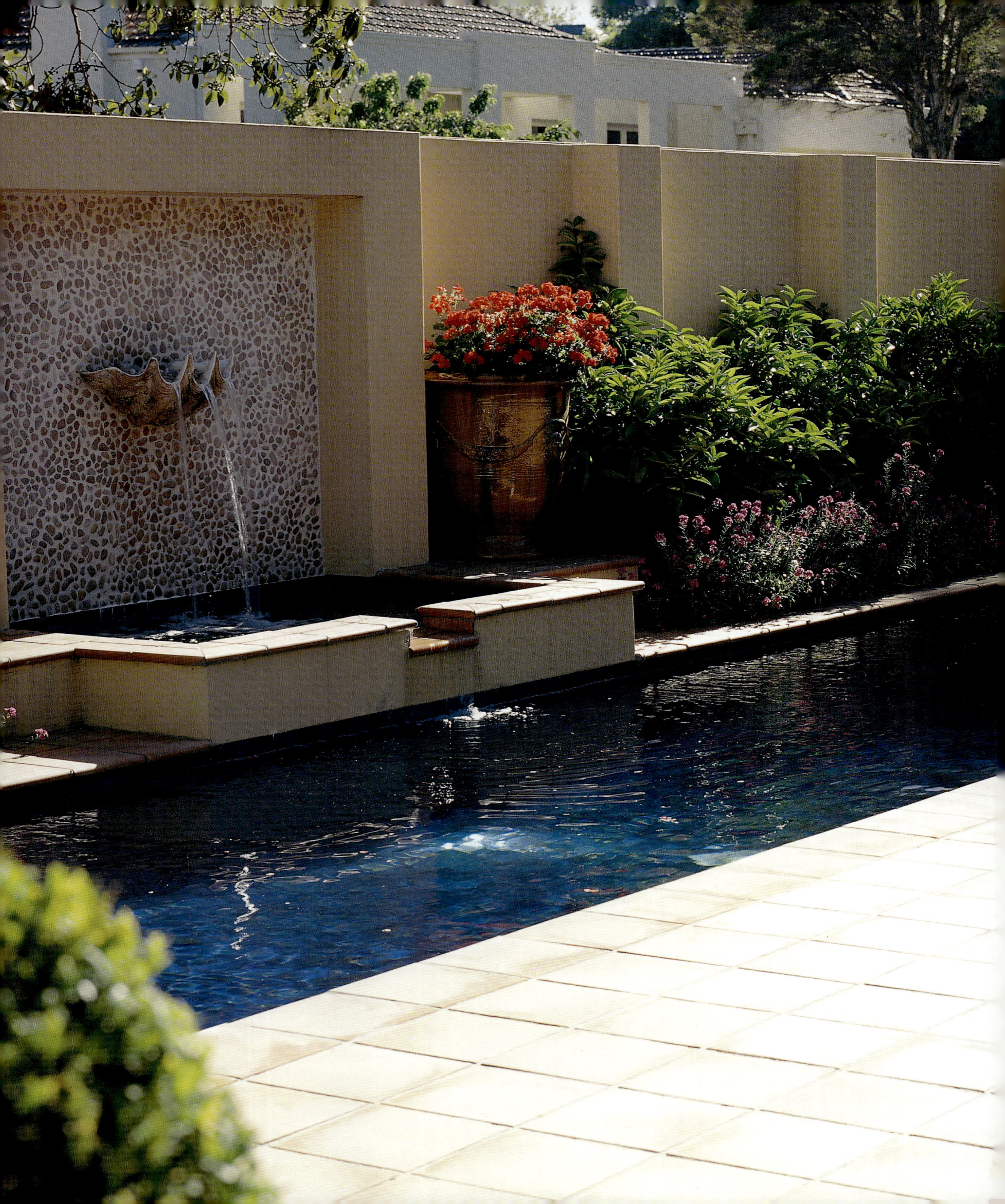

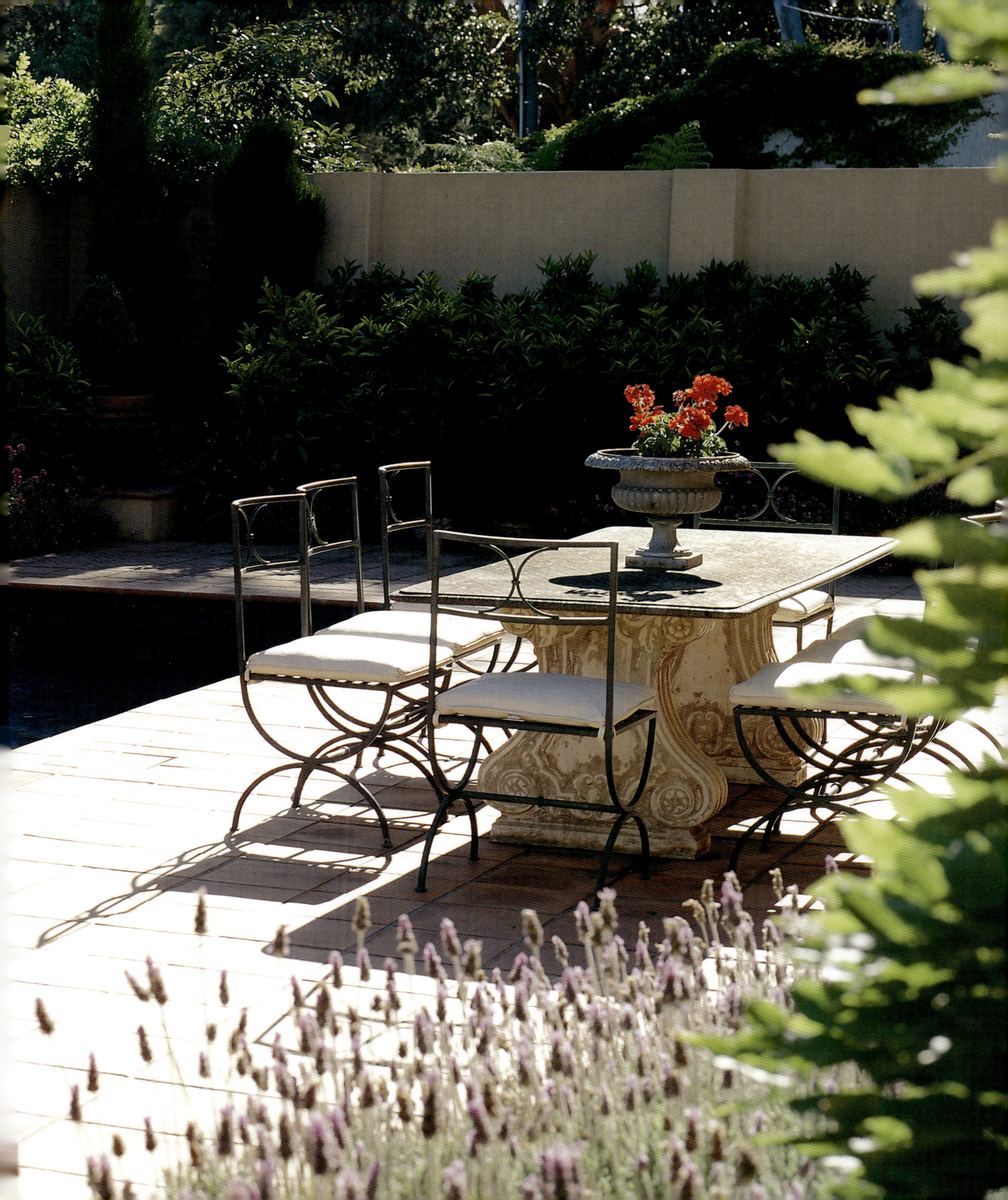

into the garden to play. There are also strict regulations about the construction of pool fences; these may vary from local council to local council, but all have the aim of ensuring that young children will not be able to climb through, under or over a fence.

In small gardens any strong division can make the space seem even smaller than it is, so you must ask yourself, too, whether it is possible to make the pool fence inconspicuous, perhaps by disguising it with a hedge if it is an ugly metal fence, or by constructing it in glass, or by building it in a material sympathetic to the house. One of the biggest mistakes that people make when space is limited is to place the fence too close to the pool so that the pool area feels like a gaol. A pool needs at least 2–3 metres of clear paving on some sides to ensure that the area provides sufficient space for people to lie on sunlounges or sit near the pool – and to ensure that the area appears balanced. The pool must look inviting if it is to entice people in: no one wants to swim in a cage. Most people want an open expanse of sparkling water and warm paving.

Finally, you will need to consider whether you have enough space for the pool area to include storage – and for you to hide it, since it is hardly something you would want to look like a feature of the garden. The pool area has to accommodate pumps, and filtration and other maintenance equipment. All of these are quite large so require a storage area of roughly 4 square metres. There are council regulations affecting pool equipment: it is not allowed to be placed on the boundary, and must be soundproofed if a neighbour's house is close by. Sometimes the equipment can be buried in a box in the garden, or storage can be located in the garage or at the side of the house; if this is not possible, a trellis or plants will disguise it – but again space is required.

My strong belief is that if you do decide you want a swimming

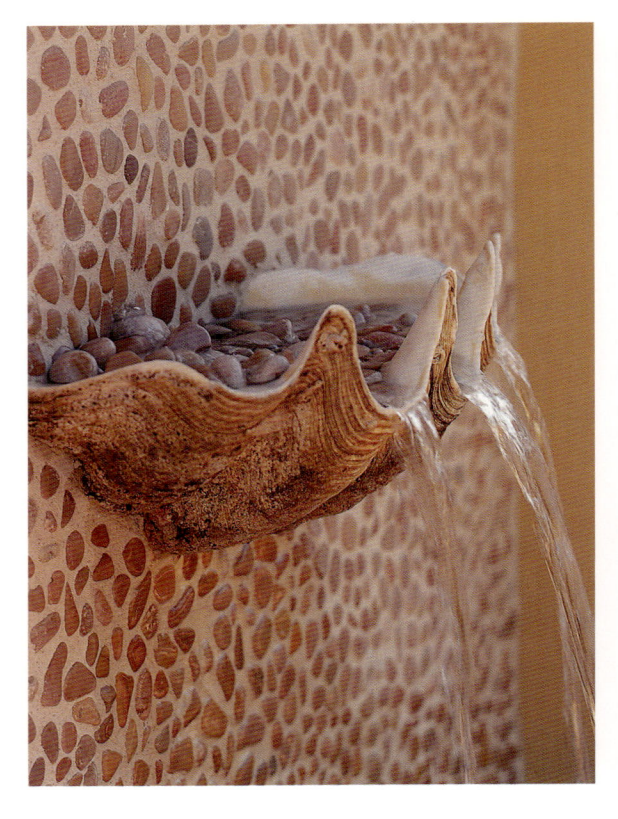

The lap pool shown on the previous pages demonstrates how swimming pools should be positioned in small gardens: its narrowness and its placement against the far wall leave maximum room for generous garden beds and a paved area broad enough to take a table and chairs, chosen in preference to sunlounges. So that the spa did not look primarily like a recreational facility, I turned it into an ornamental pool with a wall fountain. Since a Mediterranean style suited the sunny courtyard, I used just a clam shell, mounted on a pebble-inlaid panel, for the fountain (above).

pool, you should make it fit in with the overall design of your garden and the space you have, and that if your garden is very small you can only achieve this by making it appear more like an ornamental pool than a swimming pool. A pool measuring 2 metres by 2 metres is just big enough to get into and cool down, but has the great advantage that it can be made a decorative element that does not overwhelm a small area. Proportion and appropriateness are the crucial factors. Although it could be assumed that a pool should be tucked away at the end of a small garden, this is not necessarily so. A pool is often now incorporated in the design of contemporary houses, so that people sitting inside look straight through glass onto water.

The first thing to consider, when designing the swimming pool itself, is the colour of the lining (and hence the colour the water will take on). The garden offers the clue. If a pool is to be made the major feature of a stark contemporary courtyard with little planting, dark blue can be employed to stunning effect. However, if the pool is to be surrounded by luxuriant plants or perhaps a lawn, a soft green will help it to merge with the garden. Most pools are fully lined with tiles or the paving material used in the garden when that is suitable, which can be expensive. Less expensive is a pebble finish, which is a render-like finish available in a range of colours, applied to the shell of the pool: a pale colour works well with stone or artificial-stone paving.

Generally the paving used in the rest of the garden will look best in the swimming-pool area of a small garden or, if it is not suitable, a material in the same tone. Some of the softer stones such as the sandstones sometimes slightly crack or blister when exposed to chlorine or salt, but most surfaces, including lawn, can be placed in proximity to a pool. Gravel immediately beside a pool is not advisable, however, because it gets into it and is not pleasant for bare feet.

Good drainage around a swimming pool is essential, so that the water that splashes out is caught and carried away. Provided that their beds are well drained by agricultural pipes, many plants will grow beside a pool. A pool nestled among deep beds creates a serene courtyard, and weeping plants and climbers, their leaves just brushing the water, can look quite lovely. The colour of certain plants seems to intensify the colour of the water itself: olive trees, irises, lavenders and wisteria heighten the deep blue of a pool in a Mediterranean-style garden; English box (*Buxus sempervirens*) or rows of orange trees deepen the green of a pool.

A Garden Built Around Fountains

In the three courtyards of this garden, three fountains play, plants and paving unfolding gently around them. And through the open windows of the house the owners, as they pass from room to room, catch the murmur of falling water.

The owners very much liked the sound and movement of water in a garden. Their house was built in the Spanish mission style, and it lent itself to the use of ornamental water. They had moved to the property at a time of life when they felt they needed a smaller house and garden. One of the owners was a passionate gardener who had drawn immense pleasure from owning and tending a very large garden, so it was essential that her new garden reflect her tastes and ideas. She wanted a garden where much of the interest would derive from combinations of plant colours and contrasts of leaf shapes and textures. Low maintenance was not a priority — in fact, she wanted a garden that required regular care, though one on a smaller scale than her previous property.

Since each of the three courtyards was independent of the others and adjacent to different parts of the house, I decided that each could have a different fountain and a character of its own. Any fountain chosen would become the focus of its courtyard, so it was important to seek unusual pieces rather than standard ones.

The front garden is the largest of the courtyards (approximately 14 metres by 12 metres) and is overlooked by the rather imposing two-storey house. I decided therefore that its style, like that of the house, should hint at a Moorish influence. After some searching, I found a sculpture for the fountain that intrigued us: a snake-entwined Indian lingam, a symbol of fertility. Because the Moors went to India as well

The second of the three gardens built around a fountain is a small internal courtyard entered from the porte-cochère of the house and viewed from several of the upstairs and downstairs rooms (opposite). Like the first courtyard (the front garden) and the third (the back area), this courtyard is influenced by the Spanish mission style of the house's architecture. The symmetry of the courtyard, the colours and materials of its hard surfaces, its use of water and the leaf shapes of Iris pseudacorus, Acanthus mollis, *arum lilies (*Zantedeschia aethiopica*), and the cycads (*Cycas revoluta*) in pots, all hint at a Moorish garden.*

as to Spain, it seemed not inappropriate to use an Indian sculpture in this courtyard.

Visitors enter the front garden from a long driveway to one side of the house. As they pause in the gateway to the garden, their eyes are drawn to the fountain on the far wall. Water trickles from a bronze lotus bud, fashioned specially for the fountain, onto the lingam, which in its turn spills water into a low pool.

I suggested a wall fountain because the garden is enclosed by high brick walls, rendered in the same colour as the house. The sculpture was chosen first and is quite a special feature, so the other parts of the fountain needed to be in proportion to it, yet also in proportion to the garden. The pool chosen, for example, appears to be the width of the gateway when visitors stand on the threshold of the garden. The fountain-back was kept simple so that it did not compete with the sculpture. Its inset white pebbles work well with the rendered walls and give a Spanish air to the fountain.

Pebbles were repeated in the inserts of the paving laid beyond the verandah, onto which the front living rooms opened. The pebbles — dark green, to match the adjoining lawn and the terrazzo of the verandah — added strength where artificial-stone pavers alone might have seemed too bland. The owners wanted a lawn primarily for their grandchildren to play on; however, the grass stretching from the wide terrace to deep garden beds also created the illusion of spaciousness that the rather massive house façade required. Overscaling the main elements in a restrained design — that is, making them disproportionately large by conventional thinking — to suggest that the garden must be big is a trick I often employ.

To build the front garden, a huge liquidambar had to be cut down.

The front garden fountain is glimpsed from the verandah entry (below), and a gate opposite (see p. 46). The fountain-back is a blind arch, faced with white marble pebbles (opposite). Water trickles from a bronze lotus bud onto the marble lingam that forms the bowl (above left). The spout was mounted on the pebbled back (above right).

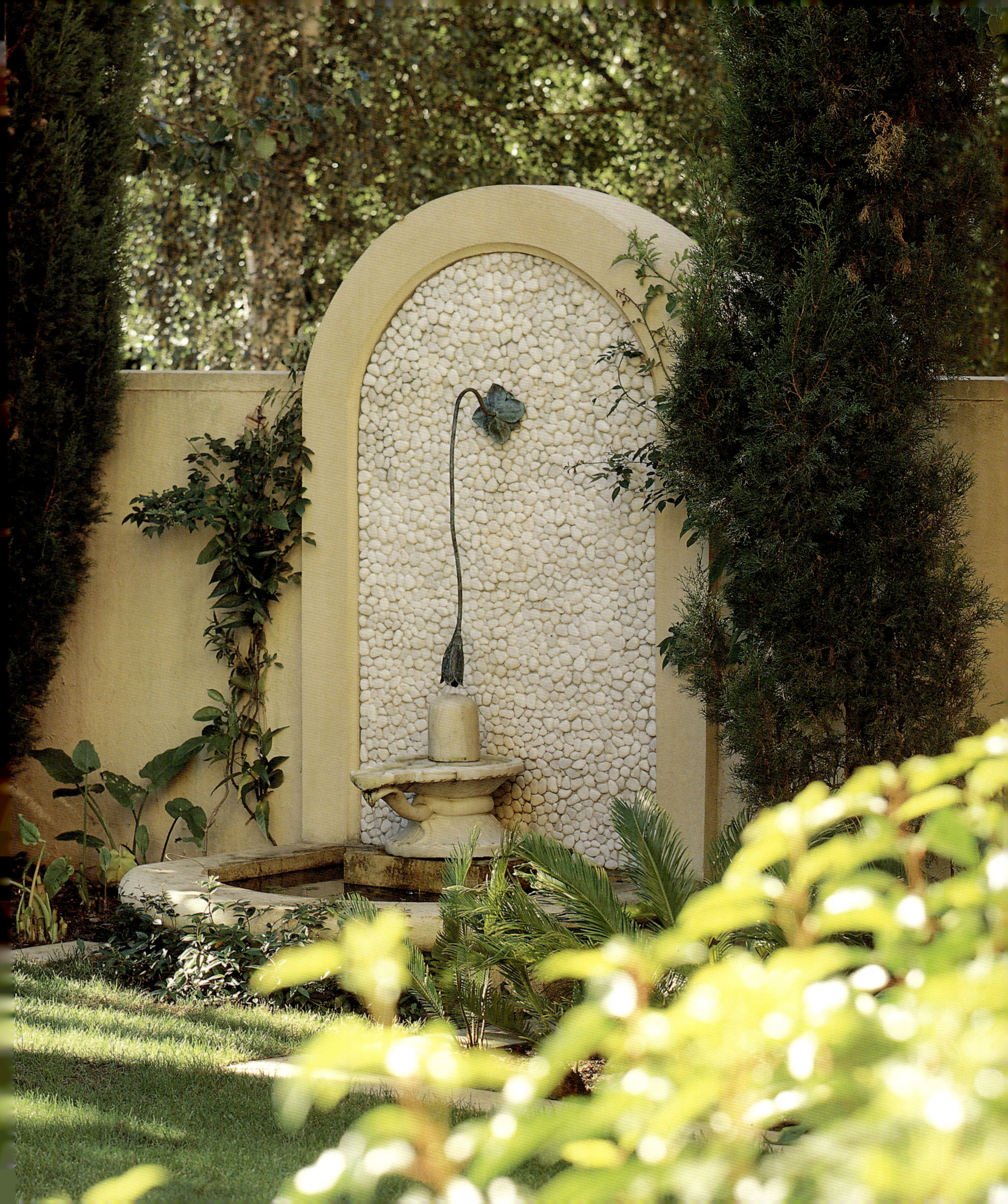

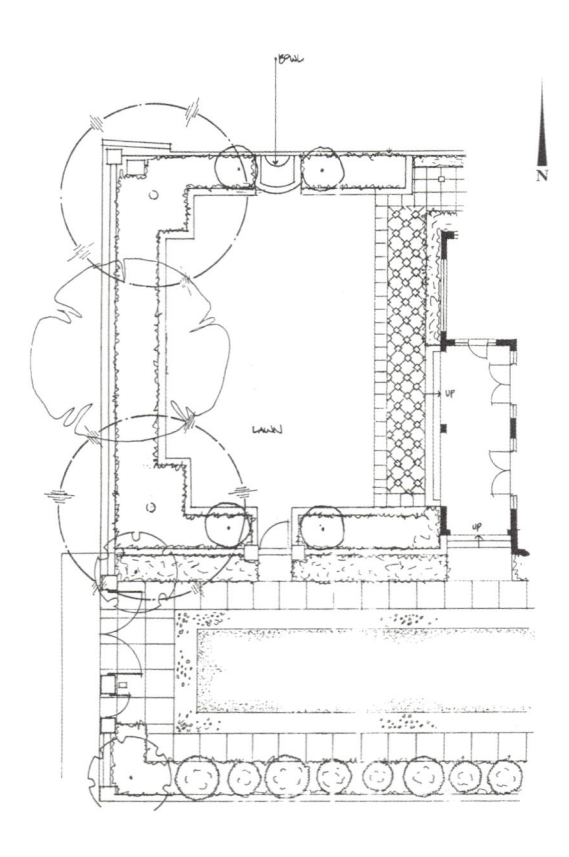

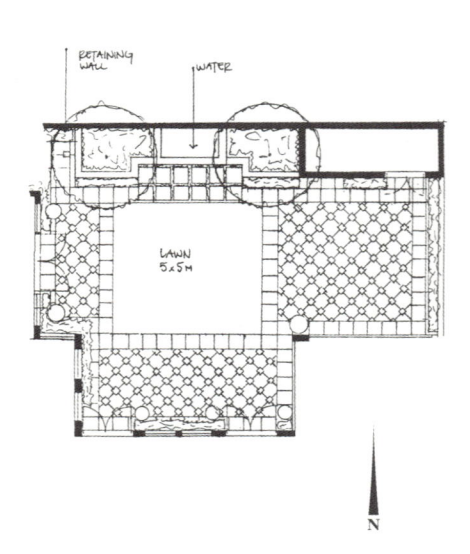

As the ground plan (left) shows, the fountain that became the central focus of the front garden was placed against the northern wall so that it could be seen from both the gateway in the garden's high southern wall and the front verandah. This positioning took advantage of the longest perspective (the frontage is 21m) and the fact that people must enter the property from the 7m wide driveway. The plan indicates the liquidambar tree, halfway along the western boundary, that was removed to make way for two better positioned and more appropriate Canary palms (Phoenix canariensis) at either end. The third, back courtyard (below left) was planned to be an extensively paved area for outdoor living, although still, like the other two courtyards, with a fountain as its focus. The fountain was designed to go against the northern wall and be recessed in a garden bed, with a Magnolia grandiflora on either side. Both the terrace on the southern side and the one on the east look across a square of lawn to it. In summer the former provides a sunny dining area, the latter a semi-shaded one. The paving pattern of the two (and of a narrow paved area on the western side) repeated that of the front terrace.

The pool of the second, internal courtyard (right) is roughly a square, bordered by bands of pavers and pebble-inlaid concrete, with at its centre a circle: a lotus-patterned marble fountain. Rills at either end of the pool run nowhere but suggest a larger water system.

[102]

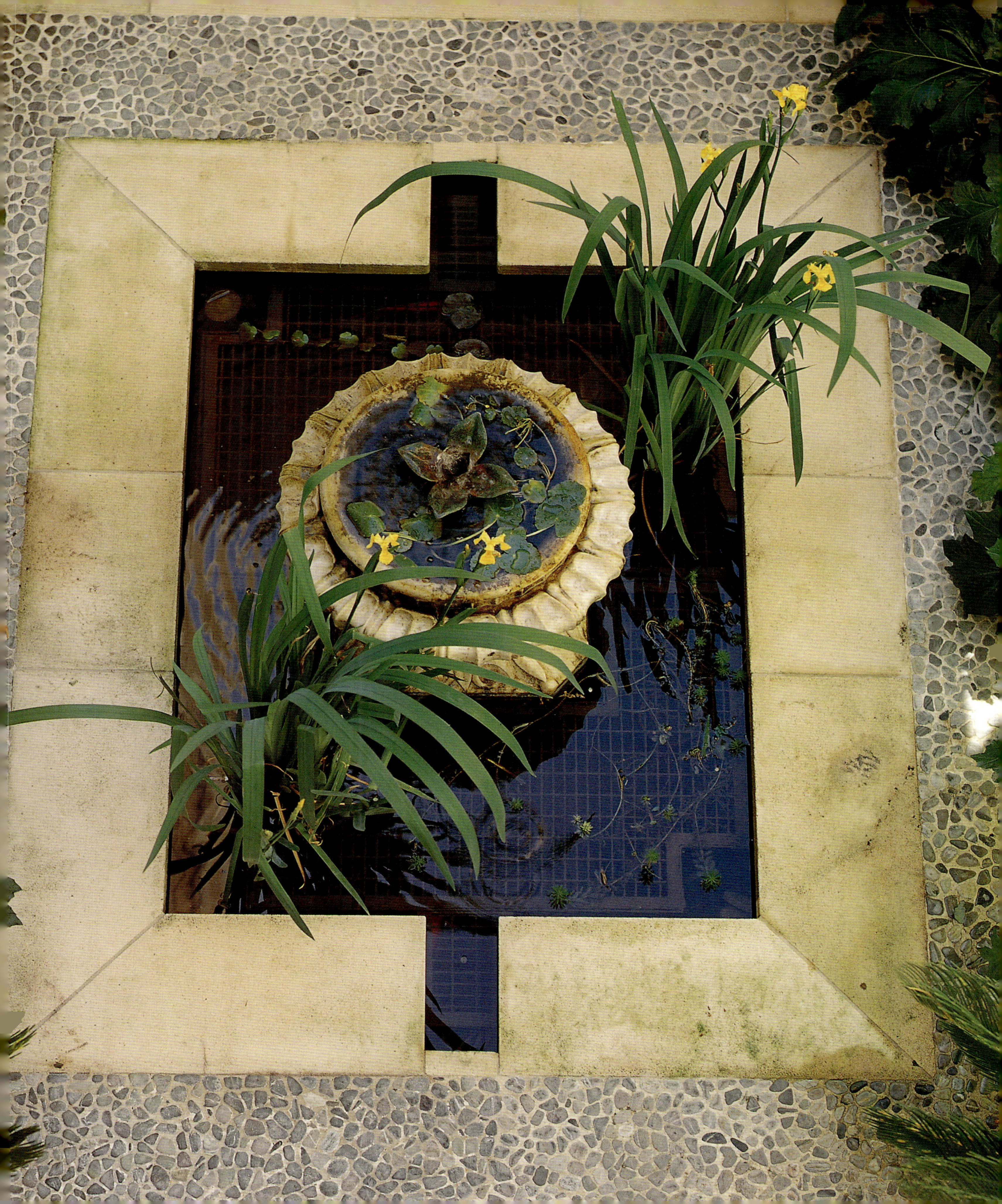

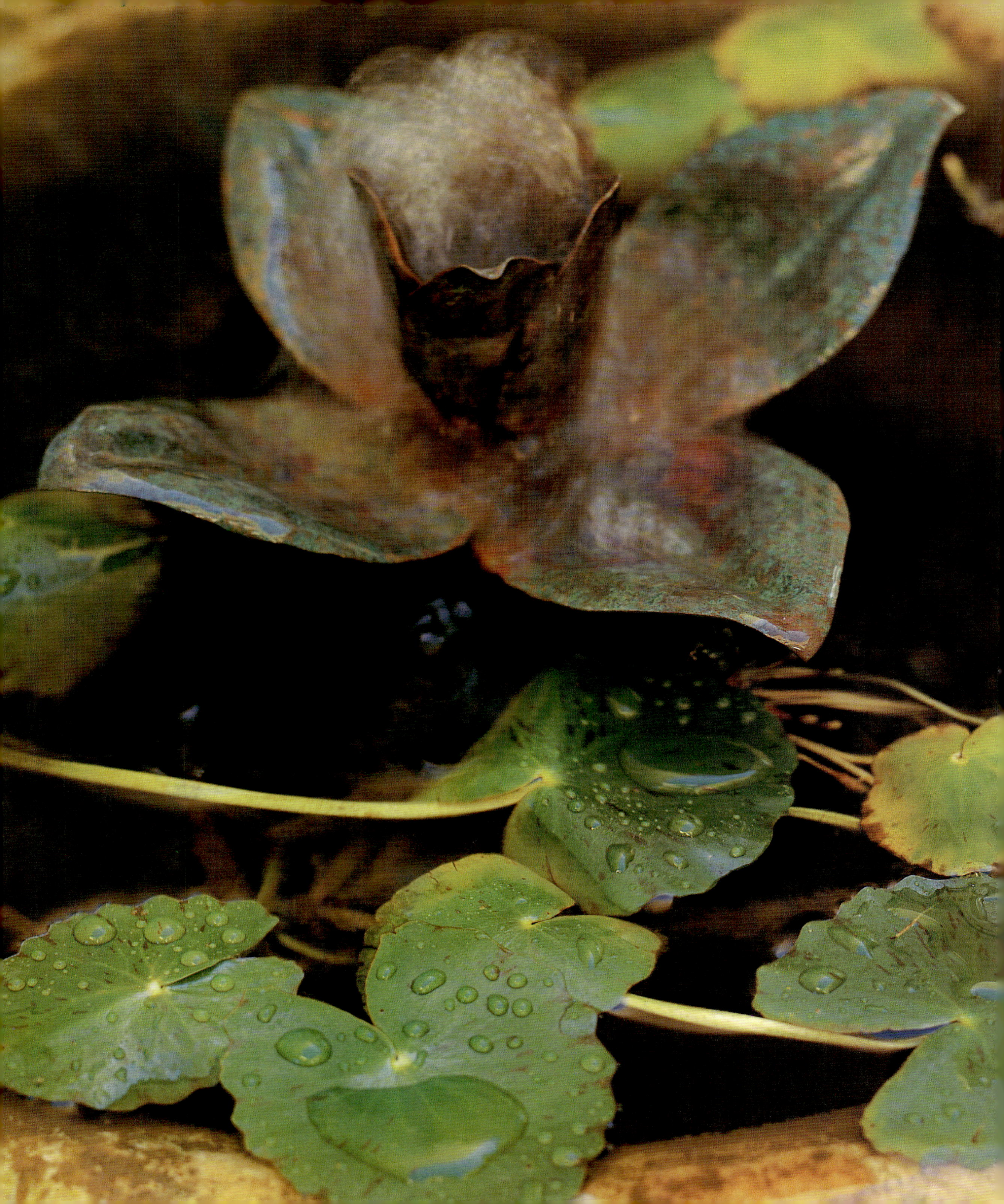

In the small fountain bowl of the internal courtyard the green leaves of Nymphoides crenata *float beside the bronze petals of the lotus-flower spout (opposite).*

Although it was an attractive tree, it interrupted the flow from house to garden beds that was vital to the design. I replaced it with two very large Canary palms (*Phoenix canariensis*), planted on either side of the garden, to match the house's architecture. This may seem strange, given that a large tree had just been removed, but provided the trees are positioned correctly in the garden such overscaling does work.

The palms were the starting point for an exotic, 'textured' planting scheme that included pencil pines (*Cupressus sempervirens* 'Stricta'), oranges in pots on the terrace, lemon trees (*Citrus limon* 'Meyer') espaliered on a wall, and lots of plants such as cycads (*Cycas revoluta*) that rely more on foliage than flowers for their effect. The result was a luxuriant garden containing some of the plants traditionally found in Spanish gardens — and others, like the cycads, that look as if they might have been. Maintenance — mowing, fertilising, pruning and clipping — is reasonably high, which makes the passionate gardener in the family happy!

The tiny internal courtyard, which measures only about 5 metres by 4 metres, is glimpsed through the windows and doors of many rooms in the house. It is visible from the front entry on the driveway side of the house, from the informal sitting room, from the kitchen, and from the formal dining room, as well as from upstairs, so the fountain chosen as the main feature needed to be one that could be viewed from all sides. Again we selected an Indian piece: a bowl, which had probably been used originally as an urn, with an edging of lotus petals. The lotus, with its echo of the fountain in the front garden, became the inspiration for the bronze fountainhead we had made specially by my brother Benjamin. To enhance the fountain's beauty, we placed it in the middle of a sunken square pool edged simply with cement pavers set flush with the courtyard's surface. A border of dark green pebbles and another of artificial-stone pavers were sufficient to display the pool and fountain. From upstairs, viewers look down on a small, perfect gem: an opening lotus bud set within a circle set within three rectangles. This is the simplest of courtyards — anything elaborate would have been disastrous in such a confined space — but its singular fountain makes it a special place.

The tiny garden experiences all the inevitable problems of an internal courtyard: lack of sunlight, lack of ventilation, lack of water. The last problem was remedied by installing a sprinkler system; the first two could only be circumvented by carefully choosing the toughest shade-loving plants. Fortunately, I did not want to crowd the courtyard: plants were very much secondary to the water feature in the design, and meant merely to soften the peripheries.

The disproportionately high walls I draped in a curtain of Boston ivy (*Parthenocissus tricuspidata*). Then I planted *Acanthus mollis* and arum lilies (*Zantedeschia aethiopica*), both of which take very low levels of light, for their broad, arching foliage and thrusting flower stems. Tall *Iris pseudacorus* stand in the pool and seem happy to be there, although they do not flower quite as well as they would in the open. And in the fountain itself the living leaves of *Nymphoides crenata* lie on the surface of the water, beside the bronze petals of the lotus. Spiky cycads, given additional height by being planted in pots, complete the rather architectural planting of the small space. Because the choice of plants was strictly disciplined, the courtyard greenery is healthy — and looks it.

The third, irregularly shaped courtyard lies at the back of the house and was designed to be the most functional of the three. This is where the owners do their outdoor entertaining and dining, and where their grandchildren mainly play when they visit. I suggested two terraces adjacent to the house, one in sun and one in part shade in summer, so that the owners would have the flexibility of choosing where they sat or dined according to the weather. Both face a small square of lawn that gives the grandchildren a soft surface to play on.

The main focal point is again a fountain — the largest of the three — in the centre of the northern wall. The fountain is recessed in a niche measuring 2 metres by 2 metres flanked on either side by two spreading *Magnolia grandiflora*, which were brought in as mature trees since they grow so slowly. A green glazed ceramic pot of water overflows into a raised trough. The fountain is a strong presence, whichever of the two terraces it is viewed from.

The two terraces match each other and another small, paved area beside the house: differentiation would have been too discordant in such a limited space. All have the same artificial-stone pavers and small diamond inserts of green pebbles — the pebbles a reminder of the other two courtyards. Both dining terraces are large enough to have their own table and chairs so the owners do not have to shift furniture from one part of the courtyard to another.

A green glazed pot was chosen for the fountain of the third courtyard, and given a single spout.

The trough of the fountain in the back garden was recessed between two raised beds that hold a Magnolia grandiflora each and star jasmine (Trachelospermum jasminoides). The base of the trough and the raised beds are skirted by T. asiaticum. The glazed pot of the fountain is in keeping with the appropriately rustic character of a courtyard designed for family entertaining.

Again, to preserve the unity of the design, the furniture of the two terraces is the same. Black wrought iron, which matches the Spanish mission style of the house's external and internal gates, was chosen because heavy furniture would have made the courtyard look cluttered and obstructed the view of the fountain from the house.

The owners wanted the fragrance of flowers all about them as they sat outside. However, plants in the courtyard were necessarily restricted to the sides of the garden, and to some degree to the vertical plane, because of the space taken up by the terraces and lawn. Nevertheless, there was room for the two *Magnolia grandiflora*, so that in summer the air is filled with the scent from their great white cups, and with the heavy perfume of *Gardenia augusta* 'Florida' also. The gardenias thrive in the warmth trapped by the courtyard and in the moisture from the sprinkler system. White star jasmine (*Trachelospermum jasminoides*) and magenta bougainvillea, so often found in Mediterranean gardens, clothe the garden walls. The bougainvillea is so at home that, encouraged by wire supports, it has climbed well above the walls to block out the view of neighbouring houses and totally enclose a perfect courtyard in which to sit and enjoy the glint of sunlight on water.

PLANTS

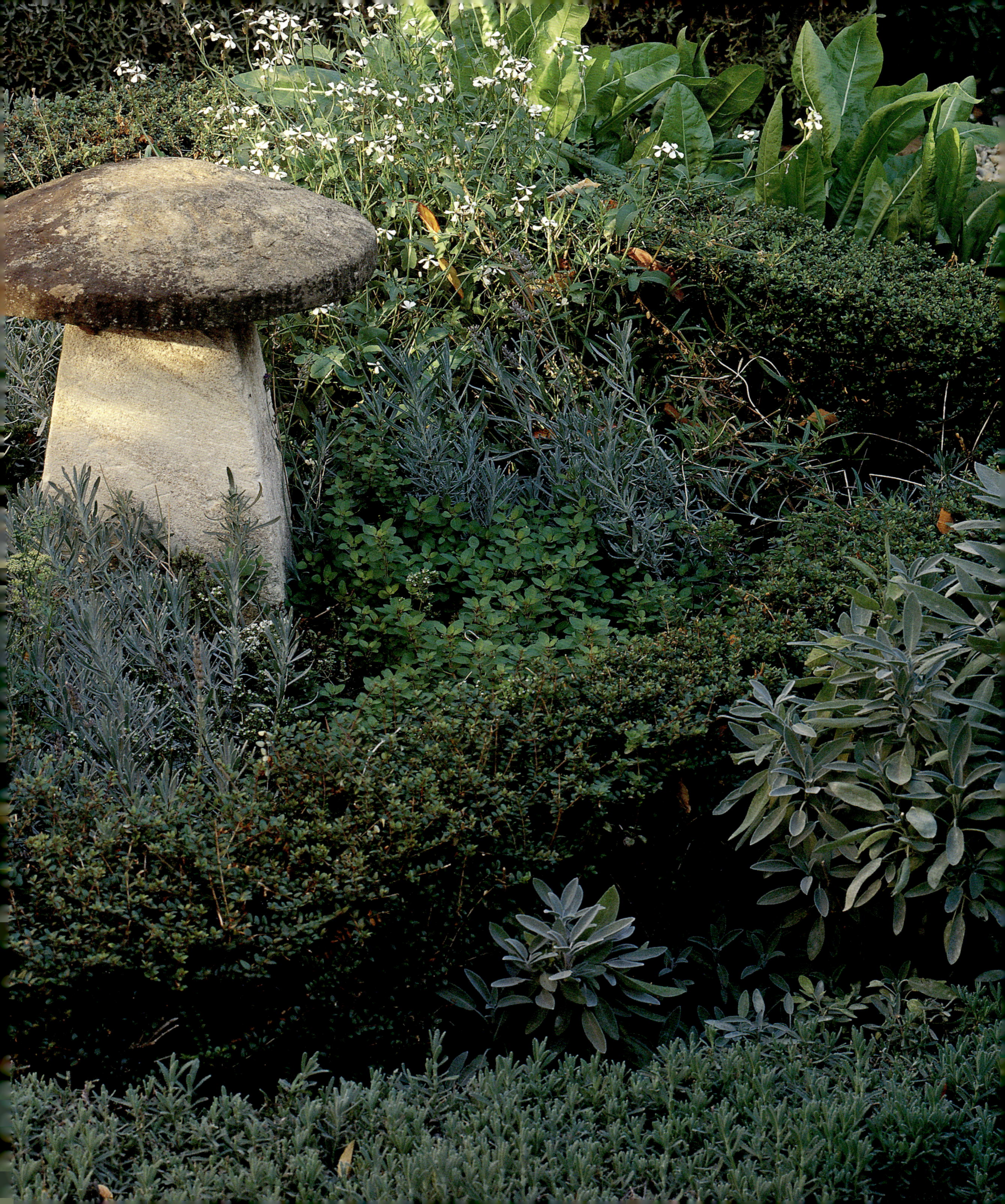

The smaller a garden is, the more disciplined the planting needs to be. To achieve the most striking effect, the planting scheme has to be kept simple and diversity limited. I also believe that the more formal the planting design is, the better the results will be in a small space. Plants that romp and ramble, spread untidily in summer then die back in winter, are exhilarating in a large area, but look messy in a small area and soon grow out of proportion to the other elements of a garden's design. Small gardens that are always on display need strong, clean lines and flourishing but controlled plantings year long.

Deciding on a planting scheme is one of the fundamental parts of the design process, to be done at the beginning of the project. As with every other aspect of developing your garden design, the starting point is establishing what style of garden best suits your house and the space available: the planting scheme follows from that decision. The garden of a house built in the English tradition should usually include some plants found in English gardens, such as roses, wisteria, lavenders and irises. The garden of a Mediterranean-influenced house will look in style filled with grey-leafed plants such as lavenders and rosemary. The garden of a contemporary house often takes dramatic foliage such as the fleshy, sometimes spiky, leaves of succulents.

As a consequence of analysing your house style and garden area, it is possible you may even decide that just a water feature and gravels of different colours or sizes, rather than plant material, will best set off

The fullness of the planting is sufficient to suggest this is a courtyard of plants, and to belie the fact that the garden bed contains only irises and roses, set against a background of pleached pear trees (Pyrus ussuriensis). It was not so important in this garden that rose bushes are at their least attractive in winter, because it is a swimming-pool courtyard. The paving, which the roses mellow, puts a safe distance between the bushes and the water of the pool.

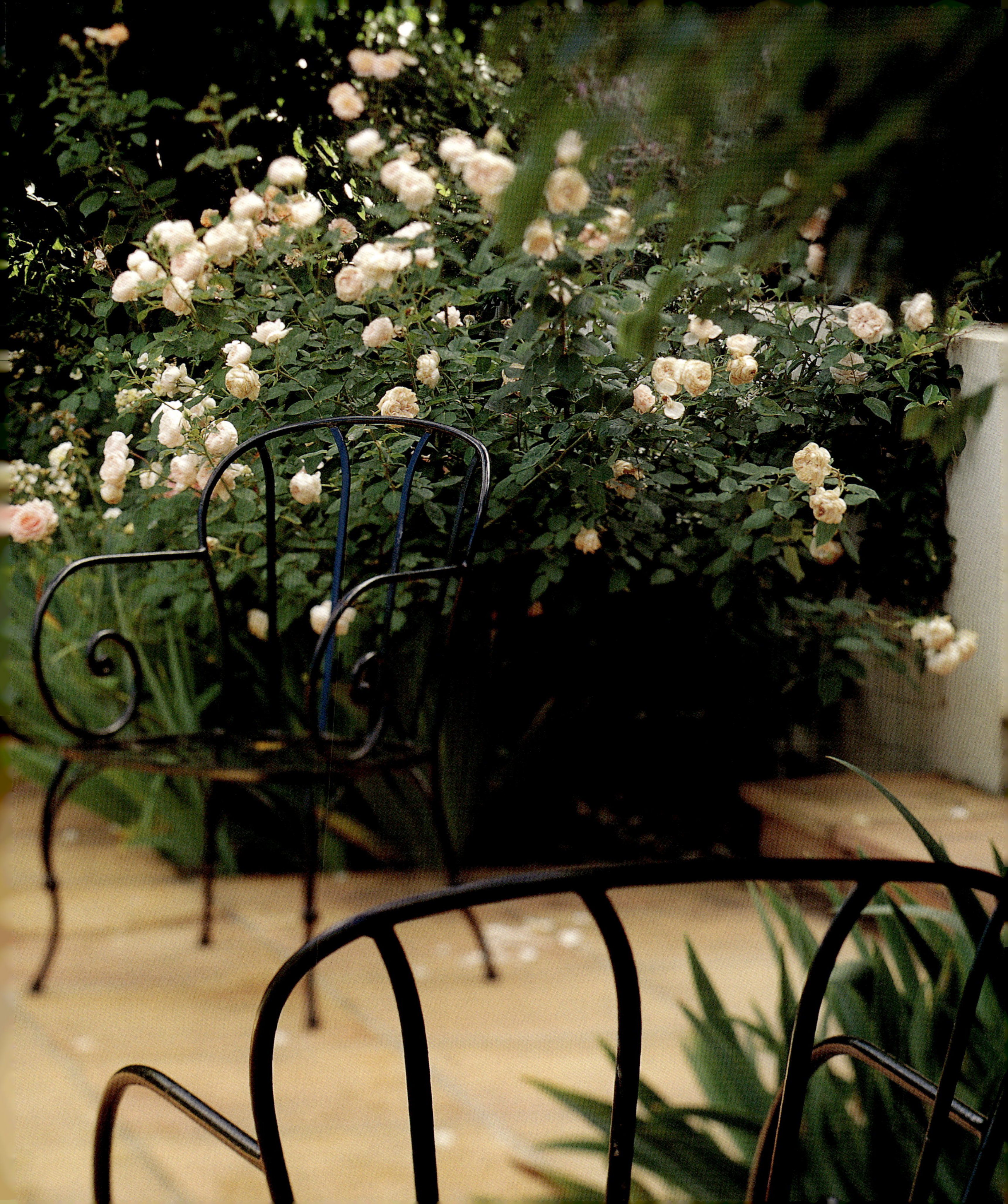

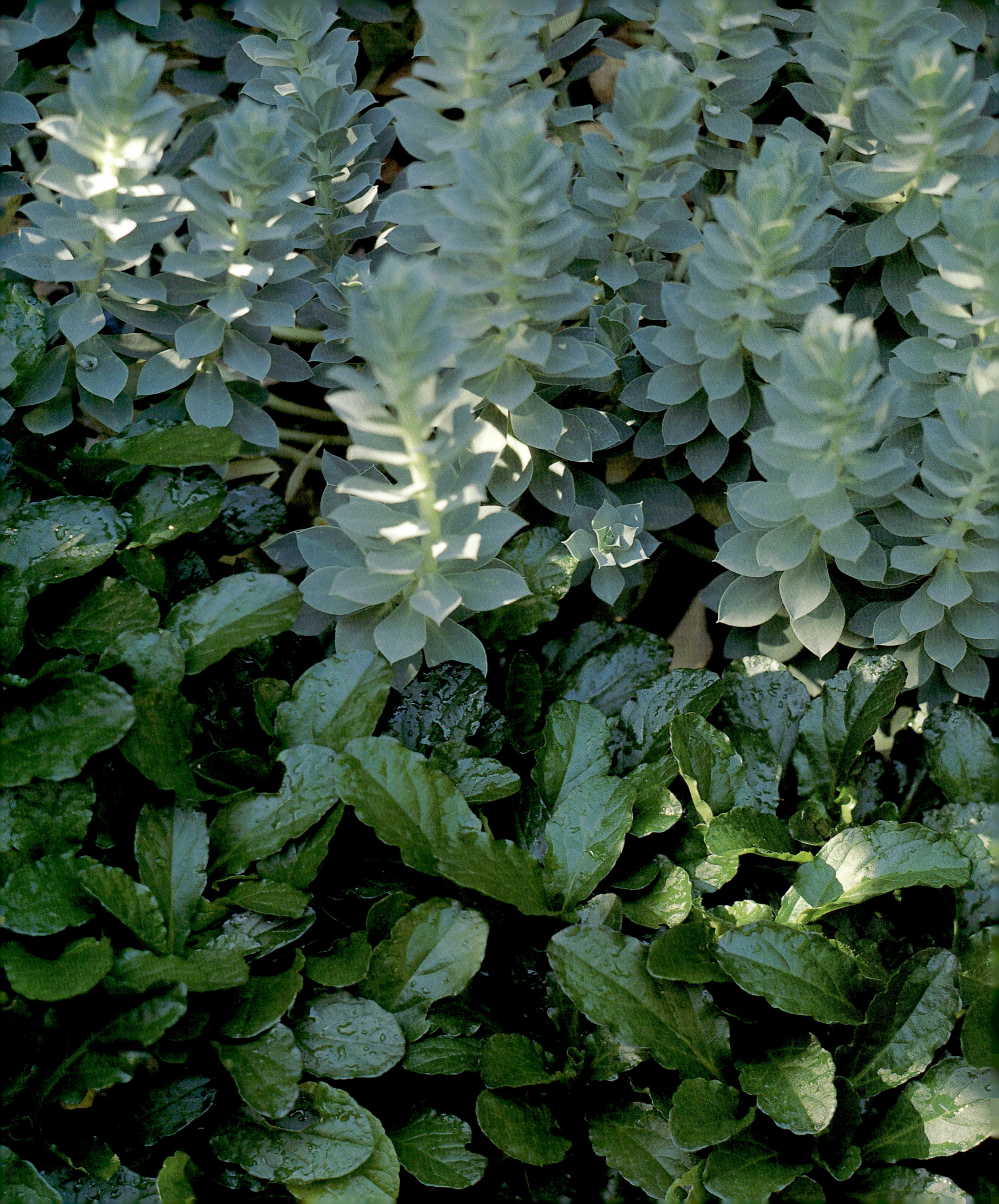

A demonstration of how effective green can be as the predominant colour in a garden, provided there is variation in tone, shape and texture: young green stems of Euphorbia myrsinites *thrust above the softer, darker green mat of the ground cover* Ajuga reptans. *However, the foliage of the euphorbia is also a foil for the spikes of blue when the ajuga is in flower. Both plants will thrive in partial shade or sun.*

the building and create sufficient interest for the eye. After all, some of the most harmonious gardens in the Japanese style rely only on rocks, pebbles and water. Again, the best design may be one in which some plants are included, but only as a minor component. Very restricted areas such as light wells and sideways may primarily need pavement to achieve some sense of space. These kinds of areas are often also difficult growing environments, and components other than struggling plants may look far more attractive.

A greater effort needs to be made to use the vertical plane for plants in a small garden, where pressure for space at ground level is more intense than in a larger one. Climbers such as wisteria, star jasmine (*Trachelospermum jasminoides*) and Boston ivy (*Parthenocissus tricuspidata*), rising above low, clipped hedges or flowering plants, add height and depth to the planting, while stealing little ground space or light from the other plants. Trained to grow around the arches and other decorative details of a trellis, they can also enhance the ornamentation of a garden.

There are suitable and unsuitable plants for a small garden. A small garden should always be given a strong framework of evergreen plants, particularly when it is an extension of the house used for many months of the year and viewed from the house all year round. A large garden overarched with bare trees can have a haunting beauty in winter; a small garden filled with leafless plants speaks of loss and desolation at a time when people most need to be reminded of life and growth. However, opting for evergreens is where discipline comes in, for you may well have favourite deciduous plants you long to see growing in your garden. And, exquisite though their flowers and scent may be, you will be disappointed with your garden for much of the year if you rely heavily on flowering plants. Few rose bushes, for example, bloom for

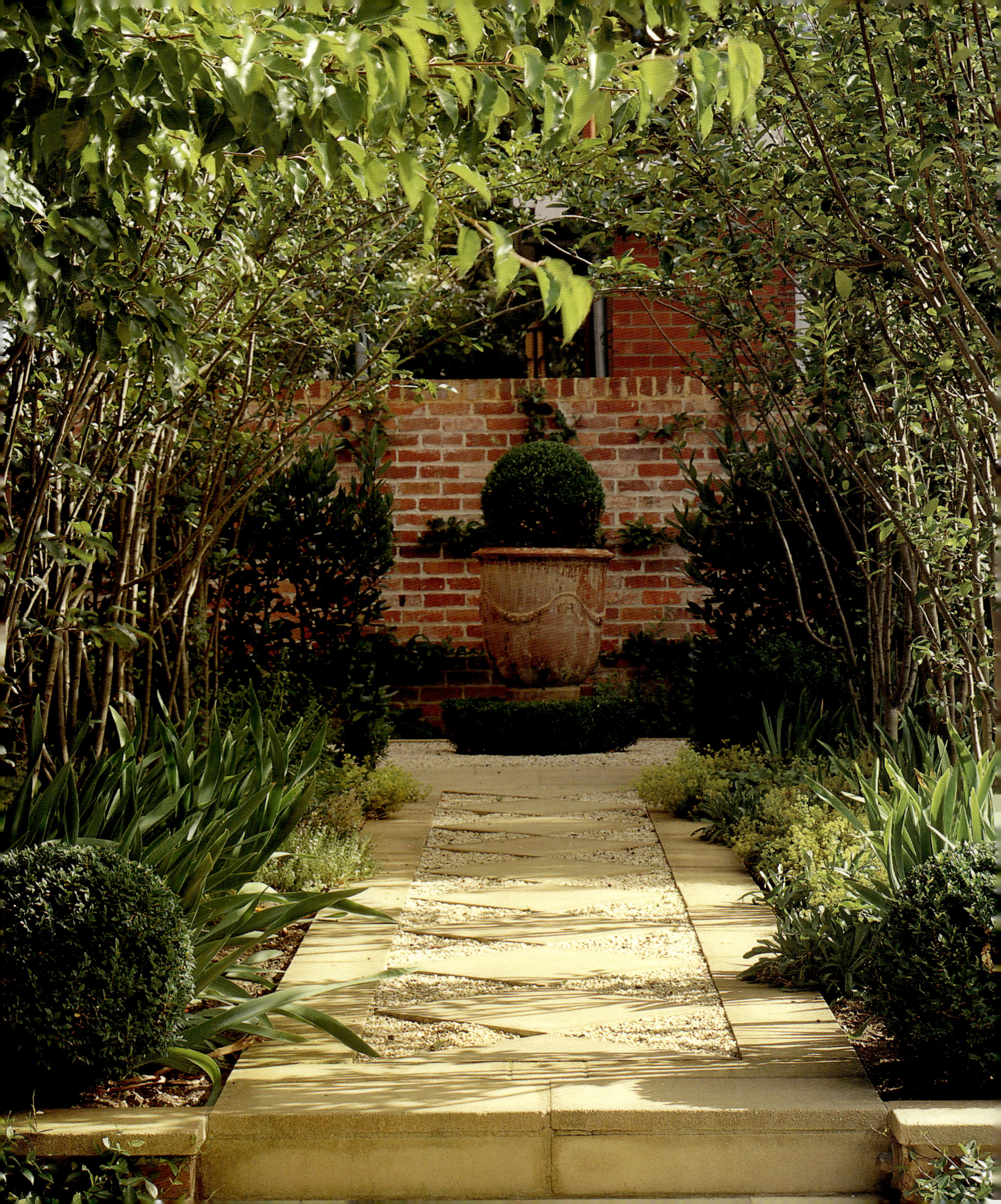

*A vista can be created even in a small garden (opposite). Two lines of six trees, with an urn at one end, turn a short path on one side of this garden into a convincing walk. In reality lines of trees were only possible because light-framed, deciduous crab apples (*Malus spectabilis*) were chosen.* Malus spectabilis *are particularly good value in a small garden because they have exquisite pink blossom in spring and yellow crab apples in autumn. The tunnel formed by the overarching branches further falsifies the perspective, and frames the richly glazed Anduze urn. For a short walk, plants are the best choice of secondary decoration. A simple sphere of English box (*Buxus sempervirens*), which matches two spheres marking the entry, gives the urn further height and solidity. Clumps of irises and a froth of Alchemilla mollis offer sufficient variety of form without compromising the unity of the walk.*

longer than one or two periods in the year, and most are bare in winter. In contrast, hedges of evergreens such as English box (*Buxus sempervirens*) or *Lonicera nitida* make an impact for twelve months of the year. This does not mean that deciduous plants have no place in a small garden: a few planted in a setting of evergreens impart a satisfying sense of the changing seasons and of decline and renewal in nature. The pale outlines of deciduous climbers and espaliered fruit trees, in particular, greatly enhance the winter garden.

One or two plants on their own have little impact, while numerous different plants grown in confusion are bewildering. Massed planting – the extensive use of one type of plant – is therefore the best style of planting for small gardens. Hedges, as much as drifts and large clumps of plants, constitute a massed planting. Cottage-garden plantings can be charming but they are not an appropriate style for small gardens. Flowering perennials and annuals require a lot of maintenance, are at their best only in the warm months and are straggly, dormant or dead for the rest of the year.

Since every plant is always on show in a small garden, the form, foliage and habit of each type chosen must be exceptional. It may be that one type of plant has beautifully shaped leaves but a lax habit, or an elegant branch structure but a tendency to shoot up to 10 metres. In addition, the different types of plants chosen must combine well to help achieve the larger effect intended in the garden design. Even the smallest garden, restricted to evergreens, requires at least subtle variation of shapes and sizes, and of shades of green or colours, to avoid monotony, and certain garden designs demand bold contrasts of form and foliage. The stimulation of an integrated planting scheme, in which every plant looks right year long, will ultimately make the rejection of a few favourites seem worthwhile.

Disciplined planning extends further: the plants chosen must be able to thrive in the environment into which they are being introduced. This means learning about the requirements of likely candidates, analysing your garden's physical characteristics quite closely before making the final selection, and providing and maintaining the conditions that the chosen plants need. No matter how desirable a plant otherwise is, don't use it if it is unsuited to the climate and soil of your area. It – and you – will only be miserable.

Special Problems

Temperature and the level of light, both throughout the day and throughout the year, are difficult to modify in any garden, and usually the best solution is to choose plants that originated in conditions similar to those prevailing in the garden. Problems of temperature and light are often magnified in small areas. High walls and neighbouring trees press around many small gardens, making them cool, shaded places for much of the day and year, while other small gardens, particularly paved courtyards enclosed by walls, soak up the sun and radiate heat from every surface. And some small gardens have one part that receives full sun and another — perhaps only a metre or two away — in heavy shade. This causes a problem for any garden design that has as its basis symmetrical planting: only the limited number of plants that grow equally well in sun or shade will provide the required uniformity.

Waterlogged soil is a potential problem in a small garden surrounded by high walls because solid structures and foundations trap water and prevent it from draining away, unless an adequate drainage system has been installed when work on the garden was first undertaken. Ventilation can also be a major problem in a courtyard: pests and diseases thrive in a windless environment. As a gentle movement of air is almost impossible to achieve in a small enclosed space, it is best to compensate for a lack of ventilation by planting only vigorous, hardy types of plants and avoiding precious plants that require constant applications of pesticides.

Correct nutrients and water are essentials for all plants, but in a small area they are of critical importance. Competition between plants is fierce. Particularly in the case of massed plantings, you are giving plants tougher growing conditions than normally prevail, so it is imperative to start with properly drained topsoil, to which a lot of decayed matter has been added, and to feed and water the plants regularly. Plants in large gardens tend to look after themselves to some extent: to feed on their own decayed leaf matter and draw water from their surroundings. Plants in a smaller garden are confronted by an essentially artificial environment: they need more fertilising and watering than they do in natural conditions. In the active months of spring and summer, and even into autumn, fertilise plants once a month, then provide another feed in winter.

The crab apple trees Malus ioensis *'Plena' were chosen for this pleached hedge to provide spring blossom and autumn colour: they have pale pink flowers and wonderful yellow autumn foliage. Crab apple trees are an excellent choice for a small pleached hedge: because they grow to only 4 or 5 m, they do not need constant clipping to keep them to a reasonable height. Their light framework, bare in winter, also makes them a good choice when the hedge is to screen, but not totally block off, one part of the garden. Pleached hedges have the great advantage that plants can be grown underneath. Here an enjoyable interplay has been set up between the loose mop-tops of the trees and the razor-sharp low hedge of English box. A planting of perennials and bulbs would be equally fitting, though more informal.*

Useful Plants

The plants listed in the following pages are the ones I have found particularly useful in small gardens, both for their hardiness and their suitability, and for their adaptability to the formal style, and its variations, that interests me. I have noted key characteristics of the plants that may influence your choice — namely, whether they are evergreen or deciduous, the colour of their flowers where appropriate, their height, and their preference for sun or shade.

Pleached Hedges and Small Trees

In the chapter 'Fundamentals' I mentioned the advantages of using a pleached hedge — a 'hedge on stilts' — in small gardens, particularly along a boundary. A pleached hedge allows plants to be grown in the bed beneath it, whereas a solid hedge may take up a long strip a metre or so in width. Although essentially a row of trees, a pleached hedge does not necessarily prevent the sun from reaching other plants: if the garden faces north or west, the hedge will not block out the light. However, if the garden faces south or east, shade-loving plants will need to be planted beneath the trees.

Although pleached hedges are usually grown to a greater height than solid hedges, like solid hedges they need to be clipped regularly. Many of the best trees for pleaching grow to a considerable height when left untouched. If these trees are allowed to grow to their full height, their canopies will become entangled and also look out of proportion with the straight, pruned trunks. Often the regular pruning required to keep the canopies neatly rounded and to a height of 5–8 metres can only be done with the aid of a cherrypicker; if this is a problem, a pleached hedge of small crab apples may be best. Before you acquire any tree for a small garden always establish what the root habit is and how far from a solid structure it needs to be planted. The following list gives the trees I have found useful for pleaching, and the heights to which they should be kept.

Alnus cordata Italian alder   deciduous, 7 m, sun
Arbutus unedo strawberry tree   evergreen, 5 m, sun
Ficus benjamina weeping fig   evergreen, 8 m, sun/shade
F. microcarpa var. *hillii* Hill's weeping fig   evergreen, 8 m, sun/shade
Magnolia grandiflora   evergreen, white flowers, 7 m, sun/shade
Malus ioensis 'Plena' Bechtel's crab apple   deciduous, pale pink flowers, 5 m, sun
Platanus × *acerifolia* London plane tree   deciduous, 8 m, sun
Populus yunnanensis Chinese poplar   deciduous, 7–8 m, sun
Pyrus calleryana   deciduous, white flowers, 6 m, sun
P. ussuriensis   deciduous, white flowers, 6 m, sun

Hill's weeping fig makes an excellent pleached hedge for the climates of Sydney, Brisbane and Perth; in Melbourne and the cooler States Italian alders, strawberry trees, pear trees and Chinese poplars are particularly suitable for pleaching. All the trees just mentioned are fast growing and therefore ideally planted as saplings. However, established trees, 4–5 metres in height, suitable for pleaching, can be purchased – at some cost – to create an immediate screen. In general, established deciduous trees are more suited to transplanting than advanced evergreens because they can be moved during their winter dormant period.

If privacy is your main aim, you may need to plant evergreens, such as Hill's weeping fig. However, quite often the branch structure of deciduous trees is sufficiently dense to provide a screen even in winter. Pear trees have only a short leafless period of about twelve weeks, at a time of the year when people are likely to be inside.

If the design and the space available lend themselves to the inclusion of a few specimen trees, there are a number of shapely, lightly structured, non-invasive ones to choose from. In the list below I have included hornbeams and lime, or linden, trees – so much a part of English and

Continental gardens – because of their form and because I have grown them successfully here, but be warned that they are very slow developers and susceptible to hot sunlight, which can burn their leaves.

Acacia melanoxylon blackwood   evergreen, yellow balls, 27 m, sun/partial shade
Carpinus betulus 'Fastigiata'   deciduous, 7 m, sun/shade
Cupressus sempervirens 'Stricta' pencil pine   evergreen, 8 m, sun/partial shade
Magnolia grandiflora   evergreen, white flowers, 10 m, sun/shade
Malus 'Gorgeous'   deciduous, white flowers, 2–4 m, sun
M. ioensis 'Plena' Bechtel's crab apple   deciduous, pale pink flowers, 5 m, sun
M. spectabilis   deciduous, pink flowers, 6 m, sun
Olea europaea olive   evergreen, 6 m, sun
Tilia × europaea lime, linden   deciduous, 30 m, sun/partial shade
Ulmus parvifolia Chinese elm   deciduous, 8 m, sun/partial shade

Hedges

To disguise a paling fence or fudge a boundary line, a solid hedge of cypress or holly may be required. However, hedges higher than 2–3 metres are overpowering in small gardens, and dense hedges take up precious space at ground level. Kept to the heights suggested, the following trees make suitable boundary hedges in small gardens.

Acmena smithii lillypilly   evergreen, 3 m, sun
Carpinus betulus   deciduous, 2 m, sun/shade
× *Cupressocyparis leylandii* Leyland cypress   evergreen, 2–5 m, sun
Ficus carica fig   deciduous, 2 m, sun/shade
Ilex aquifolium holly   evergreen, 2 m, sun/shade
Laurus nobilis bay   evergreen, 2 m, sun/shade
Ligustrum ovalifolium privet   evergreen, white flowers, 2 m, sun
Prunus lusitanica Portuguese laurel   evergreen, white flowers, 2 m, sun/shade
Viburnum odoratissimum   evergreen, white flowers, 2 m, sun
V. tinus   evergreen, white flowers, 2 m, sun/shade

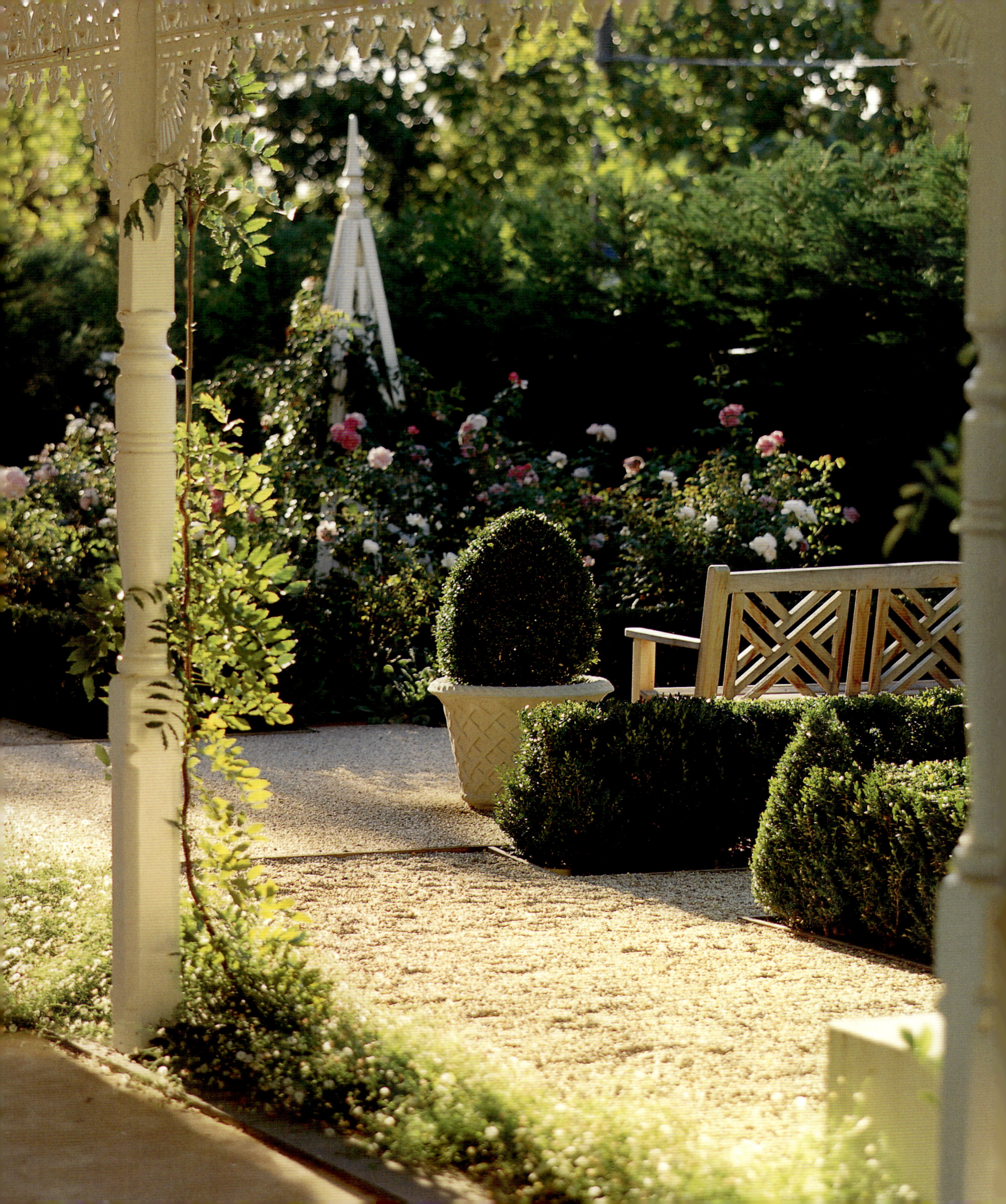

Looking towards the second rose bed (opposite) in the garden shown on pp. 68–9: this is a small garden that appears larger because of the vertical accents of wisteria-covered verandah, obelisks and cones of English box; the strong lines of the edging hedges and paths; and the rich detail of the beds and two seating bays. Pests and funguses can make growing roses a nightmare in a small courtyard, but this garden has sufficient sunlight and movement of air for it not to be a major problem. As well, David Austin roses were chosen because they are particularly resilient. In winter, when the roses are not in bloom, the English box and screening hedge of Leyland cypress (×Cupressocyparis leylandii), and the formal organisation of the design, ensure the garden still looks good.

Anyone who knows my gardens will know that English box is my favourite plant for low hedges! Its tidy form and neat, dark leaves are handsome year long, it is easy to grow, needs little maintenance other than trimming, and will take full shade or full sun. But its attraction extends beyond this. It is the perfect plant for the highly stylised hedges required in formal designs; a plant so dense and regular of form that it is almost a sculptural material, to be clipped into whatever shape is wanted; a plant whose colour is so intense and even that it seems the ideal of green.

I also frequently use *Lonicera nitida* for small hedges because it takes tough conditions and hard trimming to as low as 150 millimetres, although it needs more constant attention than English box because it grows faster. *Murraya paniculata* and *Gardenia augusta* 'Florida', with their white flowers and glossy leaves, make fragrant low hedges in the hot, moist conditions of semi-tropical and tropical zones. Gardenias are ill-suited to cool temperate climates, although murraya is more adaptable. The following list gives the evergreen plants I have found useful as low edging hedges, and suitable heights.

Buxus microphylla var. *japonica*   1 m, sun/shade
B. sempervirens English box   1 m, sun/shade
Gardenia augusta 'Florida'   white flowers, 70 cm, sun
Lavandula × *allardii*   purple flowers, 1 m, sun
L. angustifolia English lavender   purple flowers, 50 cm, sun
L. dentata French lavender   mauve-blue flowers, 70 cm, sun
Lonicera nitida   60 cm, sun/shade
Murraya paniculata   white flowers, 1.6 m, sun
Myrsine africana   60 cm, sun/shade

Border and ornamental hedges need regular clipping. People are often nervous about trimming and pruning plants — they worry that, in tackling the job head-on, they will make an irreversible mistake — but a vigorous attack is rarely necessary. Constant light clipping achieves better results than one heavy cutting-back session. The more a plant is trimmed or pruned, the more it will grow in response, and to the shape desired. However, different plants do have different trimming or pruning requirements. English box is trimmed in spring after its first flush of growth, and then trimmed every six to eight weeks for the rest of the growing season to promote thickening. Espaliered deciduous fruit trees, like deciduous fruit trees in general, need an annual pruning in winter, then only light pruning throughout the growing season.

Border Plants

My definition of a border — any bed deeper than a metre — does not fit the traditional perennial border, but there is unlikely to be room in a small garden for a bed that is up to 6 metres deep. The following shrubs, perennials and other plants are the ones I have found most useful for borders in small gardens.

Alchemilla mollis   perennial, greenish yellow flowers, 40 cm, shade
Clivia miniata   evergreen rhizome, orange/white flowers, 60 cm, shade
Cycas revoluta   evergreen cycad, 1.5 m, sun
Euphorbia amygdaloides subsp. *robbiae*   semi-evergreen perennial, green flowers, 50 cm, sun
E. myrsinites   evergreen perennial, greenish yellow flowers, 8 cm, sun/shade
E. wulfenii   evergreen perennial, green flowers, 60 cm, sun
Hosta plantaginea var. *grandiflora*   perennial, white flowers, 50 cm, shade
H. sieboldiana   perennial, white flowers, 50 cm, shade
Hydrangea arborescens 'Grandiflora'   deciduous shrub, white flowers, 1.6 m, shade
H. macrophylla   deciduous shrub, white/blue flowers, 1.2 m, shade
H. macrophylla 'Blue Wave'   deciduous shrub, blue flowers, 1.2 m, shade
Iris germanica   rhizome, blue/white/brown flowers, 60 cm, sun/shade
Lavandula dentata French lavender   evergreen shrub, mauve-blue flowers, 1.5 m, sun
Rhododendron 'Alba Magnifica'   evergreen azalea, white flowers, 60 cm, sun/shade
Rosmarinus officinalis rosemary   evergreen shrub, blue flowers, 1.5 m, sun
R. officinalis 'Blue Lagoon'   evergreen shrub, blue flowers, 1.5 m, sun
Salvia uliginosa bog sage   perennial, blue flowers, 1.2 m, sun
Santolina chamaecyparissus cotton lavender   evergreen shrub, yellow flowers, 40 cm, sun
Sedum 'Autumn Joy'   semi-evergreen perennial, green flowers turning terracotta, 60 cm, sun
Stachys byzantina lamb's ears   evergreen perennial, blue flowers, 30 cm, sun
Zantedeschia aethiopica 'Green Goddess' arum lily   perennial, green flowers, 1.2 m, shade

Sedum *'Autumn Joy'* (top left) is an excellent succulent for a dry border or a pot in a sunny position. Its toothed leaves maintain their vibrancy for most of the year, and its green flowerheads turn russet as summer wanes. Iris germanica (top right), the common bearded iris, is very hardy, but needs full sun. Although its flowers are unsurpassed, it is the verticality of its leaves and its clump-forming tendency that make it such an outstanding plant. Euphorbia wulfenii (bottom left) is another tough plant, and takes very dry conditions. Its stems of bluish green leaves need to be kept cut back, with the reward that it bears heads of yellow-green flowers for up to two years at a time. Hosta plantaginea var. grandiflora (bottom right), with its arching leaves, is ideal for a moist, shady border — where it forms large clumps — or pot.

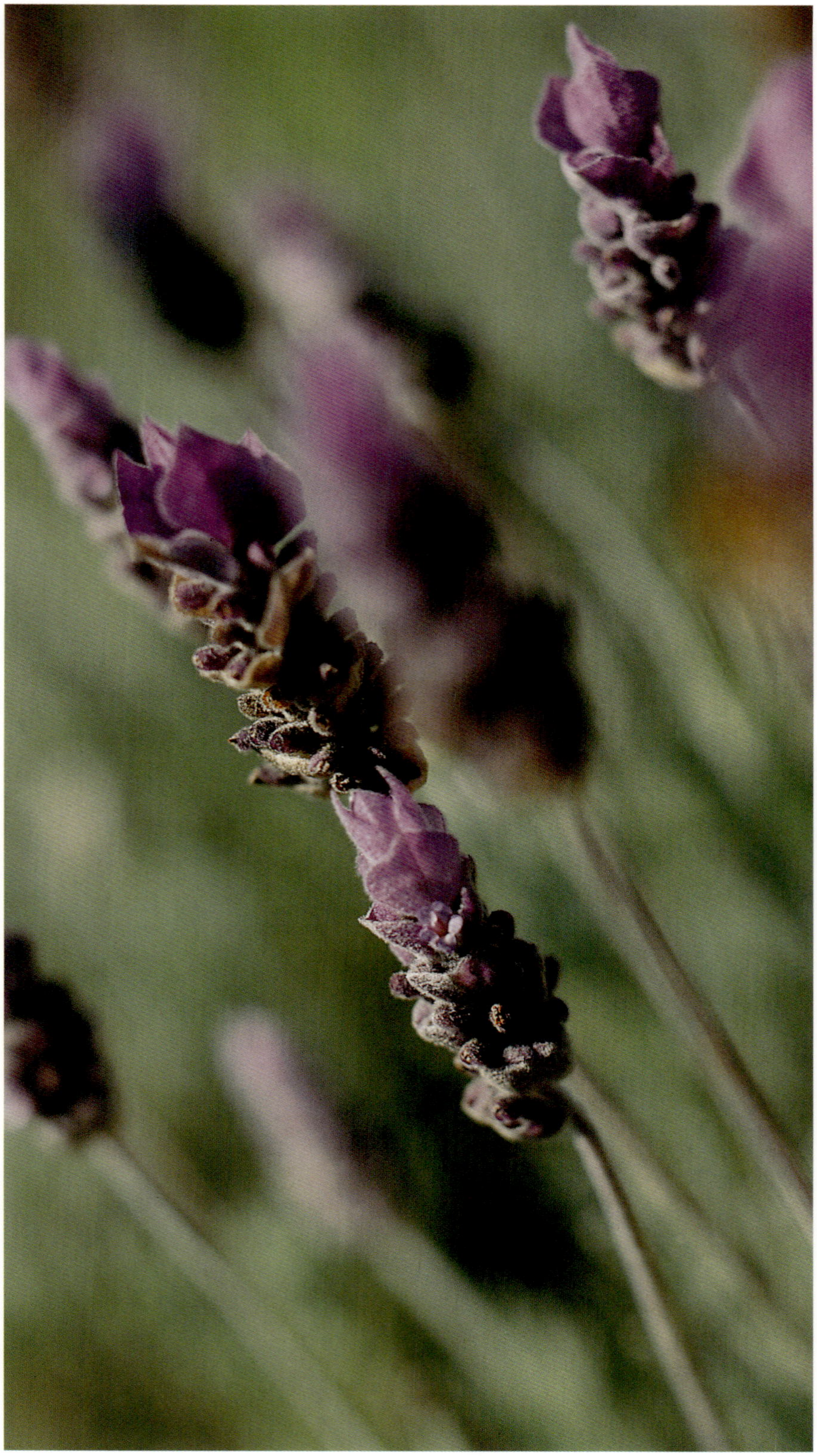

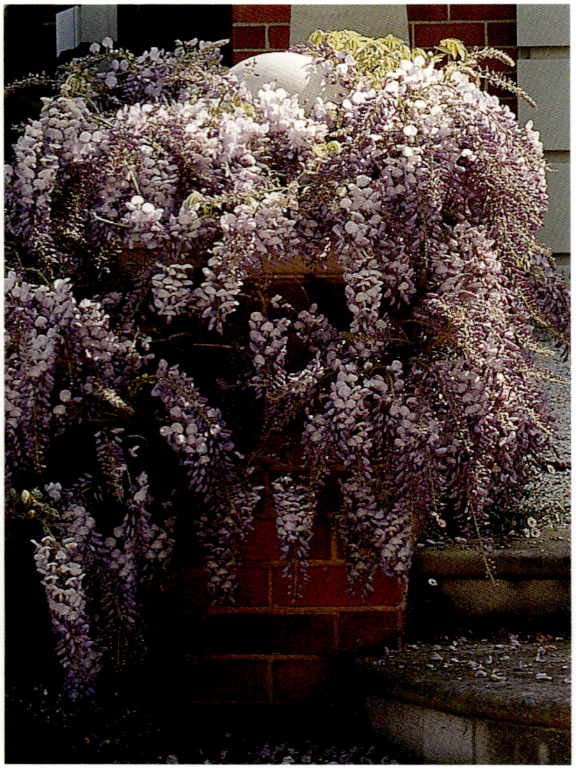

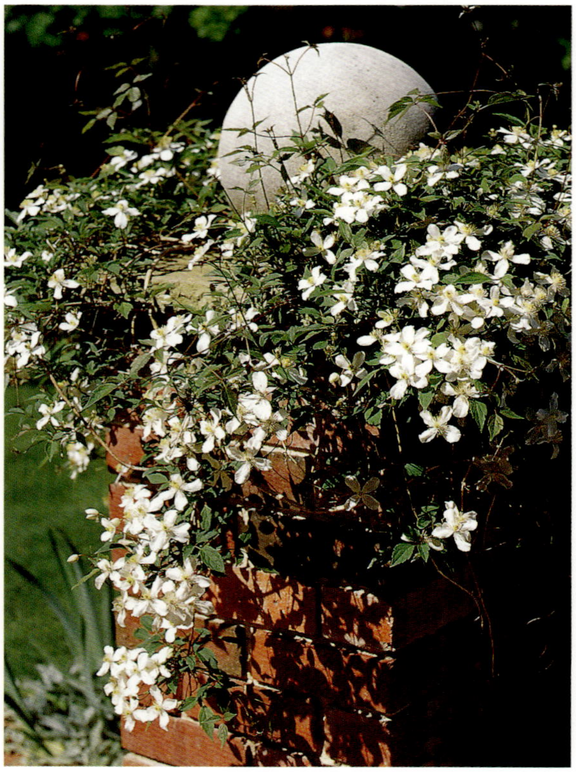

I find myself planting these flowers again and again in small gardens. French lavender, Lavandula dentata (opposite far left), with its aromatic, greyish foliage and spikes of strong mauve-blue flowers, is one of the best and hardiest plants for massed plantings or even just as an accent. It thrives in full sun and can flower for nine to ten months of the year. Wisteria sinensis (opposite top right) is my favourite climber for outlining the features of a house or decorative trellis, but it can also wonderfully drape harsh brick retaining walls and piers, provided that it is kept strictly controlled with regular pruning. Its twisted form when bare in winter has its own fascination. The deciduous climber Clematis montana (opposite bottom right) is a lighter option for a pier. In spring the sphere of a pier rises like a moon from a cloud of starry white flowers.

Climbers

Contrary to popular belief, climbers do not get into houses and destroy them; however, they can certainly clog up gutters and plant their aerial roots on paintwork. Avoid the more invasive ones — ivy, wisteria and Virginia creeper, for instance — if you do not have the time to regularly prune them, and choose instead a more delicate one such as clematis. I often effectively restrain climbers by training them around a feature such as a window or along the top of a decorative wall, using stainless-steel wires and brackets and a mechanism that allows the user to tighten the wires regularly. These are the climbers I often plant in small gardens (their mature heights have not been given because all climbers should be controlled).

Clematis montana   deciduous, white flowers, sun
Ficus pumila creeping fig   evergreen, sun/shade
Hydrangea petiolaris climbing hydrangea   deciduous, white flowers, sun/shade
Parthenocissus quinquefolia Virginia creeper   deciduous, sun/shade
P. tricuspidata Boston ivy   deciduous, sun/shade
Trachelospermum jasminoides star jasmine   evergreen, white flowers, sun/shade
Wisteria floribunda   deciduous, blue flowers, sun
W. sinensis   deciduous, blue flowers, sun
W. sinensis 'Alba'   deciduous, white flowers, sun
Rosa 'Albertine'   deciduous, pink flowers, sun
R. 'New Dawn'   deciduous, pink flowers, sun
Climbing *R.* 'Iceberg'   deciduous, white flowers, sun

Plants for Ornamental Pools

Both true water plants such as water lilies (*Nymphaea*) and *Nymphoides*, which have their roots below the water though their leaves and flowers lie on the surface, and plants that like to stand with their feet in water, such as *Iris laevigata, I. pseudacorus* and the Louisiana hybrid irises, need oxygenated water. The pools in which they are planted must contain oxygenating plants, which grow beneath the surface and are obtainable from nurseries. Apart from ensuring that the water receives oxygen and does not become stagnant, maintenance of the pool is virtually nil.

Herbs and Vegetables

Many herbs and vegetables are attractive plants as well as useful ones, so they certainly earn a place in a small garden. Often they are given their own patch or a particular place in a bed, or grown in pots. However, they can also be the basis of a formal, geometric design for the whole garden. The design is delineated by low, clipped hedges and the spaces between planted with annual herbs and vegetables, rotated according to their growing season. The hedges ensure that the pattern remains to interest viewers even when winter encroaches and annual plants decline. English box and *Lonicera nitida*, as always, make good edging plants, but rosemary and lavender also clip well and look most appropriate. Even strawberries (*Fragaria*) can edge the herb and vegetable compartments. Flowers can be integrated into a herb or vegetable garden to considerable effect – far better than herbs or vegetables into a flower garden.

Ground Covers

Ground covers have a number of uses in small gardens, conventional and unconventional: they can go beneath trees and clipped hedges, but they can also be used to form geometric patterns in a formal garden design, in the same way that materials such as gravel are used. Thyme being tough and sun-loving is ideal planted in geometric patterns and paved areas. I often use climbers such as the *Trachelospermum* species and ivies given below as ground covers; they are excellent as long as they are regularly clipped to the heights suggested. All the plants listed are evergreen.

- *Erigeron karvinskianus*   30 cm, sun/shade
- *Hedera canariensis* Canary Island ivy   30 cm, sun/shade
- *H. helix* English ivy   30 cm, sun/shade
- *Soleirolia soleirolii* baby's tears   10 cm, shade
- *Thymus serpyllum* 'Alba' wild thyme   white flowers, 10 cm, sun
- *Trachelospermum asiaticum*   white flowers, 20 cm, sun/shade
- *T. jasminoides* star jasmine   white flowers, 30 cm, sun/shade
- *Viola hederacea* Australian native violet   blue flowers, 25 cm, shade
- *V. odorata* violet   white/blue flowers, 7 cm, sun/shade

Plants for Pots

Plants for pots need to be hardy ones because their growing conditions are constricted and challenging. The sun dries out pots quickly and the plants cannot seek water. Climbers in pots have a limited life: they always seem to reach a certain height, then decline. Roses in pots need such constant feeding, watering and attention in general that I don't advise using them. However, all the following plants do well.

> *Buxus sempervirens* English box   evergreen shrub, clipped, sun/shade
> *Citrus* species   evergreen trees and shrubs, clipped, sun
> *Hosta* species   perennial, 50–150 cm, moist shade
> *Lavandula dentata* French lavender   evergreen shrub, mauve-blue flowers, 1.5 m, sun
> *Pelargonium* geranium   evergreen perennial, flowers various colours, 60 cm, sun
> *Sedum* 'Autumn Joy'   semi-evergreen perennial, green flowers turning terracotta, 60 cm, sun

Plants for Balconies

Balconies are rigorous environments for plants. The plants are buffeted by more winds than they would be on the ground, and the winds quickly dry out their pots. If it is possible to add an attractive screen to your balcony, plants will do better. Because a screen is visible from the outside of a building, permission from the local council, or from the body corporate if the balcony is part of an apartment, may be needed.

Plants are also exposed to the sun – or, on some recessed balconies, to permanent shade. Pot plants on balconies need to be watered every day, so some kind of watering system is essential if there are a lot. Plants have a very limited life in this environment, so you have to be prepared to change them quite regularly.

When a balcony is the only space available for plants, massed pots in tiers may seem the best way to achieve the effect of a garden. However, plants should never obscure the view for people sitting on the balcony or in a room that gives onto the balcony. And plants do much better if they are kept below balustrade height: any plant above that gets blown about by the wind.

The plants listed above as suitable for pots are also, with the exception of the hostas, sturdy enough for balconies. Lillypillies will grow in pots on a balcony, in either sun or shade, and provide a leafy background, but they must be shielded from the wind. English box, bays and olives are all hardy trees that can withstand some wind; they need to be kept clipped, although confined on a balcony they will grow even more slowly than they do in the ground. Olive trees require a sunny position; box and bay trees can be placed in either sun or shade.

Light Wells and Internal Courtyards

Light wells are the most difficult garden places of all. They get no ventilation and usually very little light. As space is very constricted, the climbers Virginia creeper, Boston ivy, creeping fig and English ivy (*Hedera helix*), all of which take low light levels, are valuable. A central internal courtyard is larger than a narrow light well, and may get more light, but ventilation is unlikely to be much better in most cases. As I discussed earlier, it may be wiser to restrict the design to a water feature and interesting paving or gravels than to persist with unhealthy plants.

The smaller a garden, the more attention to appearance it needs. Some of the plants hardy enough to flourish there can also take the area over, and have to be regularly cut back to prevent them swamping the other plants and spoiling the lines of the design. Small gardens are not necessarily high-maintenance gardens in terms of the total number of hours per week that have to be spent on them, but they do require consistent maintenance because they are always on view.

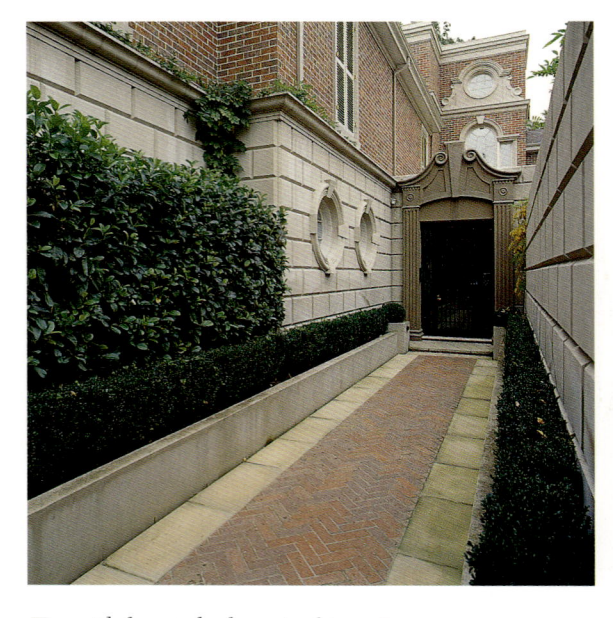

To avoid the wind, plants in this rooftop garden (opposite) needed to be kept to below the height of the balustrade. The garden can afford a severe planting because it borrows excitement from the view, and a touch of whimsy from a pair of stone lions that survey the city from two couches of English box. A long walkway (above) is a difficult space to make attractive, and a tough environment for plants. Because ventilation and light were so poor and this walkway so narrow, hedges of English box were an obvious choice. I was, however, also able to fit a taller hedge of fragrant-flowered Viburnum odoratissimum in a recess to achieve a depth of green. These shrubs hate wind so thrive in such a position. A line of wisteria drifts along the top of the first-storey moulding, able to catch some sunlight.

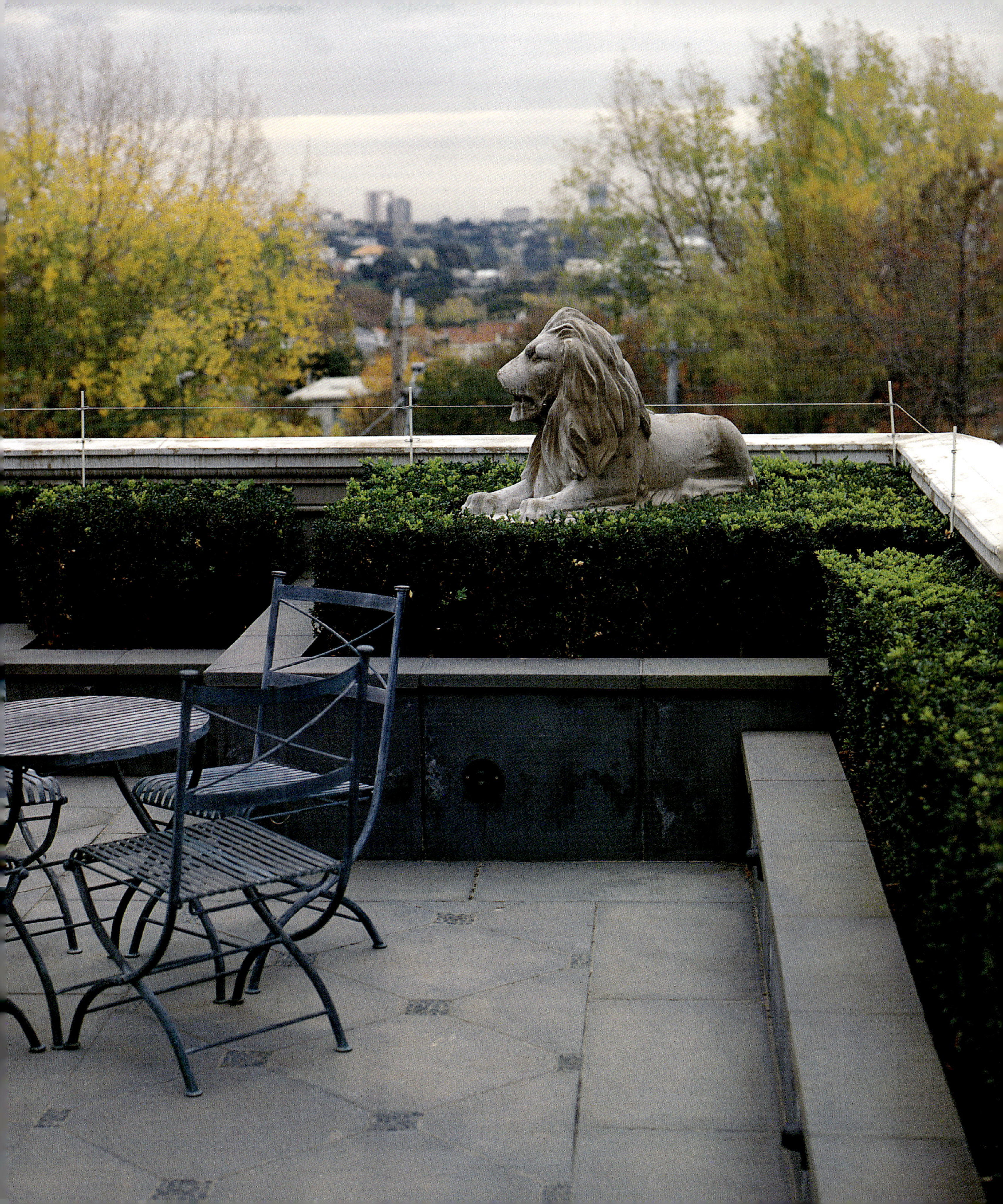

A Picking Garden

*The picking garden comprises two sections, a swimming-pool area and this lower herb and vegetable garden, which is visually the focus of the whole garden. The central bed of the herb and vegetable garden is outlined with French lavender (*Lavandula dentata*) that circles a diamond formed by* Lonicera nitida *divided into quadrants by plantings of English lavender (*L. angustifolia*). The compartments created are planted with herbs. The hub of the bed is an appropriately rustic old English staddle-stone. A seat beyond amusingly extends the use of lavender; French lavender forms the skirt and armrests, L. × allardii the back.*

The owner of this picking garden is a wonderful plantswoman with whom I have enjoyed working over a number of years. Her picking garden is a more recently designed part of the garden that I first described in The Defined Garden *(1996). An enclosed garden, running the width of the back of the house, it is divided into two parts: a swimming-pool courtyard and a sunken herb-cum-vegetable garden. The owner wanted the whole area, which is within easy reach of the kitchen, to be a functional one filled with herbs, vegetables and fruit trees; however, she also wanted it to be aesthetically pleasing because the windows of the kitchen and the living area look into it. Planting most of the intrinsically informal annuals and perennials in beds formally edged by clipped hedges, within a geometric ground plan, seemed the best way to achieve a picking garden yet avoid the problem of the space looking scruffy and formless in winter.*

The house is a two-storey, clinker-brick building with white wooden window frames and doors, in a mock-Tudor style. Visitors move from one part of the picking garden to the other through an opening between two wing walls, 600 millimetres high, built in the same brick as the house walls. On top of the piers that flank the opening between the wing walls, we placed two spheres carved from stone, in traditional European style — simple ornamentation but sufficiently strong to punctuate the entry.

French windows open directly from the informal living area onto the first section of the picking garden, the swimming-pool courtyard. Originally the couryard was dominated by a Hawaiian-style, kidney-shaped swimming pool, surrounded by wooden sleepers, which was quite unsuited to the house. We replaced the pool with a much more discreet rectangular one. Being narrower, it left the courtyard with a more functional space, which we paved in the same brick as the house.

A large evergreen hedge of bay trees (*Laurus nobilis*) wraps around the garden to help screen out the neighbours and provides the owner with aromatic leaves for cooking. Bay trees grow slowly, so mature plants were installed.

On the far side of the courtyard a narrow garden bed abuts the swimming pool, its plants actually spilling over the edge, and extends along an adjacent wall. Despite their proximity to the pool, plants thrive in the bed. The owner's family is grown up so there are rarely children splashing about in the water. The plants in the bed constantly change. If the owner sees new ones that she likes, she is not afraid to rip out the old ones. Originally angelicas, hogweed (*Heracleum giganteum*) and members of the Umbelliferae family were planted in the shady bed, highlighted by the dark green of the bay hedge, but soon they were replaced with euphorbias. Such changes are not as radical as they sound, however, for the architecture of the garden itself stays the same.

Two lemon trees (*Citrus limon* 'Meyer'), clipped into standards, were placed in 77-centimetre pots on either side of the swimming-pool terrace at its northern end. Like everything else grown in the garden, the large trees provide the owner with produce for the house, yielding over a hundred lemons every year. Though the swimming-pool courtyard is primarily for outdoor living, it decidedly fulfills the owner's vision of the whole back area as one picking garden.

People sitting around the swimming pool have the pleasure of looking through the opening formed by the two wing walls into the sunken herb and vegetable garden. The area was already lower than the house and the swimming-pool courtyard when I began constructing the garden, and I did not excavate further; however, I added brick steps in keeping with the house, the upper level and the wing walls.

The herb and vegetable garden was a small area, measuring about 5 metres by 5 metres, which I surrounded on two sides with a simple, free-standing trellis fence, 2.2 metres high. I wanted the trellis to match the trim on the house and be quite a focal point in itself, so I painted it white. To further dramatise it, I gave it a backing painted dark green. The dark colour recedes so that the boundary of the small area is blurred a little.

I decided to place a circular planting bed at the centre of the herb and vegetable garden, partly because that was an appropriately traditional design for such a garden, and partly because whenever

I design for a small square I like to incorporate a central circle of some kind — a circle is perfect for softening the hard lines of the perimeter. This was a house, too, whose brickwork had been mellowed by climbers, so it was important to construct a courtyard in keeping with that effect.

For the centrepiece of the planting bed I chose a delightful old staddle-stone imported from England, sufficiently unusual to be a focal point of the herb and vegetable garden and yet simple enough to suit the size and practical purpose of the area. Staddle-stones were originally functional, not ornamental, objects used in rural England to stop rats from devouring hay stacks. The hay was stored on timber boards supported by lines of the stones, the mushroom shape of the stones preventing any rodents from reaching the fodder.

Around the staddle-stone we planted three hedges. We did not want these to be too formal so we used a combination of *Lonicera nitida* and lavenders. The outermost, lowest hedge was a circle of French lavender (*Lavandula dentata*), within which was planted a diamond of lonicera and four spokes of English lavender (*L. angustifolia*), which radiated from the staddle-stone to join the diamond at its points — with the result that eight compartments for herbs were created within the circular bed. In these the owner plants parsley, sage and thyme and all the other traditional herbs that die and need replacing annually. She regularly changes the types of herbs planted, rotating them according to their requirements and growing seasons.

I edged the herb bed with brick to contain it and separate it from the gravel of the path that encircles it. Gravel was chosen for the softness of its effect, since there was already considerable brick paving in the swimming-pool section. A deep garden bed, edged with French lavender, runs around the perimeter of the herb and vegetable garden. The border hedges in the herb and vegetable garden are usually not allowed to flower. Lavenders make excellent hedges, particularly if they are prevented from flowering; once they have flowered they tend to become woody. The owner grows her vegetables in the perimeter garden beds. Being originally a country woman, she expects a garden to provide her with a steady supply. She also grows perennial and annual flowers and more herbs here, combining them with the vegetables in cottage-garden fashion — though the effect, given the clear geometric lines of the garden's design and its neatly hedged compartments, is quite different from that of a blousy cottage garden.

Jonathan apples (top) were trained to grow along the low wing walls separating the two sections of the garden, while golden delicious apples (bottom) were grown to frame the windows of the house. In both cases the apple boughs lend an appearance of venerability to hard brickwork.

This ground plan (not to scale) is not what the term 'picking garden' immediately conjures up (below): on the contrary, it suggests there was little space available for planting. However, by using the vertical surfaces and the perimeter areas to the full, room was found in the southern section, the herb and vegetable garden, for espaliered persimmon and Nashi pear trees on its southern and western sides, crab apple trees (Malus) in the south- and north-western corners, herbs in the compartments of the central bed, picking flowers as well as vegetables in the beds around the perimeter, and Jonathan and golden delicious apple trees on the retaining and house walls respectively. Even in the swimming-pool section there was space for a bay hedge (Laurus nobilis) on the western and northern sides and rosemary hedges (Rosmarinus officinalis) beside the retaining walls, for two large lemons in pots (Citrus limon 'Meyer') placed in the north-eastern and -western corners and for picking flowers in the long bed tucked between the pool and the hedge on the west.

Two sides of the herb and vegetable garden are marked by a trellis (right). It was designed as an open grid to support espaliered persimmon (Diospyros) and Nashi pear trees. In this instance I chose to have the (white) timberwork contrast, rather than harmonise, with the (green) background to vividly display the lines of the trees espaliered on it. The hedges of rosemary edging the wing walls inform visitors that they are about to enter a herb garden.

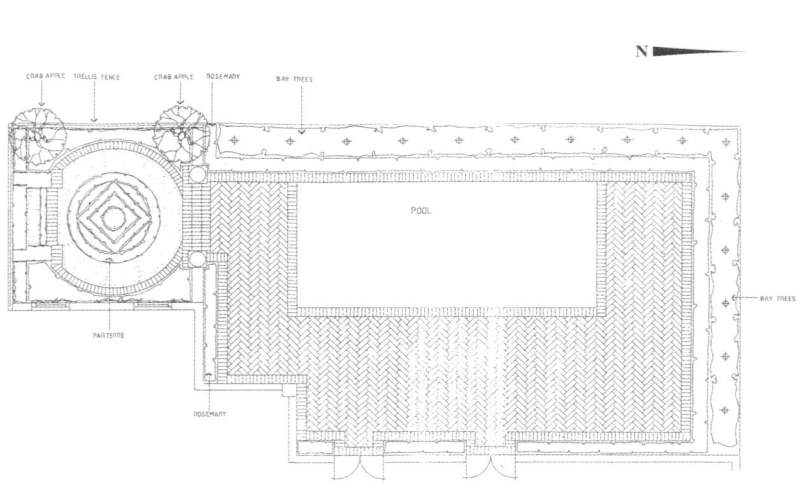

[134]

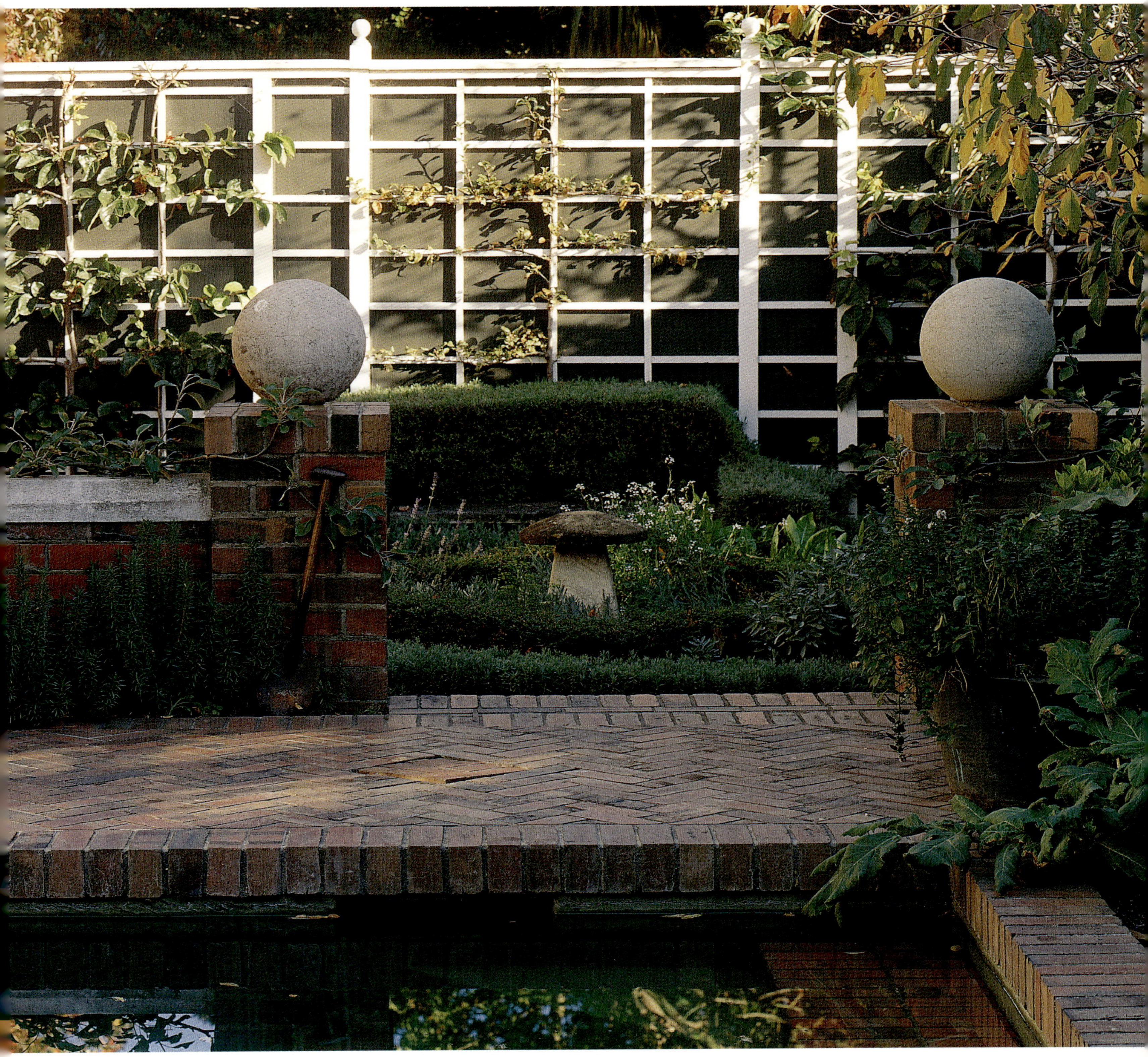

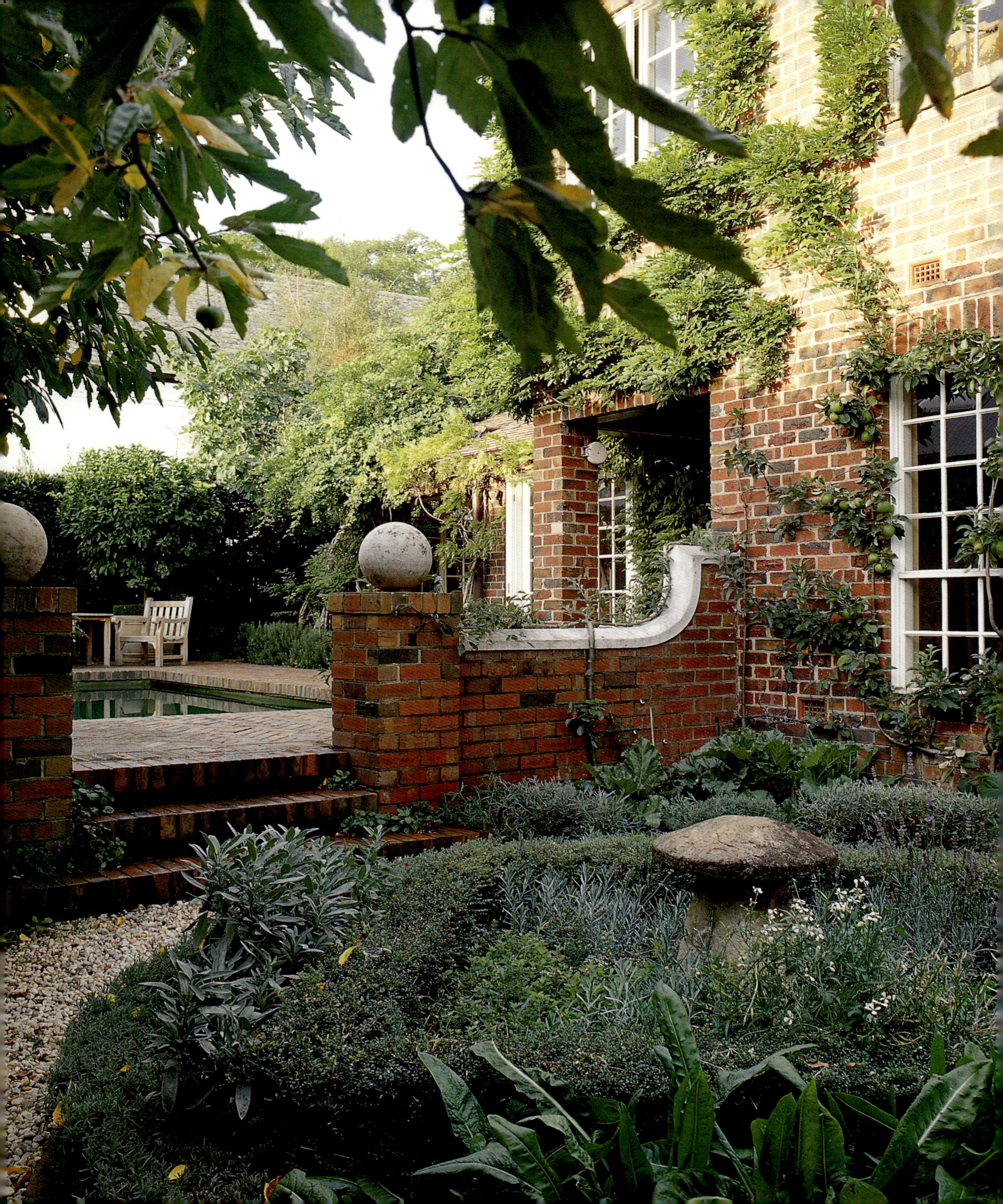

The steps that lead from the swimming-pool section to the herb and vegetable garden (opposite), like the wing walls, repeat the house's use of clinker bricks, and are softened with wild strawberries (Fragaria vesca). I added an eighteenth-century French stone ball to each of the flanking piers as a plain adornment in keeping with the functionality of the picking garden and the simplicity of the staddle-stone. Even the swimming-pool courtyard provides fruits and herbs for the kitchen, as the two potted lemon trees, clipped into semi-standards, and the hedge of bay behind them, attest. The lining of the pool was painted green to match them.

The main axis of the picking garden runs parallel to the house from the swimming-pool courtyard, through the opening between the wing walls, to a lavender seat set against the far wall of the herb and vegetable section. The seat is merely a stone slab, supported by two brick piers, with French lavender planted beneath it so that it appears to sit on top of a hedge. French lavender, too, forms the arms, while the back of the seat is created by *Lavandula* × *allardii*. The lavenders are not allowed to flower, though this does not greatly lessen their scent. Anyone sitting on the seat brushes against the lavender, immediately releasing wafts of strong perfume. The simple seat, its stone matching the staddle-stone and the spheres on top of the wing walls, its lavender matching the predominant plant in the garden, is perfect for such a small space.

Every surface in the herb and vegetable garden was utilised for planting. Even the steps were softened with wild strawberries (*Fragaria vesca*) planted between the bricks. Nashi pear trees and persimmon trees (*Diospyros*) were grown against the trellis and apple trees trained around the windows of the house and along the top of the wing walls. Restricted to walls, trees such as these are possible even when space is confined, their stature adding the depth and balance of planting essential to plant-centred gardens but often lacking in small gardens. Espalier has not only the advantage that it confines the fruit trees to the vertical plane, but also displays to perfection their superior characteristics: delicate blossoms in spring, fresh green leaves in summer, ripened fruits and brilliant leaves in autumn, shapely bare boughs in winter. The leaves of the persimmons in particular turn a spectacular red in autumn. To complete the bounty of the garden and ensure that the design did not become over-formal, we added a couple of crab apple trees (*Malus*). These were slight enough to be tucked into two corners of the garden, with herbs and vegetables at their feet. In autumn their crop makes fine jelly.

This picking garden is a high-maintenance garden. Apart from the very regular soil preparation, feeding and watering that vegetables require, and the annual replacement of many of the plants, the hedges need frequent clipping to prevent them spreading too much and growing too high for the garden design. However, because the owner has long been an ardent gardener, she happily gives her garden the constant care it demands.

LIVING IN THE

GARDEN

Small gardens can be fascinating display cases to be gazed into from the house, or vivid backdrops to life as it is lived inside from day to day. But that is only half their charm, for they can also be very special additional rooms of the house: places to sit on sunny days, places to eat on balmy evenings. The direct warmth of the sun; small movements of air; the sound of water; deep shadow and the dazzle of light on leaves; the fresh green of thriving plants — these are pleasures that no internal room can bring to living.

Deciding how much time you want to spend outdoors is fundamental before you design and build the different parts of your garden. If you only want to sit outside from time to time, perhaps having a coffee with one or two friends — or to view rather than live in the garden — then just a small paved terrace may be sufficient. On the other hand, if you want to hold outside parties or seat a lot of people around a table on the terrace, your entertaining area will need to be larger. Guests for drinks will want to move freely about the garden and from one group to the next, not be jostled as they eat and drink, and they will also want to be able to sit down now and then. At dinner parties, as at drinks parties, guests appreciate being served smoothly and inconspicuously — something not easily achieved when you are battling for space. And expansive conversations are difficult in cramped conditions.

Remember, too, that if you have permanent outdoor dining furniture, you will need to be able to walk around it comfortably in the times when you are not entertaining but simply enjoying your own garden. It is important at the design stage to think about the kind of table

Iron furniture has been chosen for the swimming-pool courtyard shown earlier on pp. 110–11, because of its lightness both physically and visually. The cushions are removed from the sunlounge when it is not in use so that it does not impede the view of the garden and the water, but rather adds its own shadow play. The elegant, dark lines of the furniture particularly suit the pink tones of paving and roses.

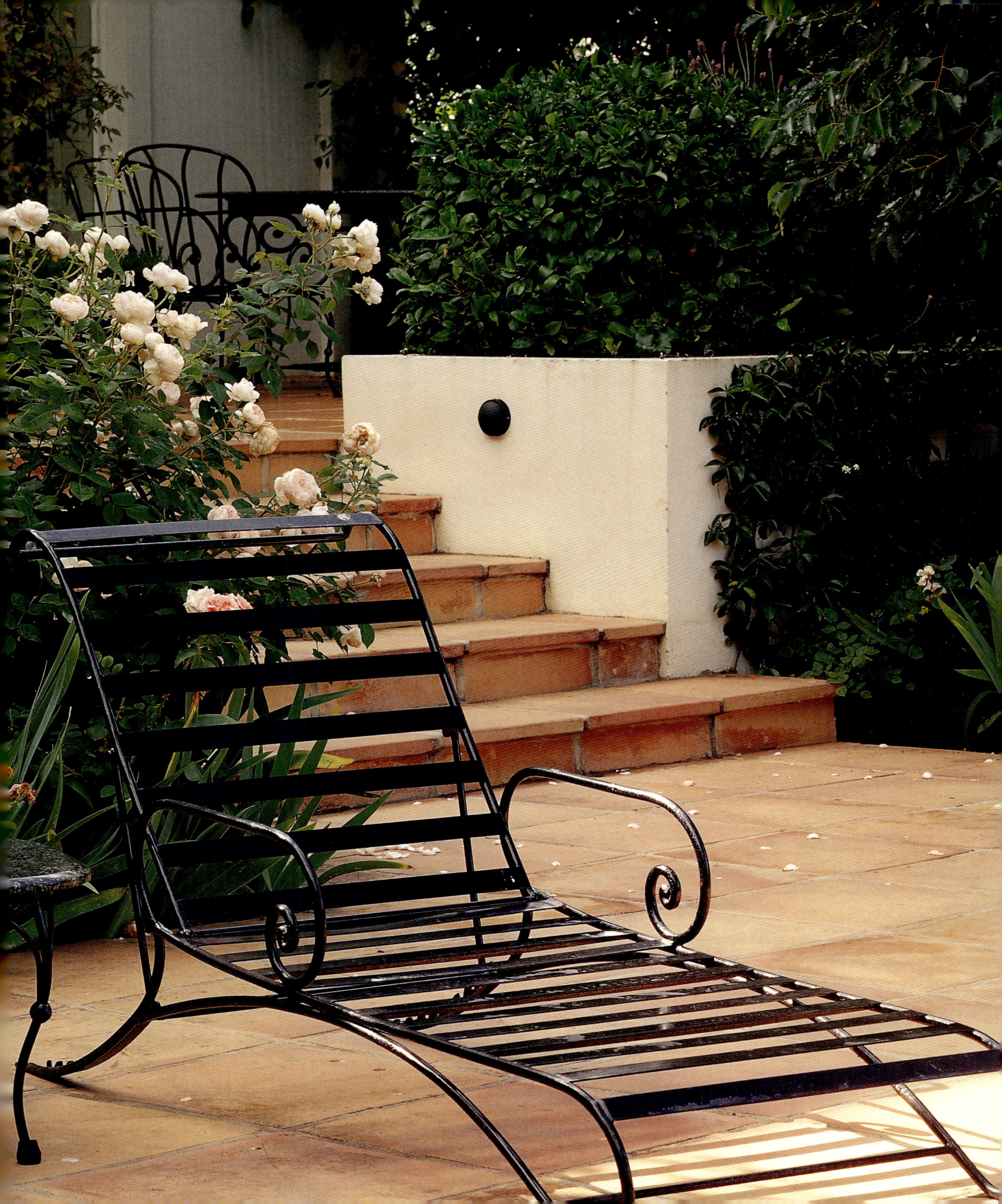

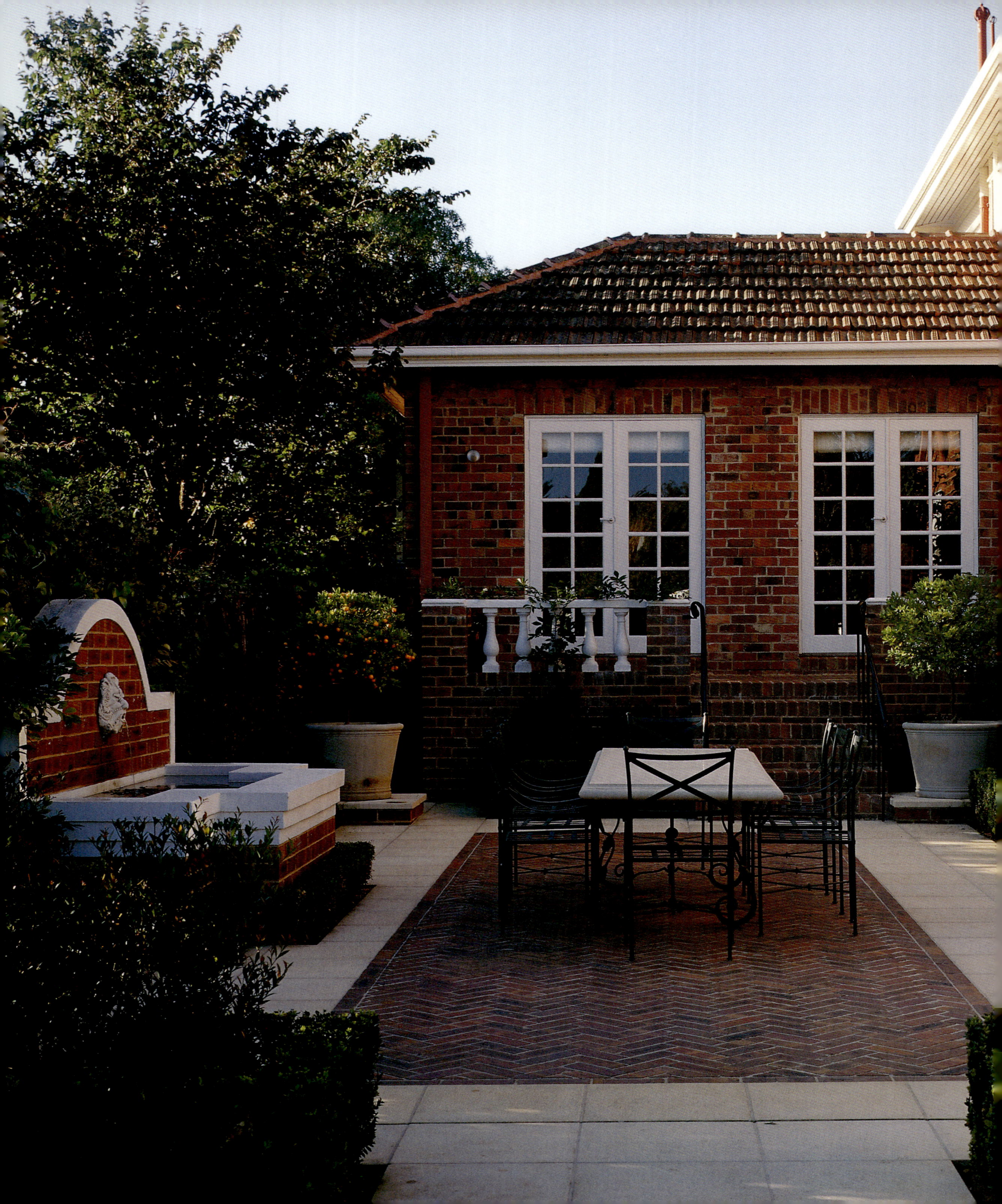

A small terrace for dining on: like all areas, it needed points of interest for the eye, but these — a fountain, and pots of kumquats (Fortunella) slightly raised on brick stands — had to be kept to the perimeter to allow sufficient room for the table and chairs. The terrace, being adjacent to the house, took the cue for its hard surfaces from the building. The restrained iron chairs and pale stone tabletop marry perfectly with the equally restrained herringbone pattern of the paving in the limited space, but also ensure — like the paving border — that the brickwork does not appear too heavy.

and chairs that would suit the garden you are planning, and then ensure that the space allotted for them will be sufficient. The rules that apply to designing a living room or dining room apply equally to designing a well-functioning outdoor room.

For practical reasons, the outside entertainment area needs to be close to the kitchen: you don't want to have to cart crockery and food a long distance. If you have the chance to plan the garden at the same time as your house or an extension to your house, consider having French windows onto the garden because, apart from allowing the house to flow into the garden, they make it easy to transport food — and furniture — outdoors. A number of American houses have a specially designed kitchen window, with an adjacent bench outside, so that food can be passed through.

Sometimes although furniture will technically fit into a space, it does not look right. Furniture rearing up just beyond the windows of the house can be quite confronting — after all, the whole art of designing a small garden is to suggest space where there is little. You need to make sure that your garden will not be so filled with permanent furniture that it looks cluttered and its main sight-lines become obscured. If there is a danger of imbalance, consider simply carrying out a table and chairs, or perhaps just the chairs, from the house whenever you want to eat in the garden, or have furniture that you can store easily and just bring out for the main weeks when you entertain. Another solution is to build benches at the side of the garden, to which you can draw up a table. Alternatively, the American idea of a bench adjacent to a kitchen window can be utilised. The bench can be made large enough to dine on, with the added advantage that people eating at it can talk to the person cooking in the kitchen. The kitchen surfaces, provided they are durable ones such as marble or granite, can be repeated on the bench to further unify the area.

Very occasionally a small garden is designed around the furniture, not the reverse. A fine old, carved-stone table may dictate a garden that is simply a fitting background to it, or determine the paving material chosen. Antique French cast-iron furniture may suggest a simple trellis-enclosed courtyard. And although it is true that permanent furniture may spoil the uncluttered lines of a garden plan, it is equally true that an expanse of paving can look more inviting if furniture is included in the design.

Outdoor Dining Furniture

Outdoor furniture needs to be in harmony with its surroundings. If the paving material of a small terrace is light-coloured natural or artificial stone, for example, a top in a similar material will make the table less conspicuous. Metal furniture goes well with terracotta tiles. Both stone and metal suit stone or rendered-brick houses. Timber furniture blends well with weatherboard houses and timber decking, and also often suits a house decorated with a timber trim.

Metal furniture is suited to small gardens because it is both light in appearance and light to shift from one part of the garden to another or from sunshine to shade. Timber is visually heavier so requires more surrounding space if the garden is not to look crowded. Always choose a hardwood timber, which is long lasting. Teak is particularly good because it does not require maintenance and weathers to an attractive grey. Teak is a rainforest timber, so it is important to buy furniture guaranteed to have been made from trees grown on a plantation. Another advantage of timber furniture is that it comes in many sizes and designs so suits different architectural styles, whereas much of the metal furniture available copies the French traditional style with its curved lines and perforated tabletops.

In contrast to metal and wooden furniture, stone furniture is permanent furniture. It is too heavy to be moved easily or often to suit the seasons or the weather. Because it looks massive, it automatically becomes a major feature wherever it is placed. A table with a stone base and top

This courtyard, shown more fully on pp. 94–5, had sufficient paving away from the swimming pool to hold a permanent table and eight seats. As a consequence the table could be an imposing stone one, although to lighten the effect refined chairs in iron — one of the few materials that go with stone — were chosen. Pale cushions, which tone with the colour of the tabletop, were necessary for comfortable dining. The table was placed so that the fountain, with its flanking Anduze vases of geraniums (Pelargonium), provides the perfect backdrop to a dinner party.

needs to be a very special piece to be considered for a small area, unless a heavily monumental garden design, based on hard landscaping rather than soft planting, is chosen.

Even when space is very limited, there are certain outdoor tables that can be kept in the garden permanently. Some small timber and metal tables come with leaves or fold-out extensions that need only be used when a number of people dine. Alternatively, small matching tables, square or semicircular in shape, can be placed on either side of the garden, so that they do not interfere with a central sight-line, and brought together for a dinner party. Inconspicuous outdoor coffee tables offer a solution for informal dining. Small slabs of stone can be easily turned into coffee tables by giving them a stone or rendered-brick base.

Always choose chairs that match your table, if possible: decorative metal, for example,

*A seat from which to view the garden is almost a necessity, and often adds a decorative element in its own right. A Chippendale wooden bench was chosen because its strong pattern was reminiscent of the house windows (above left). The waxy leaves and fruit of a lemon tree (*Citrus limon *'Meyer') felicitously frame the white seat, painted to match the house trim. The lavender seat of the picking garden featured in the 'Plants' chapter is both a traditional and a whimsical — though nevertheless dominant — feature in the garden (above right). In the warehouse courtyard shown also on p. 87 a teak sunlounge suits the overhead beams (left). The beams were kept to add their strong lines to the courtyard when the roof was removed in this section during the conversion. Hardy plants — for example, star jasmine (*Trachelospermum jasminoides*) along the fountain-back and on the wall, and pear trees (*Pyrus ussuriensis*), with arum lilies (*Zantedeschia aethiopica*) *and* Dietes grandiflora *beneath them — offer a foil for the timber.*

looks out of place with sturdy timber. Stone benches to match stone tables are available but have the disadvantage of being backless: metal chairs, which usually work well with stone tables, or a stone banquette built against a garden wall, may be better. And always try outdoor dining chairs first: comfort is essential for long hours of companionable sitting around a table, yet outdoor dining chairs, particularly iron ones, are notoriously uncomfortable. Carvers are more comfortable than armless chairs, but unfortunately take up a lot of space so are generally not suited to small gardens.

Cushions, either brought from the house or left permanently outside, improve the comfort of outdoor dining chairs. Ones covered in a waterproofed canvas or synthetic material, and stuffed with a waterproof filling, are commercially available, though in a limited number of shapes, sizes and colours. If you are happy to carry cushions in and out of the house, you can choose any fabric and colour you like: consider matching the soft furnishings of the house interior, or perhaps the colour of the exterior walls or paving. Cushions made in the traditional green-and-white striped canvas are also a reliable option.

Garden Seats

Seats can be placed in many parts of a garden. Traditionally they have been positioned at one end of a gravel or lawn walk to allow people to sit and enjoy the beauty of a major feature placed at the opposite end; however, a fair amount of space is required for this. Seats can themselves be a decorative element of the design: the most effective ornamentation in a small garden can often be a simple built-in bench or a wooden seat. Certainly the positioning of benches is usually an aesthetic rather than a functional matter. Often constructed by laying a natural or an artificial-stone slab across two brick piers, they add a strong architectural feature to a garden – and a permanent one – so getting their placement right is crucial.

Benches are not usually a free-standing structure, but rather built into or against a wall, and often flanked by garden beds. As the garden featured in the previous chapter showed, a bench can appear to float on a sea of green if a small hedge is planted below the slab; I have found lavender

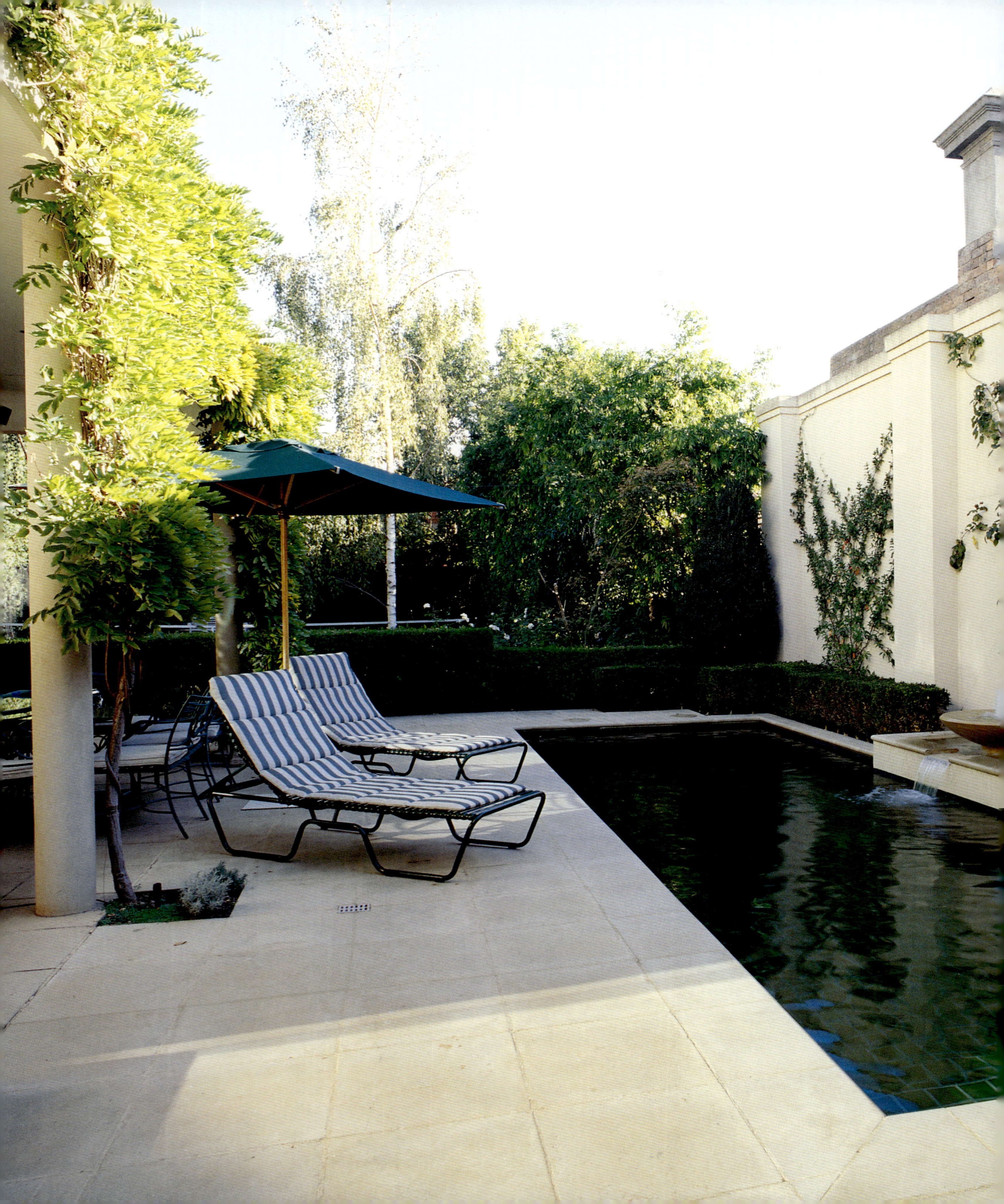

This swimming pool is only large enough for cooling off in and its courtyard is also small, but the careful limitation of poolside furniture to two plain sunlounges makes the area of paving seem greater than it is, aided by the understated pool itself. A market umbrella, in a traditional green matching the stripes of the mattresses, provides shade. Because the pool is the main feature, it required a focal point, hence the simple fountain created by placing a bowl in a rectangular trough set above the pool and using reticulated pool water. Dark green hedges, wisteria-clad columns and climber-filled recesses in the wall provide a lushness that compensates for the lack of garden beds and is picked up by the colour of the pool.

(*Lavandula*), English box (*Buxus sempervirens*) and rosemary (*Rosmarinus officinalis*) successful for this purpose. Stone benches suit a garden in which attractive masonry and paving are dominant components: they are not something that can be tacked onto just any garden. Although they invite visitors to sit and view the garden, they are too hard to be comfortable for long.

Wooden garden seats are subtle and pleasing adornments of a garden, and have the advantage over stone benches of being more portable. They can be moved from sun to shade and back again, carried to different spots as needed and removed from a lawn when it has to be mown. Although wood is intrinsically softer than stone to sit on and against, wooden garden seats often benefit from the addition of cushions: large, overstuffed ones are particularly inviting.

POOLSIDE FURNITURE

Relaxing by the water is one of the enjoyments of having a swimming pool, but put too much furniture in the pool area and it begins to look like a resort. Particularly in a small garden, if the illusion of an expanse of water set in an expanse of garden is to be kept, the poolside must be uncluttered, with two or three sunlounges at most. Low coffee tables are indispensable for keeping books, food and articles dry, but there is usually no room for a dining table.

Pool furniture is tricky to choose for it needs to meet a number of criteria. It must be durable because it will be exposed to all kinds of weather and to the water and chemicals of the swimming pool. The frames of poolside furniture are constructed of wrought iron, teak, plastic or aluminium. All the frames need mattresses or cushions,

Lighting not only allows a garden to be used at night, but also changes its atmosphere, as this courtyard, shown previously on p. 89, demonstrates. The courtyard is lit — and the weight of the columns considerably dramatised — by downlights placed at regular intervals along the beams. However, the main focus remains the fountain: the bust is uplit on either side, and five submerged lights catch the water as it gushes from the five taps.

which should be covered in canvas or a synthetic material able to withstand chlorine and salt as well as the sun's rays. Folding furniture that can be stored until needed is an advantage in a small area. Wrought-iron and some wooden furniture does not fold, but many of the plastic and aluminium styles do and are light to transport. Like the storage for the pool equipment, the storage for the furniture should be somewhere inconspicuous, such as the garage or the utility area.

Umbrellas are often a necessity: these days people are aware that they need to protect their skin from the sun's ultraviolet rays. There is a good range of umbrellas available, in all sorts of sizes. They usually have pine or teak stands and poles, and canvas tops. The most important consideration when using an umbrella is to ensure that it is properly moored. A permanent bracket or a metal slot incorporated in the paving offers a firm anchor, but is rather visible in a small garden when the umbrella has been folded away. An umbrella makes a strong statement in a small area so ideally its canvas should be beige if the paving is a similar colour, or perhaps green if there is surrounding greenery or a lawn, so that it merges with its background a little. For the same reason, over-large umbrellas are to be avoided.

Barbecues

The best barbecue in a small garden is the one you can't see: a mobile barbecue that can be stored elsewhere. Most people only barbecue food ten times or so a year yet a permanent barbecue is a dominant feature in a small garden all year long: it cannot be tucked away because the ritual of a barbecue demands that people stand around talking to the host while he or she turns the food! If a built-in barbecue is considered essential, the best solution is to set the smallest gas cook top available into a deep, attractive wall, or slide it into a recess in the masonry. European ovens — wood-fired ovens set within a chimney — are more handsome than many barbecues and enhance gardens built in a rustic Italian or Spanish style. However, their bulk automatically makes them a major focal point in any small garden, and they are really only for serious cooks who want to use them very regularly for many sorts of cooking, including baking bread.

Lighting

One of the great pleasures of having a garden is to be outside at night. The garden takes on quite a different atmosphere: familiar objects become unfamiliar; small sounds and rustlings are suddenly noticeable; the surrounding trees and shrubs seem taller and nearer; night and the garden close around. Subtle light enhances the sensuality of the night garden. It should seem a part of the night itself, its sources hidden from the observer: free-standing coach lamps belong to a streetscape or the long driveway of a mansion, not to a small garden.

Lighting should primarily draw the eye to the special features of the garden. Soft light gives ornaments and water and the forms of trees a new glamour at night. Hedges, as secondary features of a garden, usually do not need to be emphasised and in fact are quite hard to illuminate successfully: the light needs to just graze the surface for the full length of the hedge, which usually cannot be done. Visitors will want to be able to move about the garden confidently guided by lights, so steps in particular must be lit for safety; the lights can be discreetly recessed on either side of the flight. Paths, too, need to be indicated but are harder to illuminate attractively: double rows of path lights can soon make visitors feel they are on an airport runway. Often there is sufficient ambient light from sources in the garden such as highlighted trees or ornaments to illuminate the paths without the addition of specific lighting.

I prefer uplighting to downlighting: downlights often shine in people's eyes and cause glare in the garden. Lighting from below is far more exciting because it carries the eye up an object to the mysterious darkness beyond. Uplighting illuminates, for instance, the trunk of a tree rather than its canopy. Lighting from above tends to pin an object down and shut out the night. However, downlighting is essential when lights cannot be placed near the base of an object, as for example when an ornament or tree is completely surrounded by paving.

The house itself should always have external lights for safety and security. These are often placed more visibly than the ones employed in the garden, but there are numerous fittings to choose from to match the style of the house, from pendant lamps for Victorian verandahs to contemporary designs for modern exteriors. Although switches for both the garden and the exterior house lights should be installed inside, users should be able to control the lights separately. If the garden is to be viewed from inside, it may look more dramatic lit only by a few of the garden lights. If it is to be the setting for a dinner party, most of the external lights may need to be switched on — although, since much of the special atmosphere of dining outside is created by softly lit ornamentation against a dark backdrop, you may decide that exterior lights flood the garden too much and that just candles or lanterns are enough to eat by.

Lighting a special feature is as much about shadow as it is about light: it is the contrast that gives an object allure. Achieving a balance between light and shade is quite a delicate matter. Always try the effect of light from different angles — at night — before you install permanent lighting so that you ensure the light will not wash out the object. You may find you need to

With effective lighting, shadows as much as soft light create the attraction of the night garden.

position a light directly below the object or half a metre away from it: there are no hard and fast rules because each object has a different shape and size and height.

There are two voltages of electricity that can be used in a garden – 240 volts and 12 volts – and you need to decide at the planning stage which to use. A large garden with imposing trees that are to be spotlighted requires 240-volt electricity, and the cables must be laid by an electrician. Electricity of this voltage is dangerous if someone working in the garden is able to cut the cable and be electrocuted. I prefer 12-volt electricity because it is far safer. It does not require cables, and the flex can be run on top of the soil as well as underground – particularly useful when a garden is being modified. The flex does not need to be laid by an electrician, although the conversion from house power to 12 volts must be handled by one. As discussed in 'Fundamentals', a conduit through which the flex is later run can be included when the slab is laid.

Ornamental pools lit at night are magical in a garden. As water moves across submerged globes in the pool, light shimmers on its surface and the contours of the fountain, if it has one. Lights are positioned 100–200 millimetres below the surface of the water, not at the bottom because it inevitably becomes murky in time. They are attached to the sides of the pool or to bricks or long rods installed on the bottom, and are easily obtained: most large lighting shops specialise in garden lighting, including lights for pools. All fittings come with a range of globes of different wattage that operate on 12-volt electricity and are safe for underwater use.

If your budget allows, you may find specialist advice beforehand useful: a lighting expert will go over the garden and give you specific suggestions about what lights to install and where best to place them. Then you can handle the installation yourself or have the consultant arrange it.

When the construction is finished, the outdoor furniture chosen, the soft lighting installed, then there is nothing left to do but enjoy life in the garden. However small it is, if you have designed it to suit your house and your needs, constructed it soundly, planted it wisely, and given it intriguing changes of level and perspective and a few special objects for the eye to take pleasure in, your garden cannot help but be a retreat to restore the senses and lift the spirits.

An Outdoor Room

A garden with the feel of a Roman courtyard, in which to hold Friday night dinner parties: that was the owner's request. In answer (left), I built on site as the main feature a monumental rendered-brick fountain inset with marble and supporting three antique English lead dolphins.

Regularly on Friday evenings the owner of this garden holds a dinner party outdoors. His only brief to me was that I design a masculine garden in which he could frequently entertain. The whole house was built around three sides of a large courtyard, into which the glass walls of every room looked. Visitors stepping beyond the front door immediately found rooms opening out to the courtyard. The house was a featureless modern building, so the owner saw the courtyard as setting the architectural style. He had travelled often to Italy, loved all things Italian, and had had huge murals of Italy painted on the walls of his living rooms. Consequently, he liked the thought of a strong design in the Roman style.

As this drawing of the layout shows (right), the garden was wholly paved to maximise the space for outdoor entertaining; the plan was to continue the terracotta tiles of the adjacent rooms into the courtyard to make it a true extension of the house. The other main details (oil jars in the four corners and a fountain and garden beds on the northern side) were kept to the sidelines — but so brashly overscaled that no one would dare to suggest the courtyard was small!

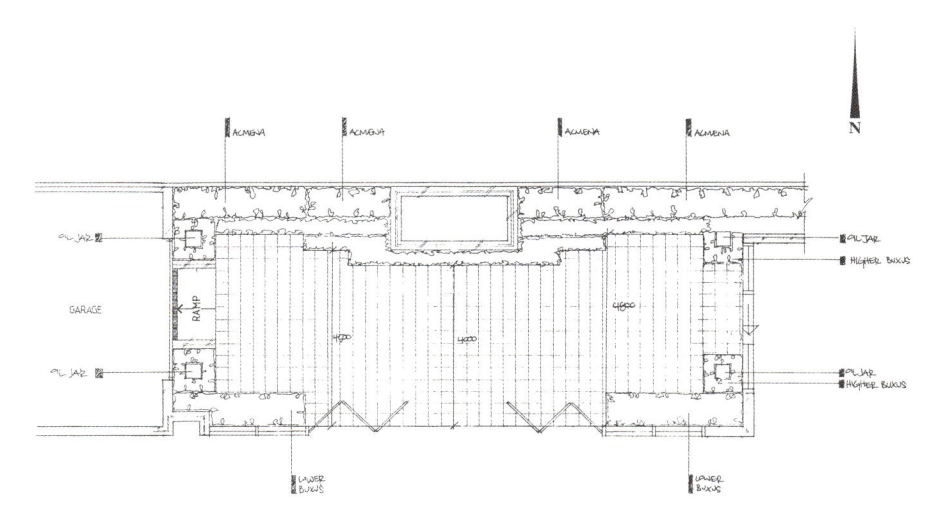

My first task was to fill in the swimming pool that had been constructed in the centre of the courtyard, since it took up too much space and prevented dining outdoors comfortably. Then I paved the courtyard with terracotta pavers to match those used in the interior of the house. In each of the corners I placed an enormous Spanish oil jar on a stand, around which I planted English box (*Buxus sempervirens*) hedging so that the jars appear to be cushioned on the box.

[155]

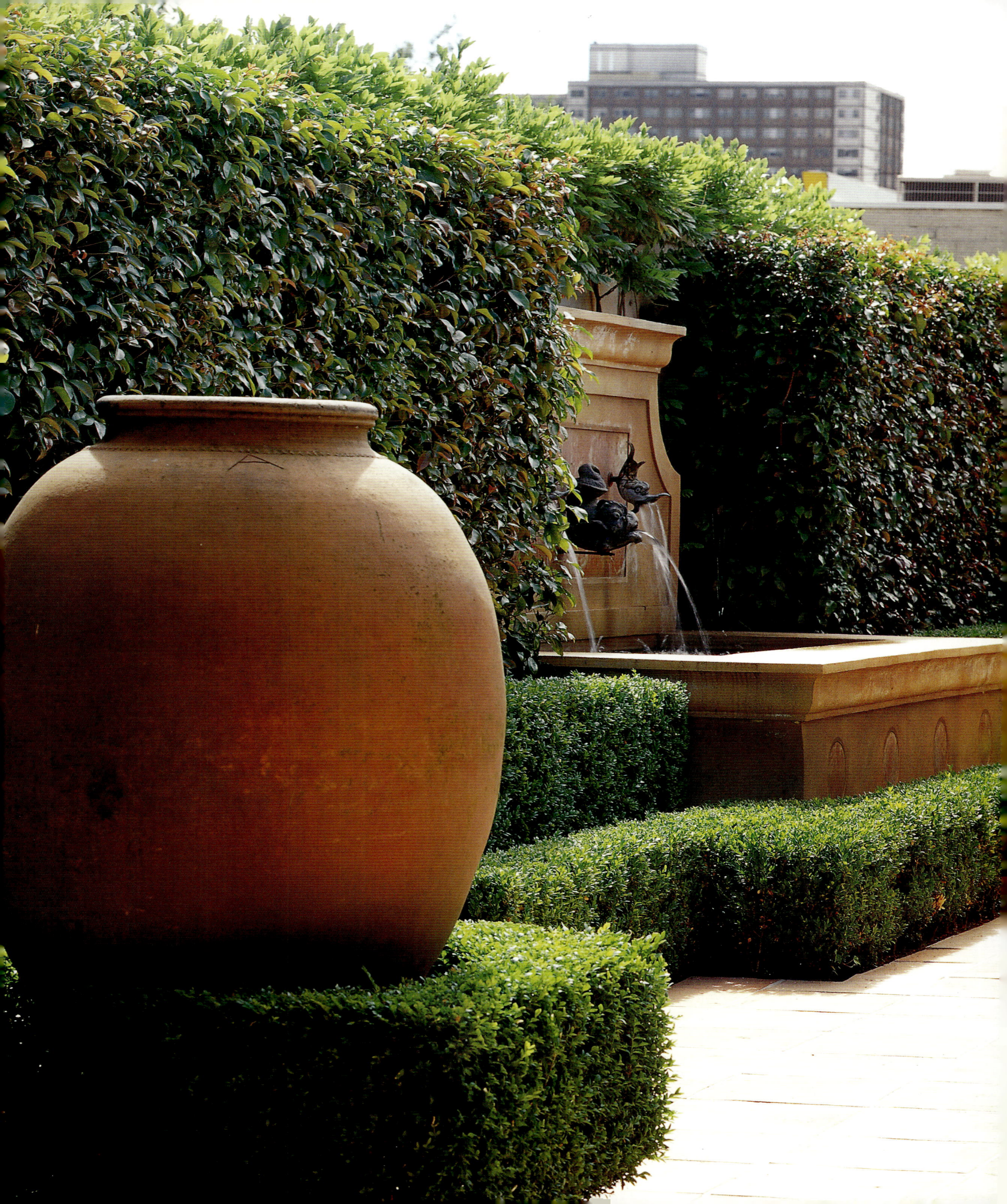

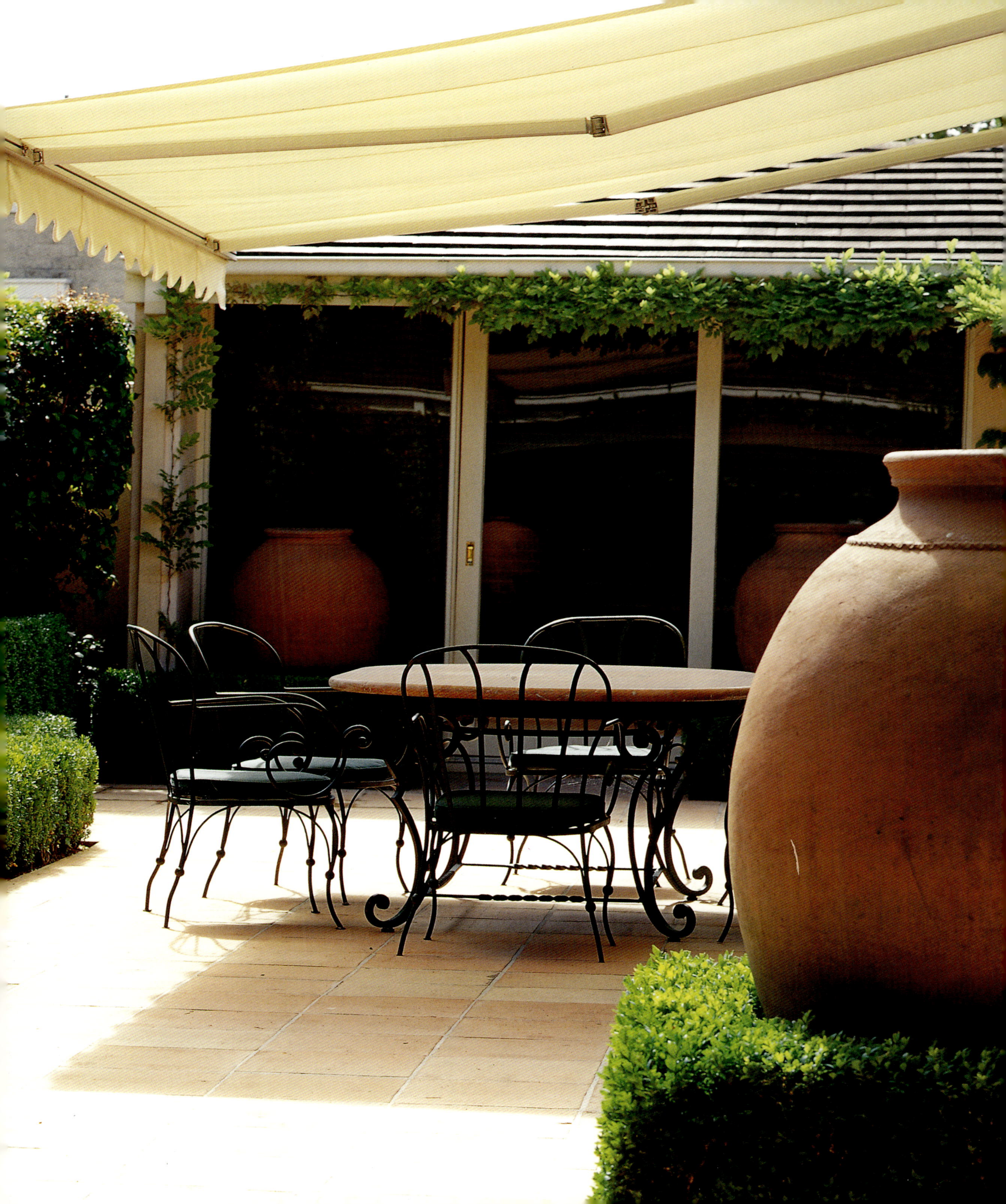

As the owner wanted a fountain, I decided to install on the far wall a substantial one that would be the main focus for both the garden and the house. I constructed a very Italianate fountain, decorated with specially chosen marble. Three lead dolphins mounted on a large marble panel splash water into a heavy trough inset with circles of marble. The eighteenth-century English dolphins – one large and two smaller in size – which I had discovered in an antique shop, had probably been taps originally and were easily converted into spouts.

The planting scheme for the garden I kept very simple: just three kinds of plants. Lillypilly (*Acmena smithii*) was used as a tall hedge on either side of the fountain to disguise the boundary. Below that were planted two tiers of box, and *Wisteria sinensis* was trained around the window frames of the house. It is a highly restricted, highly tailored scheme that underpins the masculine design of the courtyard. Apart from the racemes of wisteria in spring, the garden looks very clipped and green for twelve months of the year – though the greens themselves change from bright new growth to darker maturity as the seasons pass.

The courtyard measured 6 metres by 14 metres but several tricks made it look larger. By paving the courtyard in the same terracotta tiles as the interior – and by extending these even into the garage, which is often opened up to provide more room for outdoor parties – the inside and outside living areas were both made to look greater than they were. Secondly, the main features of the courtyard were overscaled: not just the massive oil jars and fountain, but the planted areas also. One of the mistakes that people make with a small courtyard is to assume that, because they do not have much space, a garden bed should be restricted to a narrow strip. The result is that viewers immediately read the strip as narrow and rightly conclude

A permanent oval table was stationed in the centre of the courtyard (previous pages and above). Its marble top matched the solidity of the other decorative objects, but the ironwork of its base and chairs ensured that the view was not obstructed. A retractable awning was installed to provide shade and shelter. Planting defined the perimeter of the courtyard. A line of Wisteria sinensis *runs along the top of all four walls, at the same height. A tall hedge of lillypilly (*Acmena smithii*), flanking the fountain, rises above a hedge of English box (*Buxus sempervirens*). A second, lower box hedge skirts the fountain and becomes a third layer on either side; the depth and luxuriance of planting achieved balances the fountain and makes the courtyard a buffer against the city beyond. The huge oil jars, whose bulk is needed to anchor the courtyard at its four corners, paradoxically also seem to ride lightly on magic carpets of box.*

[158]

that the garden is very small. A generous bed generously planted persuades viewers the garden is large and hides the boundary, reinforcing the inference.

The garden is very much one designed for living in. A canvas awning, which moves out on a mechanical arm, was erected to provide shade on hot days and protection during a summer downpour. Electrically operated awnings are excellent for very small areas where a verandah or pergola might offer too much permanent shade, take up precious room and look too heavy for the space. Once they retract, they are invisible and their metal box can be covered with a climber, such as the wisteria used here.

A table that could seat eight or so people was positioned permanently in the courtyard. It had a heavy stone top, but its iron base and chairs lightened the effect and did not impede the view of the garden. In fact the table was exactly right for this courtyard: its solidity added to the forceful design that was our aim and, far from seeming out of proportion itself, it helped to keep the dominant pavement in proportion. Two sets of green cushions, one striped, were made specially for the seats and to complement the interior decor.

Lighting was most important in this garden since every room looked into it. I decided to up-light the four Spanish oil jars and the lillypilly hedges, and put a number of submerged lights in the fountain so that light danced over both the water and the marble panel with its dolphins. That was all that was needed in the garden. As I have said, it is quite difficult to illuminate hedges effectively, and often unnecessary since they are usually background elements; however, in this case lighting the lines of lillypilly on either side of the fountain was manageable because they were short. The light throws all three layers of hedging into dramatic relief and intensifies the greens.

From the street there is nothing about the house to suggest such a courtyard as this exists, so that crossing the threshold to instantly behold it is always a surprise. At night, though the city is a deep purple skyline in the background, the courtyard becomes a world apart for all those who dine there, complete unto itself.

Acknowledgements

I would like to thank the following people very much for allowing us to photograph their gardens: Mr J. Baron; Mr and Mrs P. Bartels; Mr and Mrs A. Bell; Mr C. Bilionis; Mr and Mrs C. Bodsworth; Dr W. Brumley; Mr and Mrs R. Castan; Mr and Mrs R. Cooper; Ms S. Fink; Mr J. Kanis; Mr and Mrs C. Kimberley; Ms A. Lansley; Mrs J. McConnell; Ms A. Maize and Mr M. Dempsey; Mrs N. Metzner; Mrs V. Neale; Mr and Mrs R. Park; Ms M. Paspaley; Mr and Mrs R. Polk; Dr and Mrs D. Rogers; Mr J. Rossi; Mr and Mrs J. Smiley; Mr and Mrs J. Thomas.

My gratitude also to Graham Geddes for allowing us to photograph the two fine statues shown on page 65, at Graham Geddes Antiques; the Protocols and Special Events Department, Sydney City Council, for permission to photograph the 1997 Splendiflora exhibition; and *Vogue Living* for permission to reproduce the photograph that appears on pages 138–9.

A particular thank-you is owed to Simon Griffiths, for his very special interpretation and sensitive understanding of my work; Lesley Dunt, still the greatest editor in the world, whose help with the writing of the book was invaluable; Julie Gibbs, Executive Publisher at Penguin, whose enthusiasm and talents always inspire me; Tony Palmer, for the artistry of his book design, which displays Simon's photographs and my garden designs to such great effect; Emma Ferguson and Wilma Ferguson-McLellan for their enormous help in the office; Julian McCarthy and Andrew McFarland for their meticulous preparation of many of the gardens photographed; and Geoff Mance and Gardens At Night for their excellent lighting of my gardens.

Finally, I would like to acknowledge my great friends John Coote, with whom I work so closely on many projects and from whom I learn so much; Leonard Vary, whose brilliant negotiating skills, so generously exerted on my behalf, I deeply appreciate; and Will Fennell, for all his encouragement and support during the creation of this book.

INDEX

Page numbers in italic refer to photograph or ground-plan captions

Acacia melanoxylon (blackwood) 119
Acanthus mollis 90, 106
Acmena smithii (lillypilly) xi, xii, 21, 22, 25, *25*, 51, 53, 90, 119, 128, 158, *158*, 159
Ajuga reptans 39, 77, 78, *113*
Alchemilla mollis 77, *115*, 122
Alnus cordata (Italian alder) 118
annuals 70, 115, 131, 133
Arbutus unedo (strawberry tree) 118
arches 49
arum lily *see Zantedeschia aethiopica*
Australian native plants xii, 25, 48
Australian native violet *see Viola*
axis of garden ix, x, 7, *8*, *8*, 10, 13, *13*, 35, 43, 44, 58, 89

baby's tears *see Soleirolia soleirolii*
balcony gardens viii, xiii, 62, *62*, 127–8
barbecues 151
bay *see Laurus nobilis*
bearded iris *see Iris*
benches *8*, 26, *143*, *146*, 147
blackwood *see Acacia melanoxylon*
bog sage *see Salvia*
border plants 122, *123*
Boston ivy *see Parthenocissus*
box *see Buxus*
busts 5, 6, 18–19, 26, *66*, 66
Buxus (box): *B. microphylla* var. *japonica* 121; *B. sempervirens* (English box) xii, *13*, 19, 21, *21*, 22, 25, *25*, 35, 53, 54, 61, 64, 70, 71, 80, *81*, 91, 92, 97, 115, *115*, *117*, 121, *121*, 122, 127, 128, *128*, 149, 155, 158

Canary Island ivy *see Hedera*
Canary palm *see Phoenix canariensis*
Carpinus (hornbeam) 118; *C. betulus* 25, 119; *C. betulus* 'Fastigiata' 118–19
Chinese elm *see Ulmus parvifolia*
Chinese poplar *see Populus yunnanensis* 118
Citrus limon (lemon) 127; 'Lisbon' 19, 22, *25*, 26, 29, 80, 105; 'Meyer' 132, *134*, *137*, 146
Clematis montana 68, 125, *125*
climbers 45, 46, 61, 80, 113, 125, 127
Clivia miniata 122
cotton lavender *see Santolina chamaecyparissus*
crab apple *see Malus*
creeping fig *see Ficus*
× *Cupressocyparis leylandii* (Leyland cypress) 119, *121*
Cupressus sempervirens 'Stricta' (pencil pine) 46, *105*, 119
Cycas (cycad) 25; *C. revoluta* 6, 19, 22, 25, 98, *105*, 106, 122

Dietes grandiflora 146
dining area in courtyard 7, 8, 26; furniture 26, 140, 143, *143*, 145, 147
Diospyros (persimmon) 134, 137
drainage 36, 37, 43, 97
driveways 45, 78, 80, 81

English box *see Buxus*
English ivy *see Hedera*
English lavender *see Lavandula*
Erigeron karvinskianus 64, *91*, 126
espaliered trees 81, 122, 137
Euphorbia 46, 77, 132; *E. amygdaloides* subsp. *robbiae* 122; *E. myrsinites* *113*, 122; *E. wulfenii* 122, *123*
evergreen plants xi, xii, 25, 113, 115, 118, 121–2
extension of house into garden xiii, 5, 11–15, *13*, *14*, 38, 39, 53, 158

fences 45, *45*, 48, *48*, 49, 92, 96
Ficus (fig): *F. benjamina* (weeping fig) 118; *F. carica* (common fig) 80, 81, 119; *F. microcarpa* var. *hillii* (Hill's weeping fig) 118; *F. pumila* (creeping fig) 44, 125, 128
focal point 35, 43, 58
formal style ix–xii, 6, 126
Fortunella (kumquat) *143*
fountains: backs of 92, 100, *100*; as focus 7, *8*, 11, 15–16, 52–3, 58, 89–90; framing wall 10, 11, 16, 18; garden built around 99–107; lighting 26, 29, *150*, 159; matching architecture of house 89–90, *91*; proportions 16, 90, *90*; urn as 51, *51*, 52–3, *54*, 80, *81*; viewing point 89; wall-mounted 90, *91*, 92, *92*, 100
Fragaria (strawberry) 126; *F. vesca* (wild strawberry) *137*, 137
French lavender *see Lavandula*
furniture 158, *158*, 159; dining 26, 140, 143, *143*, *145*, 147; poolside 149–51, *149*; seats 136, *146*, 147, 149

Gardenia augusta 'Florida' 107, 121
gates 45, *45*, 46, *46*, 48, *48*, 49, 78, 80
geranium *see Pelargonium*
gravel 15, 37, *37*, 38, 40, 133
ground covers 39, 126
ground plan 7–10, 32, 49

hard landscape ix, x–xi, xii, 19
hard surfaces 38–43; low maintenance 51, 54, *54*; plants to soften 36, 64
Hedera (ivy) 64; *H. canariensis* (Canary Island ivy) 126; *H. helix* (English ivy) 44, 126, 128
hedges 48, 49, 117, 119, 121–2; clipped ix, xi, xii, 121, 126; clipping, pruning, trimming xi, *21*, 121–2; double 21, *21*; layered 35; lighting of 151–2, 159; plants for 21, *21*, 25, *25*, 81, 115, 119–22, 132; pleached 46, 48, 117–18
Heracleum giganteum (hogweed) 132

herbs 80, *80*, 126, 131, *131*, 134
Hill's weeping fig *see Ficus*
hogweed *see Heracleum gigantrum*
holly *see Ilex aquifolium*
horizontal and vertical surfaces xi, 32, 35, 39, 40, 53
hornbeam *see Carpinus*
Hosta 71, 77, 127, 128; *H. plantaginea* var. *grandiflora* 122, *123*; *H. sieboldiana* 122
Hydrangea 71; *H. arborescens* 'Grandiflora' 122; *H. macrophylla* 122; *H. macrophylla* 'Blue Wave' 58, 122; *H. petiolaris* (climbing hydrangea) 125; *H. quercifolia* 46

Ilex aquifolium 119
internal courtyard 84, 99, 102, 105–6, 128
Iris 77, 97, 110, *110*, *115*; *I. germanica* (bearded iris) 122, *123*; *I. laevigata* 125; *I. pseudacorus* 99, 106, 125; Louisiana hybrids 125
Italian alder *see Alnus cordata*
Italian influence x, 6
ivy *see Hedera*

kumquat *see Fortunella*

lamb's ears *see Stachys byzantina*
Laurus nobilis (bay) 119, 128, 132, *134*, *137*
Lavandula (lavender) xii, 77, 97, 110, 126, 146, 149; *L.* × *allardii* 121, *131*, 137; *L. angustifolia* (English lavender) 121, *131*, 133; *L. dentata* (French lavender) 66, 121, 122, 125, 127, *131*, 133, 137, 146
lawn 36, 37, 38, 80
lemon *see Citrus limon*
level changes x, 7, 35, *35*, 52–3, *52*, 54
Leyland cypress *see* × *Cupressocyparis leylandii*
light wells 128
lighting 26, *26*, 55, *150*, 151–3, *152*, 159
Ligustrum ovalifolium (privet) 119

[*161*]

lillypilly see *Acmena smithii*
lime, linden see *Tilia × europaea*
London plane tree see *Platanus × acerifolia*
Lonicera nitida 19, 20, 21, 22, 25, *25*, 44, 71, 115, 121, 126, *131*, 133

Magnolia grandiflora 81, *102*, 106, 107, *107*, 118, 119
maintenance 128; and formal style xi, 6, 51; see also plants
Malus (crab apple) 134, 137; *M.* 'Gorgeous' 119; *M. ioensis* 'Plena' (Bechtel's crab apple) *117*, 118, 119; *M. spectabilis* 115, 119
massed planting xii, 22, 115, 116
Mediterranean style x, 21, 45, 48, 96, 97, 107, 110
Moorish influence 6, 16, 99–100, *99*
Murraya paniculata 121
Myrsine africana 121

niches 5, 6, 10, *11*, 18–19, 66–7, *66*, 106
Nierembergia repens 39
Nymphoides 125; *N. crenata* *105*, 106

obelisks 68, *68*
Olea (olive): *O. europaea* 97, 119, 128
ornamental pools 86–7, *87*; to enhance fountain 52–3, *102*; lighting 86, 153; painted 16, 86, *90*; plants for *105*, 106, 125; proportions 16, 86, 90, *90*; reticulation system 86–7
overscaling xiii, 62, 72, 100, 105

Parthenocissus: *P. quinquefolia* (Virginia creeper) 125, 128; *P. tricuspidata* (Boston ivy) 10, 22, *22*, 106, 113, 125, 128
paving: to demarcate terraces 8; driveway 81; edging for 43; extension of house xiii, 5, 11–15, *13*, *14*, 38, 39, 53, *158*; laid on slab 43; mosaic 40, *40*, 43, *43*; patterns *13*,*14*, 15, 39, 53, *54*, *102*, *143*; softening *39*, 126; swimming-pool area 97
pear see *Pyrus*
pebbles 38; for fountain 96, 100, 105; in paving *14*, *15*, *39*, 40, *40*, *43*, 81,

106; swimming-pool finish 97; in water 16, *16*, 89
Pelargonium (geranium) 71, 127, *145*
pencil pine see *Cupressus sempervirens* 'Stricta'
perennials xii, 115, 117, 122, 131, 133
persimmon see *Diospyros*
perspective x, xii, 10, 58, *115*; false 7, 10, 71–2, 80
Phoenix canariensis (Canary palm) *102*, 105
picking garden 77, 78, 80, 81, 131–7, *131*, *133*, *134*, 137
planting scheme xi, 19, 77, 105, 110
plants 110–16, 128; for balconies 127–8; for borders 122, *123*; climbers 45, 46, 61, 80, 113, 125, 127; ground covers 39, 126; for hedges 19, 21, 21, 25, *25*, *81*, 70–1, *70*, 115, 119–22, 127, 132; herbs and vegetables 80, *80*, 126, 131, *131*, 134; for internal courtyards 106, 128; for light wells 128; for ornamental pools 125; for pleached hedges and small trees 46, 48, 117–19; for pots 21, 70–1, *70*, 127; see also maintenance
Platanus × acerifolia (London plane tree) 118
pleached hedging 46, 48, 117–18
pools see ornamental pools; swimming pools
Populus yunnanensis (Chinese poplar) 118
Portuguese laurel see *Prunus*
pots 21, 70–1; as fountain 106, *106*; plants for 70, *70*, 71, 127
privet see *Ligustrum ovalifolium*
proportion xii, 7; of ornamental pools 86–7, *87*; see also overscaling
pruning xi, 117–18, 121–2
Prunus 77; *P. lusitanica* (Portuguese laurel) 81, 119
Pyrus (pear): *P. calleryana* 118; *P. ussuriensis* 110, 118, 146, *146*; *P. salicifolia* (silver pear) 91

retaining walls 35–6, 54
Rhododendron 'Alba Magnifica' 122
rooftop gardens viii, xiii, 62, 128
Rosa (rose) 110, *110*, 113–14, 115, 121, 127, *140*;

'Albertine' 125; climbing 68, 125; David Austin 121; 'Iceberg' (climbing) 125; 'New Dawn' 125
Rosmarinus officinalis (rosemary) 110, 122, 126, *134*, 149; 'Blue Lagoon' 122

Salvia (sage) 133; *S. uliginosa* (bog sage) 122
Santolina chamaecyparissus (cotton lavender) 122
screens 45, *45*, 127–8
sculptures: background to 61, 75, 77, *77*; as focus 19, 75–81, *77*, *78*, *79*; see also busts; statues
seats 137, *146*,*147*, 149
Sedum 'Autumn Joy' 21, 22, 122, *123*, 127
sight-line 7, 8, 10, *13*, 35, 44
silver pear see *Pyrus*
soft surfaces 38, 43
Soleirolia soleirolii (baby's tears) 126
space (visual) x, xiii, 7, 35, 40; see also perspective, vistas
Spanish influence x, 16, 105, 107
Stachys byzantina (lamb's ears) 122
star jasmine see *Trachelospermum*
statues 29, 64–6, *65*
steps 7; aligning 35, *35*, 44; dimensions 10, 35, 44, 52; lighting 29; softening 21, 44, *137*
strawberry see *Fragaria*
strawberry tree see *Arbutus unedo*
sundial 66, *66* , 67
swimming pool 92, 96, *96*; furniture 149–51, *149*; lining colour 97, 137; paving around 97; planting around 97; utility area 150

terraces: formal 51–5, *51*, *52*, *54*; hedges on 19, 21, *21*; for outdoor living 8, 38, 106–7, *143*
Thymus (thyme) 126, 133; *T. serpyllum* 'Alba' (wild thyme) 126
Tilia × europaea (lime, linden) 77, 118–19
topiary x, xii, 21, 53, 70, *70*, 71
townhouse gardens viii, xiii, 75
Trachelospermum: *T. asiaticum* 75, *107*, 126; *T. jasminoides*

(star jasmine) 61, 70, 78, 80 *107*, *107*, 113, 125, 126, *146*
trees: on canes 21, *25*; espaliered 81, 122, 137; as focus 77; in picking garden 137; lighting 152; planting choices 118–19; pleached 46, 48, 117–19
trellis: backdrop for 72; colour of 72, *78*; along driveway *45*, 78, 80; for false perspective 71–2, *72*, 80; as garden divider *134*; on top of wall 48; for vertical plane *45*, 113

Ulmus parvifolia (Chinese elm) 119
urns: as focus 58, 62–4, *63*, *115*; as fountain 51, *51*, 52–3, *53*,*154*, 80, *81*

vegetables 126, 134
vertical and horizontal surfaces xi, 32, 35, 39, 40, 53
vertical plane 5, 6, 32, 35, 45, 53, 89, 113, 137
Viburnum: *V. odoratissimum* 75, 119, *128*; *V. tinus* 119
Viola: *V. hederacea* (Australian native violet) 126; *V. odorata* (violet) 126
Virginia creeper see *Parthenocissus*
vistas x, 58, *115*

walkways 46, 128
walls 6, 10, *11*, 12, 45–6, 48–9; for fountains 10, 11, 16, 18, *18*, 92; to match house 54; retaining 35–6, *54*
warehouse gardens viii, xiii, 87, 146
water, ornamental 84–107
water channel 8, 15, 16, *16*, 26, 87, 89
water lily see *Nymphaea*
weeping fig see *Ficus*
wild strawberry see *Fragaria*
wild thyme see *Thymus*
Wisteria 72, 92, *93*, 97, 110, 113, 121, 128, 149, 158, *158*, 159; *W. floribunda* 125; *W. sinensis* 5, *5*, 19, 21, 22, 26, 61, 78, 80, 91, 125, *125*; *W. sinensis* 'Alba' 125

Zantedeschia aethiopica (arum lily) 99, 106, *146*; 'Green Goddess' 122